So you <u>really</u> want to learn

Maths

Book 3

Serena Alexander B.A. (Hons.), P.G.C.E.

Edited by Louise Martine B.Sc. (Lon.)

Independent Schools
Examinations Board

GALORE PARK

www.galorepark.co.uk

Published by ISEB Publications, an imprint of
Galore Park Publishing Ltd,
19/21 Sayers Lane, Tenterden, Kent TN30 6BW
www.galorepark.co.uk

Typography and layout by Typetechnique, London W1
Cover design by GKA Design, London WC2H
Printed by Replika Press, India

The publishers would like to thank David Hanson once again for his
enormous dedication and help during the production of this book. Thanks are
due also to Mark Potter and Moira Laffey for their valuable comments.

ISBN-13: 978 1 902984 34 6

First published 2005, reprinted 2007, 2009, 2011

Details of other Galore Park publications are available at
www.galorepark.co.uk

ISEB Revision Guides, publications and examination papers may also be
obtained from Galore Park

Author's introduction

This book completes the ISEB Common Entrance and Scholarship syllabus for those taking Level 3, or Scholarship papers. It also covers most of the additional topics for Key Stage 3 and is therefore suitable for pupils in Year 8 or Year 9.

As in *So you really want to learn Maths* Books 1 and 2, topics that have been introduced earlier are revised before new work is introduced. The end of chapter extension exercises reflect the level of difficulty of Scholarship questions and are designed to test thinking skills as well as knowledge of the curriculum. It is hoped that students will also be exposed to a range of other puzzles and activities that allow them to use their imaginations and challenge their investigative skills.

Topics continue to be cross-referenced to the history of mathematics and, in this book, pupils will discover the magical Eye of Horus fractions and learn how lost manuscripts and mistranslation led to use of the word 'Sine'. Other topics are more recent and pupils can learn about fractal geometry and make their own stunning designs, or even just relax by playing random cricket.

It is traditional at this point to remember one's own teachers and there is one who encouraged me to spend my own teenage weekends learning how to solve the Sunday Times Brainteaser, researching Magic Square theory and making hexaflexagons, and that is my father, Giles Kirby. He, in his turn, was inspired by one William Hope-Jones, who is reputed to have written the following:

The Archimedeans' anthem
All praise to Archimedes, who weighed the royal hat,
Displacing quarts of h. and c., upon the bathroom mat.
For that unending decimal we mortals know as pi,
He found three-and-one-seventh was just a bit too high.
All praise to Arthur Eddington, who proved I don't know what,
Except that ev'rything you think's exactly what it's not.
He knows what Albert Einstein's equations are about;
And that's where he has you and me, and Einstein, up the spout.

This, I think, only goes to prove that for truly inspirational teaching a mere text book is not enough. I hope that those who use this book as a resource for their classes will also take the time to impart their own wit, humour and enthusiasm to their pupils.

New 2010 Common Entrance syllabus

When first publishing the series the intention was that 11+ topics would be covered in Book 1, all 13+ topics in Book 2, and all extension and scholarship topics in Book 3. Since then the ISEB Common Entrance syllabus has undergone two major revisions, in 2008 and 2010. The result is that while the requirements of the syllabus remain completely covered by the course, the division of the books no longer matches up precisely with that of the syllabus levels.

As of 2010, the 13+ syllabus has been re-categorised into three levels.

- Level 1 has been introduced as a new 'foundation' level that draws heavily on the 11+ syllabus
- Level 2 is the new name for Papers 1 and 3
- Level 3 is the new name for Papers 2 and 4

In summary, the books match the new levels as follows:

- 11+ is covered in its entirety in Book 1
- 13+ Level 1 is covered in Book 1, with the exception of these topics that are covered in Book 2:

13+ Level 1 topic	SYRWTL Maths Book 2 chapter
Multiply out brackets in straightforward examples, such as $3 (x + 4) = 3x + 12$ $2(a + b) = 2a + 2b$	11
Candidates should be able to take out a common factor in simple cases, e.g. $2a + 4b = 2(a + 2b)$ $3x + 12 = 3 (x + 4)$ $x^2 + 2x = x(x + 2)$	11

13+ Level 1 topic	SYRWTL Maths Book 2 chapter
Simplify numerical and algebraic fractions, such as $$\frac{4x}{12} = \frac{x}{3}$$ $$\frac{3c}{c} = 3$$	11
Candidates should be able to solve problems using angle properties of intersecting and parallel lines.	8
Candidates should be able to draw conclusions from scatter diagrams, and have a basic understanding of correlation.	19
When dealing with a combination of two experiments, candidates should be able to identify all the outcomes, using diagrammatic, tabular or other forms of communication.	4

- 13+ Level 2 is covered in Book 2, with the exception of this topic that is covered in Book 3:

13+ Level 2 topic	SYRWTL Maths Book 3 chapter
Candidates formulate and solve linear equations with simple fractional coefficients.	6

- 13+ Level 3 is covered in its entirety in Book 3.

Acknowledgements

My thanks must go to the team at Galore Park, especially Louise, who have continued to be incredibly supportive; to David Hanson for checking everything with painstaking care; to my colleagues, particularly Sanja and Sue; and to all of you who have been so encouraging about the earlier books. Most of all my thanks must go to the students of Colet Court, St Paul's School, Newton Prep and Devonshire House who have diligently worked their way through many of these exercises.

Serena Alexander, July 2005

About the author

Serena Alexander has taught Mathematics since 1987, originally in both maintained and independent senior schools. From 1999 she taught at St. Paul's School for Boys, where she was Head of Mathematics at their Preparatory School, Colet Court, before moving first to Newton Prep as Deputy Head and recently to Devonshire House. She is an ISI inspector and helps to run regular Mathematics conferences for prep school teachers. She has a passion for Maths and expects her pupils to feel the same way. After a lesson or two with her, they normally do!

Contents

Chapter 1: Working with numbers 1

  Natural numbers (also called cardinal numbers) 1

  Long multiplication and long division 2

  Integers 5

  Fractions 5

  Factors and multiples 7

  Prime numbers 7

  Prime factors 7

  Product 8

  Highest common factors and lowest common multiples 9

  Using a calculator 11

  The mode 13

  Negative numbers 13

  Brackets 14

  Second functions 14

  Using the memory 15

  Simple index functions 16

  Calculator problems 16

  End of chapter 1 activity: Calculator puzzles and games 23

Chapter 2: Decimals **26**

  The Penny and the first taxation 26

  Calculating with money: Adding and subtracting 28

  Multiplying 29

  Dividing decimals 30

  Dividing by decimals 31

  Working with other metric units 33

  More about area 34

  Estimating 36

  Degree of accuracy 37

  Revision of decimal places and significant figures 37

  Using your calculator 39

  End of chapter 2: The national elf problem 41

Chapter 3: Fractions **43**

Writing fractions today 44

Adding fractions 47

Subtracting fractions 49

Mixed addition and subtraction 50

A fraction of an amount 52

Multiplying fractions 54

Dividing with fractions 56

The reciprocal 57

Mixed operations 59

Fractions on the calculator 60

End of chapter 3 activity: Fraction, decimal and
percentage dominoes 65

Chapter 4: Index numbers **66**

Negative indices 69

Solving equations with x^2 71

Squares and square roots 71

Using prime factors to find square roots 73

Other roots 74

Using the index functions on the calculator 74

Second function 76

Index functions 76

Using the memory 78

Writing answers 79

Large and small numbers 79

Standard index form 82

Standard index form and the scientific calculator 83

Roots as indices 86

Calculating with roots and powers 86

More about square roots 87

End of chapter 4 activity: Chain letters 91

Chapter 5: Percentages **93**

    Rules of conversion 94

    Forming a percentage 94

    Finding a fraction of an amount 95

    Percentage as a decimal 97

    Percentage increase and decrease 99

    Calculating percentage increase and decrease 100

    Income tax 102

    Percentage change 104

    Finding the original amount 106

    Compound interest 108

    End of chapter 5 activity: The trading game 112

Chapter 6: Equations and inequations **115**

    Using algebra to solve problems 117

    Equations with fractions 122

    Equations with two fractions 124

    Inexact answers 126

    Solving inequalities 127

    End of chapter 6 activity: Polyhedral numbers 133

Chapter 7: Indices and algebra **135**

    Multiplying 135

    Division 136

    The power 0 136

    Negative index numbers 136

    Powers 137

    Index numbers as fractions 138

    Combining multiplication and division 139

    Indices and brackets 141

    Factorising 143

    Trial and improvement 144

    More about square roots 149

    End of chapter 7 activity: My Great Uncle's bequest 152

Chapter 8: Sequences **155**

    Sequences based on a times table 156

    Sequences based on square numbers 156

    Sequences based on triangle numbers 157

    Sequences based on a Fibonacci type number pattern 157

    Sequence notation 160

    Working to a rule 161

    More about quadratic sequences 162

    Geometric sequences: An introduction to fractals 168

    Geometric sequences and numbers 170

    End of chapter 8 activity: 3D fractals 176

Chapter 9: Using formulae **178**

    What is a formula? 178

    Substituting into formulae 180

    Area and volume formulae 183

    Finding an unknown quantity 185

    Polygon formulae 187

    Distance, speed and time formulae 189

    Average speed 192

    Rearranging formulae 194

    Units of formulae 195

    Rearranging formulae with factorising and roots 197

    End of chapter 9 activity: Perigal's dissection 200

Chapter 10: Pythagoras' theorem **202**

    Finding the hypotenuse 204

    Finding a side other than the hypotenuse 208

    Isosceles triangles 212

    Special triangles 213

    Mixed problems 217

    Pythagorean triplets 221

    End of chapter 10 activity: Truthful twins? 223

Chapter 11: Area and volume **226**

Circles 226

Parts of circles: Perimeter 227

Finding the radius 229

More circle problems 230

More about volume 234

Volume of a cylinder 237

Surface area of a cylinder 239

Units of area and volume 242

More volume problems 243

Longer problems using area and volume formulae 245

End of chapter 11 activity: Packaging the litre 251

Chapter 12: Simultaneous equations **253**

What is an equation? 253

Writing equations in two variables 253

Using graphs to solve problems with two variables 254

What are simultaneous equations? 257

The graphical method 259

The elimination method 261

The scale factor method 263

The re-arrangement and substitution methods 264

Solving problems with simultaneous equations 265

End of chapter 12 activity: A literary genius 272

Chapter 13: Graphs **273**

Travel graphs 273

Everyday graphs 277

From equations to graphs 280

Graphs of curves 282

Points of intersection 285

The reciprocal curve 287

Other curves 287

End of chapter 13 activity: Experiments and graphs 291

Chapter 14: Equations and brackets **293**

Factorising algebraic expressions 294

More brackets 295

Two sets of brackets 297

Squares and the difference between them 299

Solving equations by factorising 301

Solving problems with factorising and brackets 302

End of chapter 14 activity: The dragon curve or
Jurassic Park fractal 308

Chapter 15: Probability **311**

Calculating probability 311

Using theoretical probability 313

Probability with two events 315

Possibility space for combined events 318

Drawing diagrams to help solve problems 321

End of chapter 15 activity: Probability experiments 324

Chapter 16: Transformations **329**

Transformation geometry 330

Reflections 330

To construct a reflection of a line PQ in a line AB 331

Rotations 333

Rotational symmetry 335

Translations 336

Enlargements 339

Transformations on a grid 340

Finding a general rule for a transformation 344

End of chapter 16 activity: Hexaflexagons 347

Chapter 17: Ratio and proportion **349**

Comparing area and volume 349

Volumes of enlargements 352

More questions on area and volume 353

More ratio questions: Proportion 357

End of chapter 17 activity: Fibonacci and the Golden Ratio 361

Chapter 18: Introducting trigonometry **365**

What is trigonometry? 365

Terminology 368

Calculating the tangent 369

Calculating the angle 369

Finding the opposite side 370

Finding the adjacent side 372

Finding the angle 375

Angles of elevation and depression 377

End of chapter 18 activity: The cube root trick 381

Chapter 19: More trigonometry **383**

Sine and cosine 384

Where does the word 'sine' come from? 386

Calculating the sine and cosine 387

Calculating the angle 387

Finding opposite and adjacent sides using sine and cosine 388

Finding the hypotenuse 392

Finding the angle 393

Solving problems using trigonometry 396

End of chapter 19 activity: Binary arithmetic 402

Chapter 20: Looking at data **404**

Charts and diagrams 404

Pie charts 405

Bar charts 407

Scatter graphs 409

Mean, median and mode 411

Finding the total 414

Working with grouped data 417

Drawing bar charts 418

End of chapter 20 activity: Data collection 423

Index **425**

Chapter 1: Working with numbers

By now you should know a great deal about numbers. You should know that there are many different ways of working with them, particularly when the numbers get very large or very small.

Before we get stuck into this book it is worth making sure that we all agree on certain definitions.

Natural numbers (also called cardinal numbers)

Natural numbers are the numbers used for counting: one, two, three, four etc. They can be added, subtracted, multiplied and divided. You can of course use a calculator to conduct calculations with natural numbers; however, it is worth remembering that you can save a great deal of time if you can do simple arithmetic in your head. Try this first exercise. Write down only the answer to each question. It should take you not more than 10 minutes!

Exercise 1.1

Number your page from 1 to 60 before you start. Make a note of the time as you start and see how long it takes you to complete the exercise. Remember write down only the answers:

1.	7 × 5	**7.**	3 × 8	**13.**	72 ÷ 12
2.	8 × 9	**8.**	24 + 74	**14.**	68 − 43
3.	36 + 123	**9.**	36 ÷ 9	**15.**	5 × 7
4.	42 ÷ 7	**10.**	38 − 17	**16.**	39 − 23
5.	32 − 11	**11.**	18 + 22	**17.**	11 + 35
6.	14 + 7	**12.**	7 × 9	**18.**	24 ÷ 8

19. 8×7

20. $29 + 11$

21. 25×3

22. $32 + 9$

23. $125 \div 5$

24. $42 - 6$

25. 13×3

26. $19 + 24$

27. $33 - 17$

28. $72 \div 3$

29. $180 - 56$

30. 90×3

31. $127 + 53$

32. $144 \div 8$

33. $35 - 19$

34. $47 + 39$

35. 45×7

36. $72 \div 36$

37. $27 + 28$

38. $200 - 137$

39. 35×6

40. $39 + 47$

41. $225 - 180$

42. $225 \div 45$

43. $225 \div 15$

44. 19×6

45. 19×9

46. $200 - 79$

47. 99×2

48. 99×8

49. $128 + 52$

50. $207 + 153$

51. $305 - 125$

52. $288 \div 12$

53. 13×13

54. 15×15

55. 75×3

56. 25×9

57. 125×4

58. 20×500

59. $3600 \div 90$

60. $100\,000 \div 80$

Long multiplication and long division

The questions above could be answered using simple arithmetic. When calculations become too difficult many people may want to use a calculator. However, there are often situations when you do not have a calculator to hand and the calculations have to done using a pencil and paper. You should be able to add and subtract quite easily now. Make sure that you can carry out long multiplication and long division as easily.

Remember that for **long multiplication** we break the smaller number into a multiple of ten and a unit.

For example: 23 becomes 20 + 3
                  We can then write: 125×23 as $125 \times (3 + 20)$

Example:

125 × 23

Th	H	T	U
	1	2	5
	×	2	3
	3	7	5
2	5	0	0
2	8	7	5

Step 1: 125 x 3

Step 2: 125 x 20 – drop the zero into the answer row and continue with the 125 × 2 calculation.

Step 3: finally add 375 + 2500 (125 x 3 + 125 × 20)

Long division is done in the same way as short division, but all the working out is shown. This is so that the remainders can be calculated clearly and accurately.

Example:

851 ÷ 23

You can check by multiplying over here

		H	T	U		
			3	7		
2	3	8	5	1		
		6	9			
		1	6	1		
		1	6	1		
		-	-	-		

```
  2 3          2 3
×   3        ×   7
  6 9        1 6 1
```

Exercise 1.2

Calculate the following, showing all your working clearly:

1. 27 × 36
2. 47 × 29
3. 89 × 47
4. 68 × 91
5. 124 × 72

6. 391 ÷ 17
7. 989 ÷ 23
8. 703 ÷ 19
9. 1302 ÷ 31
10. 1247 ÷ 29

11. 213 × 69
12. 1161 ÷ 43
13. 713 × 43
14. 1363 ÷ 47
15. 999 ÷ 37

Exercise 1.3: Solving problems

Answer the questions below, showing all your working clearly. Take particular care with any remainders.

1. There are 365 days in a year and 24 hours in a day. How many hours are there in a year?

2. How many minutes are there in a year? How many seconds are there in a year?

3. In the imperial system of weight there are 16 ounces in a pound and 14 pounds in a stone. How many ounces are there in 7 stone?

4. The Americans talk about their weight in terms of pounds only. If my friend weighs 118 pounds, what is this in stones and pounds?

5. 'Julius Caesar said with a smile
    There are one, seven, six , 'oh' yards in a mile.'
    How many yards are there in five and a half miles?

6. What is 8000 yards in miles and yards?

7. A fast food shop sells on average 176 hamburgers each hour.
    How many hamburgers does the shop sell in a seventeen hour day?

8. There are 22 pupils in my class and we all have milk at breaktime. Milk comes in cartons containing one third of a pint. If a school term lasts 12 weeks and there are five days in each week, how many pints of milk does my class drink that term?

9. Rough books come in cartons of 500
    How many classes of 22 does one carton supply if every pupil needs one rough book?

10. My teacher is photocopying our maths exam. The exam is on four sheets of paper and there are 92 pupils taking the exam.

    (a) How many sheets of paper is that?

    (b) The photocopier copies 24 sheets in a minute. How long does it take my teacher to photocopy the exam for all the pupils?

11. I earn £6 an hour. I work 8 hours a day, five days a week and there are 52 weeks in the year. How much do I earn in a year?

12. From my earnings I save £25 a week towards a holiday. If the holiday costs £672, how many weeks must I save for?

Integers

A whole number is an integer and so natural numbers are all integers. Integers, however, also include 0 (zero) and negative numbers such as −3, −2 and −1

Fractions

A fraction is any number that is not a whole number (an integer) but includes a 'bit' (a fraction) of a whole number.

Proper fractions are fractions that are less than one, such as $\frac{1}{2}$, $\frac{3}{4}$ and $\frac{27}{33}$

Improper fractions are fractions greater than one, such as, $\frac{3}{2}$, $\frac{7}{4}$ and $\frac{127}{33}$

Decimal fractions are fractions written in decimal form, such as 1.25, −3.72 and 14.67

These are usually called just 'decimals'.

Recurring decimals are decimals whose numbers after the decimal point recur in a regular pattern such as 1.333 333 333... and 0.181 181 181 181...

We will have a closer look at fractions and decimals in Chapters 2 and 3

Negative integers are the set of integers (whole numbers) that are less than zero. Negative numbers can be added, subtracted, multiplied and divided in a similar fashion to natural (positive whole) numbers. Remember what happens when using negative numbers.

For example: $4 - 4 = 0$ but $4 - (-4) = 8$

It can help to draw a number line to see what is happening.

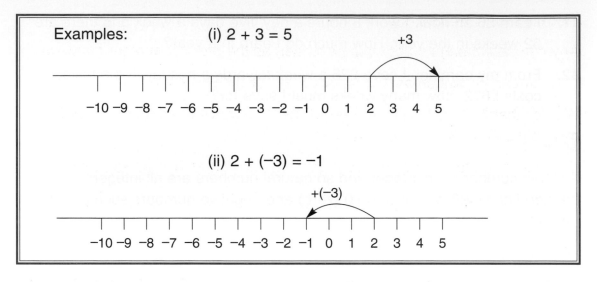

Examples: (i) 2 + 3 = 5

(ii) 2 + (−3) = −1

So   2 + 3 = 5   but   (−2) + 3 = 1   and   2 + (−3) = 2 − 3 = −1
similarly   5 − 3 = 2   but   3 − 5 = −2   and   5 − (−3) = 5 + 3 = 8
            2 × 3 = 6   but   2 × −3 = −6   and   (−2) × (−3) = 6
            6 ÷ 3 = 2   but   6 ÷ (−3) = −2   and   (−6) ÷ (−3) = 2

Exercise 1.4

Calculate these. Write down the question, any working out and the answer:

Example: −3 − (−7) = −3 + 7
                            = 4

1. −3 − 4
2. 5 − 8
3. 3 + (−6)
4. (−4) × (−4)
5. 3 × (−3)
6. −8 + 5
7. −13 − 9
8. (−3) × 7
9. 12 ÷ (−3)
10. (−24) ÷ (−8)

11. 3 × (−4)
12. 12 − (−5)
13. 14 − 8
14. −4 − 8
15. −4 − (−8)
16. 5 × (−2)
17. 16 ÷ (−4)
18. 7 − (−5)
19. −25 ÷ 5
20. (−5) × (−5)

21. 4 − 9
22. 7 − 3
23. 4 × (−3)
24. 12 ÷ (−6)
25. 5 + (−6)
26. (−5) + (−2)
27. 8 − 3
28. −8 × (−2)
29. −24 ÷ 8
30. 100 ÷ (−10)

Factors and multiples

Any natural (whole) number can be written as the product of other numbers:

24 can be written as 1 × 24, or 2 × 12, or 3 × 8 or 4 × 6

We say that 1, 2, 3, 4, 6, 8, 12 and 24 are all **factors** of 24, and that 24 is a **multiple** of 1, 2, 3, 4, 6, 8, 12 and 24

If we had to write the multiples of 5 that were less than 30 we would write:

5, 10, 15, 20, 25

Prime numbers

A prime number is a number whose only factors are itself and one, so the set of prime numbers starts: 2, 3, 5, 7, 11, 13, 17, 19, 23, 29 ...

(Note that 'one' only has '1' as a factor and so does not qualify as a prime number. It is a very special number with other properties that mean that it cannot be prime.)

Prime factors

A number can be broken down into factors that are prime numbers by successive division. These prime numbers are called the prime factors.

Example:	Find the prime factors of 210

	2	2	1	0
	3	1	0	5
	5		3	5
	7			7
				1

210 = 2 × 3 × 5 × 7

Product

A product is the **result** of a multiplication. If you are asked for **the product of 5 and 6** the answer is 30

When 210 is written like this: $210 = 2 \times 3 \times 5 \times 7$

it has been written as the **product of its prime factors.**

Exercise 1.5

1. Which of these numbers are prime numbers?
    5   17   25   27   32   37   48

2. Which of these numbers are factors of 36?
    1   2   3   4   5   6   7   9   10   36   72   360

3. Which of these numbers are multiples of 12?
    1   2   3   4   5   6   8   12   24   36

4. Which of these numbers are prime factors of 42?
    1   2   3   6   7   14   21   42

5. Which of these numbers are prime factors of 20?
    1   2   4   5   10   20

6. Which of these numbers are prime factors of 17?
    1   2   5   17   34

7. (a) What is the product of 12 and 7?
    (b) What is the sum of 13 and 3?
    (c) What is the product of 6 and 7?

8. Continue the list of prime numbers given on page 7 as far as 50

9. List all the factors of:
    (a) 65   (b) 101   (c) 19   (d) 72

10. Write the following numbers as a product of their prime factors:
    (a) 504   (b) 136   (c) 1000   (d) 945

11. (a) List all the factors of 24 and all the factors of 42
    (b) Which factors do they have in common?
    (c) Which is the highest?

This is known as the **highest common factor (H.C.F.)** of 24 and 42

12. Find the highest common factor of each of the following pairs of numbers:
    (a) 8 and 10   (b) 20 and 30   (c) 100 and 360

13. List the first 10 multiples of 4

14. List the first 10 multiples of 6

15. List the first 10 multiples of 10

16. Look at the above lists. What is the lowest number that is a multiple of:
    (a) 4 and 6   (b) 4 and 10   (c) 6 and 10

These numbers are called **lowest common multiples (L.C.M.)** of each pair of numbers.

17. Find the lowest common multiple of each of the following pairs of numbers:
    (a) 8 and 10   (b) 20 and 30   (c) 100 and 360

Highest common factors and lowest common multiples

In the previous examples H.C.F.s and L.C.M.s were quite easy to find. They could be found by inspecting the various factors and multiples. For larger numbers this is not always as simple.

Consider the question: What is the highest common factor of 210 and 375?

To answer this question each number must be broken down into its prime factors.

Example: What is the H.C.F. of 210 and 375?

2	2	1	0
3	1	0	5
5		3	5
7			7
			1

3	3	7	5
5	1	2	5
5		2	5
5			5
			1

$210 = 2 \times \mathbf{3} \times \mathbf{5} \times 7$

$375 = \mathbf{3} \times \mathbf{5} \times 5 \times 5$
$\quad\quad = 3 \times 5^3$

The common factors are 3 and 5 and so the H.C.F. is $3 \times 5 = 15$

Exercise 1.6

1.   Using your answers to q.10 in the previous exercise find the H.C.F. of each of the following pairs of numbers:
     (a) 504 and 945
     (b) 136 and 504
     (c) 945 and 1000
     (d) 136 and 945

2.   Find the H.C.F. of 330 and 175

3.   Find the H.C.F. of 132 and 165

4.   Find the H.C.F. of 812 and 638

5.   What is the largest number that divides exactly into both 1000 and 3600?

6.   Peter picks 480 apples and Piper picks 600 apples. They pack their apples into identical boxes, with no apples left over. What is the largest number of apples that each box could take?

Suppose we had been asked to find the **lowest common multiple** of 210 and 375

It is not a simple matter of looking at the first few multiples. We need to look at the prime factors again.

Example:

Find the lowest common multiple of 210 and 375

$$210 = \underline{2} \times \underline{3} \times \underline{5} \times \underline{7} \qquad 375 = 3 \times 5 \times \underline{5} \times \underline{5}$$

$$\text{L.C.M.} = 2 \times 3 \times 5 \times 5 \times 5 \times 7$$
$$= 5250$$

The lowest common multiple is the **smallest product** of the **prime** factors, repeated as necessary, of **both** numbers.

---

7.   Using your answers to q.10 in Exercise 1.5, find the L.C.M. of each of the following pairs of numbers (you can use your calculator):
     (a) 504 and 945
     (b) 136 and 504
     (c) 945 and 1000
     (d) 136 and 945

8. Find the L.C.M. of 330 and 175

9. Find the L.C.M. of 132 and 165

10. Find the L.C.M. of 812 and 638

11. What is the smallest number that is a multiple of both 20 and of 36?

12. (a) Ollie and Millie count at the same speed. Millie calls out every fourth number and Ollie every seventh number. What are the first four numbers that they call out at the same time?

    (b) Tom, Dick and Harry play the same game. Tom calls out every 20th number, Dick every 15th number and Harry every 25th number. What is the first number they all call out together?

Using a calculator

From now until your GCSE examination you will need a scientific calculator. If you do not have one already, you should ask your mathematics teacher for help in deciding which is best for you. If that is not possible, go to a shop with a large selection of calculators and ask the advice of the assistant. Make sure that you stress that you want a scientific calculator suitable for GCSE examinations, not for A levels. Some calculators do so much that they are expensive and complicated to use. Your calculator needs to have **bracket functions**, **fraction buttons**, **trigonometric** and **index functions**.

Keep your calculator manual in your Maths file!

Modern calculators are changing all the time, so you cannot expect your teacher to know exactly how each calculator works and where all the necessary buttons are. You will need to refer to the manual when you are exploring some new areas of mathematics.

Your calculator will probably look something like this:

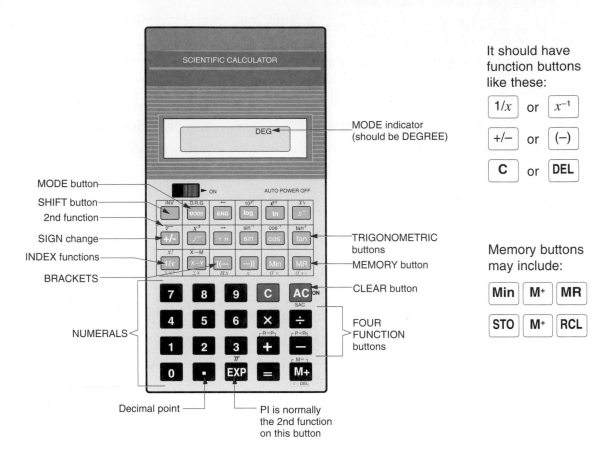

It should have function buttons like these:

$1/x$ or x^{-1}

+/− or (−)

C or DEL

MODE indicator (should be DEGREE)

MODE button
SHIFT button
2nd function
SIGN change
INDEX functions
BRACKETS
NUMERALS

TRIGONOMETRIC buttons
MEMORY button
CLEAR button
FOUR FUNCTION buttons

Memory buttons may include:

Min M+ MR

STO M+ RCL

Decimal point
PI is normally the 2nd function on this button

Exercise 1.7

Follow these simple steps to get to know your calculator. If you are stuck consult the manual and then, if you are still stuck, ask your teacher. Use the worksheet with this exercise.

1. Turn your calculator ON. Now turn it OFF, now turn it ON again.
2. Calculate 45 + 16   Write down the answer.
3. Calculate 34 537 − 12 529   Write down the answer.
4. Calculate 4 ÷ 99   Write down the answer.
5. Calculate 45 234 × 416   Write down the answer.

You have now used the four basic functions with simple calculations. Now you need to know more about your calculator.

The mode

The only mode you need to know about is normal, or computational. You will need to refer to your manual. For slightly older models pressing the mode button and then 0 leaves you in the correct mode. For newer models press the mode button and then the number under COMP. If you are in the correct mode the only **letters** on the display will be DEG. If this is not the case, ask your teacher. If you ever get peculiar answers to your calculations, then you are probably in the wrong mode!

Negative numbers

First let us see how to calculate with negative numbers.

On your calculator you should find a button like this: $\boxed{+/-}$ or $\boxed{(-)}$. The 'change sign' button $\boxed{+/-}$ changes the sign of a number just entered. The 'negative' button $\boxed{(-)}$ is pressed before a number is entered, to make it negative. These must not be confused with the $\boxed{-}$ button which is used **only** for the subtraction operation.

To answer the next two questions on the worksheet for Exercise 1.7, you need to follow one of these four key sequences, depending on the type of calculator you have:

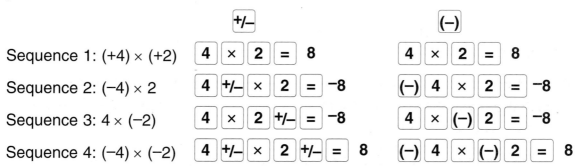

6. Calculate −45 + 16
   What is your answer? Compare this to your answer to q.2

7. Rework Exercise 1.4 using your calculator. Check that your answers agree with the answers you worked out before.

Brackets

A scientific calculator has an in-built bracket function. It will always multiply and divide before it adds and subtracts. If you want to do the calculation $4 + 5 \times 7$ you might expect the answer to be 63 but you will see that your calculator gives you 39

The calculator has calculated 5×7 and then added 4

To make the calculator work in the order of operations as written, it helps to write the calculation using brackets: $(4 + 5) \times 7$

Find the $\boxed{(\cdots}$ button or $\boxed{(}$, which is the 'open brackets' button, and press this before entering $4 + 5$

Then press the 'close brackets' button $\boxed{\cdots)}$ or $\boxed{)}$ before entering $\times 7$

This time you should obtain the answer 63

8. (a) $(3 + 6) \times 5$ (c) $(5 + 6) + (3 \times 5)$ (e) $20 \div (6 + 4)$
     (b) $9 \times (2 + 4)$ (d) $(5 - 7) \times 5$ (f) $(20 \div 5) \div (5 \times 4)$

With more complicated calculations you may need to nest brackets within brackets.

For example to calculate $2 \times \{3 \times (4 + 7) + 5\}$ you would need the following sequence of keys:

$\boxed{2}\ \boxed{\times}\ \boxed{(\cdots}\ \boxed{3}\ \boxed{\times}\ \boxed{(\cdots}\ \boxed{4}\ \boxed{+}\ \boxed{7}\ \boxed{\cdots)}\ \boxed{+}\ \boxed{5}\ \boxed{\cdots)}\ \boxed{=}$

to get the answer 76

9. (a) $4 \times \{5 \times (3 \times 6) + 5\}$ (c) $2 \times \{(5 + 6) + (3 \times 5)\}$
     (b) $9 \times \{2 + (24 \div 4) + 1\}$ (d) $20 \div \{(15 \div 5) + 2\}$

Second functions

Second functions are the functions written above the actual function button. Typically, the index functions are second functions and we will look at these in more detail in Chapter 3. Some memory buttons are also second functions.

Using the memory

When you have complicated calculations it helps to use the calculator's memory function.

To put a number in the calculator's memory you press the M+ button. To delete it press M− and to recall the number in the memory press MR. Finally to clear the memory press MC or MCl. Some of these may be second functions. You may have slightly different memory buttons on your calculator, your calculator manual should tell you about them.

The questions below (and on the worksheet) may either be answered using the calculator's memory or by using the brackets. Try doing them both ways and make sure that you get the same answer both times. If the answers are not whole numbers write down the full display on your calculator.

For example suppose you have the calculation: $\dfrac{25}{7} - \dfrac{13}{5}$

By using brackets this calculation can be rewritten as $(25 \div 7) - (13 \div 5)$

To use the memory you may follow the following steps, depending on your particular calculator:

- check the memory is clear (no M on display)
- calculate $25 \div 7$ and press M+
- calculate $13 \div 5$ and press M−
- press MR to give you the answer 0.971 428 571

Remember to clear the memory when you have finished.

10. $\dfrac{100}{12} + \dfrac{98}{6}$

11. $(312 \div 25) - (17 \times 16)$

12. $\dfrac{312 + 251}{23 \times 45}$

13. $\dfrac{158 + 753}{214 - 196}$

14. $\dfrac{451 \times 5}{263 \times 37}$

15. $\dfrac{312}{23} - \dfrac{420}{81}$

16. $\dfrac{31 \times 26}{81 - 62}$

17. $\dfrac{311}{204 \times 146}$

Simple index functions

18. Find these squares: (a) 3^2, (b) 17^2, (c) 21^2, (d) 144^2

19. Find these square roots: (a) $\sqrt{64}$, (b) $\sqrt{361}$, (c) $\sqrt{676}$, (d) $\sqrt{64\,516}$

20. Calculate $\frac{1}{8}$. (Use the reciprocal button either $\boxed{\frac{1}{x}}$ or $\boxed{x^{-1}}$. It may be a second function.) Now push the reciprocal button again, then again and again. What do you notice? Try this with some other numbers.

Calculator problems

For some questions working out has to be done in stages. When you are using a calculator it is important that each stage of your working out is written down clearly. Although the calculator will calculate correctly, it will only calculate according to your instructions. Therefore, if you enter the wrong sequence of key presses, the calculator will give the wrong answer!

Exercise 1.8

1. Write out your 17 times table. To do this put 17 in the memory, (17 $\boxed{M+}$) and then $2 \times \boxed{MR}$ =, $3 \times \boxed{MR}$ = etc.

$1 \times 17 = 17$
$2 \times 17 = 34$
$3 \times 17 = ...$
$4 \times 17 = ...$

2. The number 66 can be made by adding 4 consecutive numbers. What are they?

3. The number 1716 is the result of multiplying 3 consecutive numbers. What are they?

4. Without doing the calculations what size of answer would you expect for the following (choose A, B or C)?

(a) 98×48

A: About 5000
B: About 4000
C: About 2000

(b) $72\,954 \div 24$

A: about 300
B: about 3000
C: about 4000

(c) $11\,532 - 7312 + 534 - 1826$

A: Between 10 000 and 12 000
B: Between 2000 and 4000
C: Between 1000 and 2000

Now work them out properly and see which estimates were best.

5. It is easy to press the wrong button. You need to check that the answer is about the right size and starts or ends in the correct digit. In the four calculations below, state how you know that the answer must be wrong:
    (a) $321 \times 3 \quad = 1926$
    (b) $1234 - 692 = 1926$
    (c) $80\,892 \div 24 = 1926$
    (d) $241 \times 9 \quad = 1926$

6. The most common mistake is to press an adjacent key (for example 4 instead of 1) or to switch round two digits (for example press 21 instead of 12). Can you find which mistake was made in each of the four calculations above?

7. Using the memory efficiently can save you a lot of time. Here is a number pattern to investigate. The pattern uses the same calculation in every line. If you store the answer to that calculation in your memory [M+] and then recall it [MR] to use it again, you will save time:
    $137 \times 1 \times 73 =$
    $137 \times 2 \times 73 =$
    $137 \times 3 \times 73 =$
    $137 \times 4 \times 73 =$

    How far can you continue the pattern until the pattern in the result changes? Predict your answer and then test it.

8. Here is a similar pattern. Investigate this one:
    $143 \times 1 \times 7 =$
    $143 \times 2 \times 7 =$
    $143 \times 3 \times 7 =$
    $143 \times 4 \times 7 =$

    How far can you continue this pattern until the pattern in the result changes? Predict your answer and then test it.

9. Consider this calculation: $\dfrac{515 + 139}{342 - 124}$

    There are two ways of calculating this on your calculator:
    (a) Use the memory function: Subtract the bottom two numbers, then store the answer in the memory. Add the top numbers together and then divide by the number in the memory.
    (b) Use the brackets function by calculating $(515 + 139) \div (342 - 124)$

    Did you get the same answer both times?

10. (Use the worksheet for this question.) Captain H_2O has a new challenge! He has to visit various space stations. He must visit them in the correct order if he is to complete the challenge successfully. If he does not, then he fries! His instructions are in the form of mathematical calculations. Starting from Earth he has to calculate the correct answer. The answer will tell him where to go next. Can you help him complete the challenge?

Most calculators have a **constant function**. This repeats a function over and over again every time you press the = sign.

Try entering 17 then + and + again, now push = again and again. If your calculator does not do this try entering 17 × 1 =, store the answer by pressing ANS and then type + 17, now punch = again and again. You should have the 17 times table you worked out in q.1

11. **Famous chess board problem**

A philosopher helped his ruler in a time of great difficulty and was offered anything he wanted as a reward. The philosopher said he simply wanted one grain of rice on the 1st square of a chessboard, two grains on the second, four on the third, eight on the fourth and so on, doubling each time. The ruler laughed and was pleased that he did not have to pay out lots of money. Use the constant function (x2) to work out how many grains of rice were on the 20th square, and why the ruler soon stopped laughing!

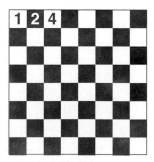

12. If you had a piece of paper 0.15 mm thick and folded it in half 50 times how high would it be?

Exercise 1.9: Extension questions

Let us look a bit more at the reciprocal button and see how it can help us solve problems.

1. Look at the calculation $\dfrac{1}{3^2 + 4^2}$

Work this out first using either the memory or the brackets function on your calculator.

Now try just working out the bottom line. You should get the result 25

Now press the reciprocal button $\boxed{\dfrac{1}{x}}$. Your answer should be the same as before.

> Your working for the above should look like:
>
> either $\dfrac{1}{3^2 + 4^2} = 1 \div 25$ or $\dfrac{1}{3^2 + 4^2} = \dfrac{1}{25}$
>
> $= 0.04$ $= 0.04$

As your calculations become more complicated it is a good idea to write down each stage as you go through it. Record any results your calculator gives you in case you need to use them again.

2. Try calculating the following in two ways. Use the reciprocal button for one of the ways.

    (a) $\dfrac{1}{5 \div 25}$ (b) $\dfrac{1}{0.2 \times 0.4}$ (c) $\dfrac{1}{0.1 - 0.06}$

3. For a calculation such as $\dfrac{5^2}{3^2 + 4^2}$ you should work out the bottom line first,

    $3^2 + 4^2$ and then find its reciprocal $\dfrac{1}{3^2 + 4^2}$

    Finally multiply by the top. What is the answer?

4. Try calculating these with the reciprocal button.

    (a) $\dfrac{5}{5 \div 25}$ (b) $\dfrac{8}{0.2 \times 0.4}$ (c) $\dfrac{4}{0.1 - 0.06}$

5. Sometimes we need to find the reciprocal of a reciprocal like this:

    $\dfrac{1}{\frac{1}{4}}$ Try this for other numbers.

6. What is special about the reciprocals of multiples of 11?

7. The ancient Egyptians found reciprocals very useful because they could write only **unit** fractions such as $\frac{1}{5}$ and not multiple fractions such as $\frac{3}{5}$

$\frac{3}{5}$ had to be written as the sum of **unit** fractions.

Can you find which 3 **different** unit fractions add up to $\frac{3}{5}$?

Slopes are given as a fraction, so a slope of $\frac{1}{10}$ means a slope of 1 in 10

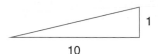

For every 10 you go along, you will go up 1

8. From a papyrus written in about 1650 BC we are told that the slope of one pyramid is $\frac{1}{2} + \frac{1}{5} + \frac{1}{50}$

What is the value of this?

9. Look at this reciprocal series: $\quad 1, \quad \dfrac{1}{1+1} \quad \dfrac{1}{1+\dfrac{1}{1+1}} \quad \dfrac{1}{1+\dfrac{1}{1+\dfrac{1}{1+1}}}, \quad \ldots$

Work out the value of each fraction. Try continuing the series. Write down your answer each time to 3 significant figures. Stop when you get the same answer every time. What is the answer?

As speed increases then the time taken to travel the same distance, or to do the same action, decreases.

10. I am filling a tank with a pipe that will fill the whole tank in 10 minutes. After 1 minute the tank is $\frac{1}{10}$th full.

(a) If I use a different pipe to fill the tank – a pipe that would fill the tank in 5 minutes – how full will the tank be after one minute?

(b) If I turn on both pipes write down how full the tank will be after:
(i) one minute.
(ii) two minutes.

(c) How long does it take to fill the tank (from empty) using both pipes?

(d) If the first pipe fills the tank in x minutes and the second in y minutes, write an expression in x and y to give the time it takes to fill the tank.

11. An intergalactic traveller is trapped in an ancient water torture tank. The evil alien switches on two taps. One fills the tank on its own in 9 minutes, and the other fills the tank on its own in 6 minutes. It takes the intergalactic traveller 3 minutes and 30 seconds to inflate his oxygen-making mask. Is he in time or does he drown first?

Exercise 1.10: Summary exercise

Answer the questions 1-10 mentally:

1. $52 + 33$

2. $65 - 41$

3. 12×8

4. $144 \div 12$

5. $134 + 59$

6. $124 - 38$

7. 108×4

8. $116 \div 4$

9. 148×3

10. $138 \div 6$

11. Answer these without a calculator. Write down the question and any necessary working:
(a) $-7 + (-4)$
(b) $4 - (-7)$
(c) $(-3) \times (-4)$
(d) $14 \div (-2)$
(e) $-4 + 12$
(f) $3 + (-8)$
(g) $15 \times (-5)$
(h) $6 - 9$
(i) $-3 + (-9)$
(j) $(-18) \div (-6)$

12. Which of these numbers are prime numbers?
1   4   5   9   13   24   31   99

13. Write down all the factors of 28

14. Which of these are multiples of 6?

    1   2   3   4   6   12   15   30

15. Write down the H.C.F of: (a) 16 and 24   (b) 252 and 714

16. Write dow the L.C.M. of: (a) 8 and 10   (b) 168 and 462

Write down your working clearly for the next three questions 17-19. Do not use a calculator.

17. On an intergalactic expedition I have packed 25 space pods weighing 12 kg each, 38 space suits weighing 28 kg each and 9 extra-terrestrial repellent missiles weighing 135 kg each. Have I packed more than the 2500 kg limit?

18. (a) The mass of one astronaut plus his kit is 84 kg. The total mass allowance on the space station is 4000 kg. If there are 23 astronauts how much mass allowance is there left?

(b) One quarter of that mass allowance is for food. Each astronaut is allowed 1 kg of food per day. How many days can the astronauts survive on their food allowance?

You may use a calculator for the remaining questions.

19. $\dfrac{319}{29} - \dfrac{420}{19}$

20. $\dfrac{35 - 17}{25 + 47}$

21. $\{2(74 - 26) - 3(25 + 17)\}$

22. $2 \times \{5 \times (6 + 17) - 4\}$

23. $\dfrac{214 + 672}{32 \times 45}$

24. $\dfrac{1412 - 987}{612 - 284}$

End of chapter 1 activity: Calculator puzzles and games
Guess the number

Ask a friend to think of a number between ten and ninety-nine. Ask them to write it down. Then, using a calculator, tell them to:

Double it	× 2 =	
Add 6	+ 6 =	
Divide by 2	÷ 2 =	
Add 2	× 2 =	
Multiply by 8	× 8 =	
Subtract 40	− 4 0 =	

Now ask them the result. On your calculator enter the result and then just divide by 8   You will have the original number!

Down to zero

Find the random number button on your calculator (usually a second function marked RAN). If this a three figure decimal then multiply by 100 to make a three digit number.

The game is to see how many stages it takes you to reach zero. At each stage you can add, subtract, multiply or divide by a **single** digit number (the result at each stage must be a whole number).

Example:

	0.471
× 1 0 0 =	471
÷ 3 =	157
− 4 =	153
÷ 9 =	17
− 9 =	8
− 8 =	0

Try a race with a friend. You will have to record every stage of your calculation!

Countdown

Make 14 cards. Mark one of the following numbers on each card: 100, 75, 50, 25, 10, 9, 8, 7, 6, 5, 4, 3, 2, 1

Pick 6 of them at random. Then use the calculator to give you a three figure random number. Can you make that number from your six numbers on the cards by adding, subtracting, multiplying or dividing as necessary? Can you beat the rest of the class?

Finding remainders

Your teacher has asked you what the remainder is when you divide 1760 by 19

Because you are not very good at long division you secretly use your calculator.

But you get the answer 92.631579 which is not much help.

Here's what you do:

subtract the whole number answer	$(- 92 =)$
multiply the decimal remainder by the divisor	$(\times 19 =)$
you get the remainder !	(12)

Try this for some other long division questions. You should nearly always end up with a whole number answer (or you could check with long division of course!)

Calculating Easter

As you know Easter does not always fall on the same date. It may seem to be chosen randomly but it is actually based on the phases of the moon. The Sun, Earth and Moon line up once every 19 years.

The date of Easter Saturday is worked out like this:

To find which phase the moon is in: **Divide the year by nineteen**

Let the answer be *A* and the whole number remainder be *B*

Find which century the year is in: **Divide the year by 100**

Let the answer be *C* and the whole number remainder be *D*

Check for leap years: **Divide *C* by 4**

Let the answer be *E* and the whole number remainder be *F*

Calculate (*C* + 8) ÷ 25

Let the answer be *G* and ignore the remainder   **Calculate (*C* + 1 − *G*) ÷ 3**

Let the answer be *H* and ignore the remainder

Calculate (19 x *B*) + (*C* + 15) − (*E* + *H*)

Let the answer be *J*   **Calculate *J* ÷ 30**

Ignore the answer but let the whole number remainder be *K*   **Calculate *D* ÷ 4**

Let the answer be *L* and the whole number remainder be *M*

Calculate (2 x *F*) + (2 x *L*) + 32 −(*K* + *M*)

Let the answer be *N*   **Calculate *N* ÷ 7**

Ignore the answer but let the whole number remainder be *P*

Calculate *B* + (11 x *K*) + (22 x *P*)

Let the answer be *Q*   **Calculate *Q* ÷ 451**

Let the answer be *R* and ignore the remainder

Calculate (*K* + *P* + 114) − (7 x *R*)

Let the answer be *S*   **Calculate *S* ÷ 31**

Let the answer be *X* and the whole number remainder be *Y*

X is the month and *Y* plus 1 is the day!

(wheeew!)

Chapter 2: Decimals

In the last chapter our calculations involved whole numbers. However, in reality, calculations rarely involve just whole numbers.

In the real world we come across numbers when we consider distances, weights, time and money. Money, as we know, involves decimals, and if we are going to be able to deal successfully with our own money then we need to be able to calculate with decimals.

The Penny and the first taxation

The decimal currency we use today in Britain was introduced in 1971. Before that we had 20 shillings to the pound and 12 pennies to the shilling, as well as other coins such as florins and half crowns. However the basic unit of currency was still the penny.

The name *penny* comes from the Old English *pennige* which shares its roots with the German *pfennig*. The coins were similar in size and weight to the continental *deniers* of the period, named after the Roman denomination *denarius*. It was for this reason that the abbreviation for the penny was a *d*.

The silver penny was introduced to England, probably by Offa, the powerful King of Mercia, about 755/780 AD, though early pennies also exist of the two-little known kings of Kent, Heacberht and Ecgberht, of about the same period. Anglo-Saxon silver pennies were the currency used to pay the Danegeld, the money paid to the Vikings by Britain to stop them ravaging the country.

Interestingly Danegeld was not paid once, but several times, and more Anglo-Saxon pennies of the decades around the first millennium have been found in Denmark than in England. It is estimated that the total amount of silver paid in Danegeld between 990 and 1015 was about 93 tons of silver, worth about £250 000 at the time and equivalent to over a billion pounds in today's money.

Even when the Vikings had stopped invading, subsequent kings of Britain continued to collect gelds, or taxes, from the population. Sadly the taxes we pay now are counted in thousands of pounds, not pennies!

Before 1971, a single penny was always known as one penny. In 1971 the penny became **one new penny** and there were **100 new pence** to the **pound**. The **new** was eventually dropped.

You may come across some other words for amounts of money. Some are the names of coins and notes and some are slang. Here are some of the most common – you could impress your grandparents by knowing these (and they might reward you with a copper, or two!)

Copper:	An old penny (also, any bronze coin – farthing or halfpenny)
Groat:	A considerable sum of money in Edward III's to Henry VI's time (originally a fourpenny piece!)
Tanner:	Sixpence
Bob:	Shilling (12 pence)

And here are some other references to the old money, some of which we still use today:

Quid:	£1
Guinea:	21 shillings (this is still used today in horse racing)
Fiver:	£5
Tenner:	£10
Pony:	£25
Half a ton:	£50
Ton:	£100
Monkey:	£500
Grand or 'k':	£1000

Calculating with money: Adding and subtracting

Remember when adding and subtracting money to make sure you keep the decimal points underneath each other!

Exercise 2.1

1. I am sent to buy a loaf of bread costing 65p and a cake costing £1.57
   What change do I have from a £5 note?

2. I have saved £24.75
   How much more do I need in order to buy a computer game costing £39.99?

3. It costs £45.56 more to travel from London to Leeds by train than by coach. If the coach price is £19.99, how much is it by train?

4. In a sponsored walk Patsy raised £25.87 more than Priscilla. If Patsy raised £65.42, how much did Priscilla make?

5. My three friends and I turn out our pockets. Between us we have three 20p pieces, four 50p pieces, five £1 coins and one £2 coin plus fifteen 2p coins and three 1p coins. How much do we have altogether?

6. My change from a £2 coin after buying 'Gamebusters' magazine was 83p. How much was the magazine?

7. I started with £10, spent £2.79 on a Smileymeal and then hired a video. I went home with £4.64
   How much was the video hire?

8. A basic pizza is £4.25, and extra toppings are 36p each. If I order a pizza with three extra toppings how much change will I have from £10?

9. To send my grandfather his birthday present I bought a padded envelope costing £1.56, and three stamps. I have £2.72 left from my £5
   How much were the stamps?

10. Before going on the school ski trip I buy sun cream costing £4.35, toothpaste costing £1.42 and a pair of socks costing £5.39
    How much change do I have from a £20 note?

Multiplying

Usually when we multiply we expect to get a larger answer. After all, if one ball costs £1.25 then three balls will cost £3.75

Now consider the following problem:

Find the area of a rectangle 40 cm by 30 cm.

The answer is 1200 cm², but suppose the question had asked for the answer to be given in square metres.

First of all we change the units to metres, and the calculation becomes:

Area $= 0.4 \times 0.3$
$= 0.12$ m²

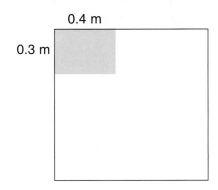

0.4 m

0.3 m

The area is 0.12 square metre, or 12 hundredths of the whole square metre.

If we multiply a positive number by a number less than one, we get a smaller answer.

- If we multiply tenths by tenths, we will get hundredths.

- If we multiply tenths by hundredths, we get thousandths etc.

Another way of thinking about this is to look at the number of numbers after the decimal point. In our example we had:

Area $= 0.4 \times 0.3$ m
$= 0.12$ m²

There are 2 digits after the decimal point, so there are 2 digits after the decimal point in the answer

If you use this rule, remember to be careful when multiplying by 5:

$0.4 \times 0.5 = 0.20$ but we write this as 0.2

Exercise 2.2

Find the answers to these multiplications:

Examples:	(i) $0.25 \times 5 = 1.25$
	(ii) $0.35 \times 0.3 = 0.105$
	(iii) $1.5 \times 1.2 = 1.80 = 1.8$

1. 0.4×0.6

2. 0.5×0.06

3. 0.02×0.006

4. 0.07×3

5. 0.5×0.2

6. 0.11×0.4

7. 0.26×0.3

8. 0.52×3

9. 0.12×5

10. 2.4×0.4

11. 1.4×1.2

12. 2.7×0.4

13. 3.5×2

14. 0.5×0.4

15. 2.5×6

16. 4.8×5

17. 5.5×0.12

18. 2.01×0.07

19. 0.005×0.4

20. 0.305×0.3

Dividing decimals

When we divide a decimal by a number, we follow the same principles as used in normal division:

Here is a straightforward division: $14 \div 2 = 7$
And here is one with a decimal: $1.4 \div 2 = 0.7$

Sometimes we have to put in extra zeros, so that we can keep dividing until we have a final answer.

Example:

$$0.2 \div 4 = 0.20 \div 4$$
$$= 0.05$$

Dividing by decimals

Dividing by a decimal needs more thought:

How many halves are there in 4
i.e. What is $4 \div 0.5$?
We know the answer Is 8
We can work this out simply because we know that $40 \div 5$ is 8

When the question is more complicated (for example $40 \div 0.005$), it is very difficult to work out exactly where the decimal point goes in the answer.

Is it 0.08, 0.8, 8, 80, 800, 8000 or 80 000?

Because dividing by a decimal is difficult, it is better if we try to make it simple by first eliminating the decimal point. Here is an example to show you what we mean:

Firstly, write $40 \div 0.005$ as $\dfrac{40}{0.005}$

Now eliminate the decimal point by multiplying 0.005 by 1000 to make 5

Remember that whatever you do to the bottom of the fraction, you must also do to the top. So, now multiply the 40 by 1000 as well.

$$\text{Example:} \qquad 40 \div 0.005 \qquad = \frac{40}{0.005} \times \frac{1000}{1000}$$

$$= \frac{40\,000}{5}$$

$$= 8000$$

That's much easier!

Exercise 2.3

Do the first 10 in your head but check by multiplication that your decimal point is in the right place.

$$\text{Example: } 6 \div 0.2 = 30 \qquad \text{Check } 0.2 \times 30 = 6$$

1. 18 ÷ 0.3

2. 0.24 ÷ 0.4

3. 1.5 ÷ 0.03

4. 3.6 ÷ 0.12

5. 0.042 ÷ 0.07

6. 3.2 ÷ 0.8

7. 320 ÷ 0.08

8. 0.0049 ÷ 0.07

9. 180 ÷ 0.06

10. 240 ÷ 0.008

You may need to write the working out in full for the following:

13. 2.04 ÷ 0.6

14. 0.000 204 ÷ 0.06

15. 320 ÷ 0.5

16. 0.402 ÷ 0.006

17. 280 ÷ 0.007

18. 0.0603 ÷ 0.09

19. 4.005 ÷ 0.015

20. 0.0036 ÷ 1.8

21. 480 ÷ 0.6

22. 0.001 08 ÷ 0.12

Now that you have practised the arithmetic try this next exercise:

Exercise 2.4: More money problems

1. I earn £4.50 a week by washing Dad's car. What do I earn in 12 weeks?

2. 5 of us share £19 equally. How much money does each of us get?

3. I buy 6 cans of cola at 45p each and 3 hot dogs costing £1.24
    How much do I spend in total?

4. I save 45p each week. What do I save in a year? (There are 52 weeks in a year.)

5. My Mother bought 6 bargain packs of pork chops at £2.35 each. What change did she have from a £20 note?

6. I had £1.64 change after buying 8 identical pencils with a £5 note. How much did each pencil cost?

7. What is the total cost of 0.3 kg of tomatoes at £2.40 a kilo and 0.6 kg of potatoes at £1.25 per kg?

8. How many cans of limeade costing 45p can I buy with a £10 note? If I buy as many as possible how much change will I get?

9. My Dad puts 31 litres of petrol in the car's tank. The petrol costs 98p per litre. How much change does he have from a £50 note?

10. At the school fete my class sold 15 large cakes at £2.45 each and 56 small cakes at 45p each. How much money did we make in total?

11. We bought a pack of 24 cans of drink for £9 and sold them at 60p each. How much profit did we make?

12. There was a broken window in the classroom. No one owned up to breaking it, so we had to divide the cost of a replacement window equally between all of us. There were 24 of us in the class and the replacement window cost £69.60. How much did each of us have to pay?

13. We all went to an amusement park. The total entry cost for 5 of us came to £24   Later on, 4 of us, including myself, had an ice cream costing £3.24 in total. Three more friends joined us for lunch and we spent £42 in total. What was my share of the cost of the day out?

14. I started with £20, bought four drinks costing 80p each and then five tickets for the cinema. I had 80p change. How much was each cinema ticket?

Working with other metric units

As we know, the metric system is based on the number 1000 such that:

- We measure length in **metres (m)**
10 millimetres (mm)	= 1 centimetre (cm)
100 centimetres (cm)	= 1 metre (m)
1000 millimetres (mm)	= 1 metre (m)
1000 metres (m)	= 1 kilometre (km)

- We measure mass in **grams (g)**
1000 milligrams (mg)	= 1 gram (g)
1000 grams (g)	= 1 kilogram (kg)
1000 kilograms (kg)	= 1 tonne (t)

- We measure volume in **litres (l)**
1000 cubic centimetres (cm^3)	= 1 litre (l)
1000 millilitres (ml)	= 1 litre (l)
100 centilitres (cl)	= 1 litre (l)

Exercise 2.5

1. I pour the contents of 4 jugs equally into 100 glasses. Each jug contains 5 l of liquid. How many centilitres of liquid are in each glass?

2. How many boys each weighing 45 kg does it take to balance an elephant weighing 3.6 tonnes?

3. There are approximately 400 peanuts in a kg. How many peanuts does it take to balance a car weighing 1.5 tonnes?

4. Which is further, 4 laps of 3.5 km or 20 laps of 700 m?

5. I decide to stand some objects on top of each other. I first put a box of height 0.5 m on the floor. On top of this I lay a book of thickness 3.7 cm, and on top of the book I place a magazine, of thickness 9 mm. How high is the magazine from the floor, in cm?

6. What is better value, 500 ml of shampoo costing £2.25 or 120 ml of shampoo costing 60p?

7. My car travels 46 kilometres on 1 litre of fuel. How far will I be able to travel after I spend £30 filling it up with fuel costing 92p per litre?

8. I reckon that we need to each have 175 millilitres of water for our trip. If 40 of us are going and water comes in bottles of 2.5 litres, how many bottles must I buy?

9. If a female elephant stands 2.4 m high, how much taller is she than a mouse, 18 mm high? Give your answer in mm.

10. When keeping goldfish, the rule of thumb is that you need about 1.6 litres of water to every cm length of fish. If you went mad and decided to keep a blue shark of length 4 metres, how many litres of water would you need in its tank?

More about area

Earlier (on page 29) we looked at the area of a rectangle 0.4 m by 0.3 m and saw it was 0.12m² in area. Now try to answer the questions in the next exercise:

Exercise 2.6

1. A rectangle 0.2 m by 5 m has an area of 1 square metre. What other rectangles have an area of exactly 1 square metre? Can you find five?

2. Write down the measurements of 5 rectangles each with an area of 2 m².

3. A rectangle with an area of 4 m² has one side of 0.5 m. What is the length of the other side?

4. A rectangle with an area of 4 cm² has one side of 20 cm. What is the length of the other side?

5. A square has an area of 0.09 m². What are the lengths of its sides?

For the following questions you need to remember the formula for the area of a triangle:

$$\text{Area of a triangle} = \frac{bh}{2}$$

Remember to check the units of measurement. Before you calculate the area of anything, you must make sure the units are the same. If you have a question where you need to write the answer in different units from those you are given, it is much easier to change the units first.

6. A triangle has a base of 40 cm and a height of 1.2 m. What is the area of this triangle, in m²?

7. Find the height, in cm, of a triangle with an area of 14 cm² and a base of 7 cm.

8. Find the base, in cm, of a triangle with an area of 12 cm² and a height of 4.5 cm.

9. Find the base, in cm, of a triangle with an area of 2 m² and a height of 40 cm.

10. Find the height, in cm, of a triangle with an area of 2.4 m² and a base of 250 cm.

Estimating

There are times when an exact answer to a problem is not needed.

For example, if I had a 1 metre plank and wanted to cut it into 3 equal pieces, I would calculate an exact measurement for each length of 0.333333 m.

In reality, however, it would be very difficult to cut a plank to a huge degree of accuracy, so I need only calculate the length to a sensible number of decimal places. In this example, a length to the nearest millimetre would be sensible, so the answer is 0.333 m.

Exercise 2.7

Use your calculator to work out the solutions to each of your answers. Give each answer to a sensible degree of accuracy.

1.   A length of ribbon 2 metres long is cut into 9 equal pieces. How long is each piece of ribbon?

2.   A class of 25 is divided into 3 groups, of about the same size, for a class outing. How many pupils are in each group?

3.   I have a jug containing 2.4 litres of squash. It needs to be shared between 18 boys. How much does each boy get?

4   A commercial traveller drives about 400 miles each day. How many days will it take him to travel round his distribution network of 3500 miles?

5.   Revise your answer to question 4 to take into account that the commercial traveller only works 5 days a week. At the weekend (Saturday and Sunday) he has to stay in a hotel. Assuming he starts his travels on a Monday, how many days will it take him to complete his journey?

6.   A delivery of 10 000 kg of builders sand is divided between 12 houses. How much sand is delivered to each house?

7.   If there are 39.375 inches to a metre, and 12 inches in a foot, how many metres are there in 10 feet?

8. When I leave the top off a bottle of cleaning fluid, about 8% evaporates in 1 hour. If I start with 240 ml, how much is left 1 hour later?

9. The population of the country of Geramania has increased by 7% over the last decade. If the population was 1.5 million 10 years ago, what is it now?

10. The local electrical shop is advertising 15% off everything in its sale. If a personal CD player cost £79 before the sale, what will it cost now?

Degree of accuracy

When you have an answer to a problem that is not exact, it is important to say how accurate your answer is.

There are two possible ways of doing this, either by using significant figures or decimal places. In some cases it may be sensible to give the answer to the nearest whole number or to the nearest 100, 1000 and so on.

Revision of decimal places and significant figures

Decimal places

The 1st decimal place is the first number after the decimal point.
The 2nd decimal place is the 2nd number after the decimal point, and so on.

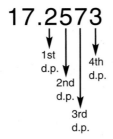

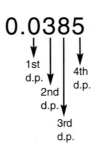

Significant figures

The 1st significant figure is the first non-zero figure.
The 2nd significant figure is the next number, whatever its value, the third is next and so on.

17.2573

1st s.f.
2nd s.f.
3rd s.f.
4th s.f.

0.000 452

1st s.f.
2nd s.f.
3rd s.f.

When rounding to a number of decimal places or significant figures we use the same rule as rounding to the nearest ten, or to the nearest 2 decimal places.

First consider the figure required. If the number to the right of this figure is 5 or more, then the figure is rounded up; if it is 4 or less, it stays the same.

17.2573 = 17.3 (to 1 d.p.)   17.2573 = 20 (to 1 s.f.)
17.2573 = 17.26 (to 2 d.p.)   17.2573 = 17 (to 2 s.f.)
17.2573 = 17.257 (to 3 d.p.)   17.2573 = 17.3 (to 3 s.f.)
                                   17.2573 = 17.26 (to 4 s.f.)

0.0385 = 0 (to 1 d.p.)   0.0385 = 0.04 (to 1 s.f.)
0.0385 = 0.04 (to 2 d.p.)   0.0385 = 0.039 (to 2 s.f.)
0.0385 = 0.039 (to 3 d.p.)   0.0385 = 0.0385 (to 3 s.f.)

Exercise 2.8

Write these numbers to the decimal places or significant figures specified:

1. Write 516.1528 to:
    (a) 1 s.f.   (b) 1 d.p.   (c) 3 s.f.   (d) 3 d.p.

2. Write 0.13 652 to:
    (a) 2 s.f.   (b) 2 d.p.   (c) 4 s.f.   (d) 4 d.p.

3. Write 9.3568 to:
    (a) 1 s.f.   (b) 1 d.p.   (c) 3 s.f.   (d) 3 d.p.

4. Write 0.083 27 5 to:
    (a) 1 s.f.   (b) 1 d.p.   (c) 4 s.f.   (d) 4 d.p.

5. Write 1.9999 to:
    (a) 1 s.f.   (b) 1 d.p.   (c) 3 s.f.   (d) 3 d.p.

6. Write 10.909 09 to:
    (a) 2 s.f.   (b) 1 d.p.   (c) 4 s.f.   (d) 3 d.p.

Using your calculator

When you are using your calculator it is very easy to miss out a '0' or the decimal point. So, before you do anything, it is good practice to **estimate** the expected answer. When you then do your calculation on the calculator, you should be able to spot any error immediately.

The easiest way to estimate is firstly to write each number to one significant figure and then to work out the answer. Give your estimated answer to one significant figure.

Examples:

(i) Estimate: $0.48 \times 3212 \approx 0.5 \times 3000$
$$\approx 1500$$
$$\approx 2000$$

using the calculator: $0.48 \times 3212 = 1541.76$

which is 1542 to the nearest whole number

(ii) Estimate: $\dfrac{34.12}{621 \times 0.048} \approx \dfrac{30}{600 \times 0.05}$
$$\approx \dfrac{30}{30}$$
$$\approx 1$$

using the calculator: $\dfrac{34.12}{621 \times 0.048} = 1.1446 \ldots$

In example (ii) above, it is important that the calculator keys are pressed in the correct sequence. This is how it should be done:

$34.12 \div 621 \div 0.048 =$ or $34.12 \div (621 \times 0.048) =$

It is very easy to make a simple error using a calculator, so be careful!

REMEMBER
The calculator will only give the correct answer if you enter the correct calculation.

Exercise 2.9

Estimate the answer to each of the following questions. Show all your working clearly and give your estimated answer to one significant figure. Then calculate the accurate answer using your calculator.

1. $925 \times 0.00\,521$

2. $348 \div 0.056$

3. 0.053×0.9873

4. $0.836 \div 38$

5. $\dfrac{291}{0.721 \times 0.683}$

6. $\dfrac{38.3 \times 5.42}{0.0572}$

7. $\dfrac{3.450 \times 24.98}{0.721 \times 382}$

8. $\dfrac{9.34}{0.251} + \dfrac{361}{0.732}$

9. $\dfrac{0.0053}{0.921} - \dfrac{16.8}{59\,132}$

10. $\dfrac{34.12 \times 0.671}{0.045} + \dfrac{0.0124}{0.681 \times 37.3}$

11. $\dfrac{21.7 \times 3.8}{0.47 \times 0.51} - \dfrac{0.69 \times 312}{0.71 \times 381}$

12. $\dfrac{0.31 \times 481}{38} \div \dfrac{491}{0.68 \times 415}$

Exercise 2.10: Summary exercise

1. I buy 8 lemons at 45p each and then 2 ice creams at 99p each. How much change do I have from a £10 note?

2. (a) 0.3×0.4 (b) 0.5×0.06 (c) 1.2×0.03 (d) 0.05×0.4

3. (a) $20 \div 0.4$ (b) $3 \div 0.6$ (c) $32 \div 0.8$ (d) $2.4 \div 0.04$

4. I buy 4 goldfish, each 2.2 cm long. If I need 1.6 litres of water for each cm of fish, how many litres of water should the tank I buy hold?

5. Give the measurements of 5 rectangles each with an area of 1.5 m².

6. (a) What is the area in m² of a triangle, with a base of 40 cm and a height of 1.1 m?
   (b) What is the base in cm of a triangle, with an area of 1 m² and a height of 25 cm?

7. Give these numbers to (i) 2 d.p. (ii) 3 d.p.
   (a) 4.254 9   (b) 12.045 83   (c) 4.009 99

8. Give these numbers to (i) 2 s.f. (ii) 3 s.f.
    (a) 143 342   (b) 0.045 673   (c) 49 999

9. (a) Estimate your answers to the following, showing all your working
        clearly. Give your answers to one significant figure.

    (i) $\dfrac{34.8 + 51.2}{0.49 \times 39.9}$ (ii) $\dfrac{312.3 \times 0.789}{41.3 \times 0.052}$

    (b) Now work out the answer to (i) and (ii) exactly. Give the full values
        shown on your calculator.

End of chapter 2 activity: The national elf problem

You might not know this but there is a national shortage of elves. Santa is
having a real problem. His recruitment drive is not bringing them in. Why can
he not recruit more elves?

Santa and Rudolph decide to go on an elf drive and find out how many elves
there actually are.

Here is the result of their first survey of a typical elf residential area:

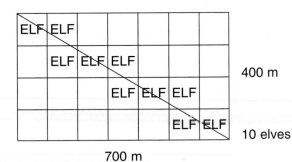

400 m

10 elves

700 m

They found that elves are peculiar people. They like being near one or two other elves but not too close to too many. Santa and Rudolph discovered that they find a rectangle of land which they then divide into a grid of 100 m squares. They then lay an elf communication line in a diagonal from the top left to the bottom right of the rectangle. One elf then lives in every square crossed by the communication line.

Here is a smaller elf gathering:

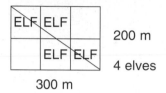

200 m

4 elves

300 m

Write down how many elves live in a rectangle:
    (a) 200 m by 200 m
    (b) 300 m by 400 m

Now investigate the problem further and find how many elves live in a rectangle:
    (c) 800 m by 900 m
    (d) $100x$ metres by $100y$ metres.

(Government Elf Warning: This does not have a straightforward answer!)

Chapter 3: Fractions

Fractions have been around for centuries. In *So you really want to learn Maths Book 2* we learnt about how the Babylonians and Egyptians used fractions.

The Egyptians had a particularly interesting way of writing fractions based on the following myth:

Horus was the son of two of the main gods in Egyptian mythology, Isis (the nature goddess) and Osiris (the god of the underworld). He was considered the god of the sky, of light, and of goodness. Horus had an evil uncle (Seth) who murdered his father, Osiris. Horus battled with Seth to avenge his father's murder. During the fight, Seth plucked out Horus' left eye and tore it apart. Thoth (god of wisdom and magic) found the eye, pieced it together, as if it were just a cracked grain of barley, and added some magic. He returned the eye to Horus, who in turn gave it to his murdered father Osiris, thereby bringing him back to life. Thereafter Horus defeated Seth.

Each part of the eye became a hieroglyphic sign for a fraction used in measuring out bushels of grain:

◁ for $\frac{1}{2}$; ○ for $\frac{1}{4}$; ⌒ for $\frac{1}{8}$; ◿ for $\frac{1}{16}$; ↺ for $\frac{1}{32}$; ⥾ for $\frac{1}{64}$.

When the fraction symbols are put together, the restored eye looks like this:

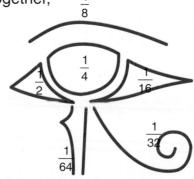

(Notice that if you add up the fractions, your answer is not quite 1

The missing fraction is the bit of magic needed for a dead eye to shine again with life!)

The Eye of Horus (or 'udjat') became a powerful symbol of health in ancient Egypt. It was worn as an amulet to ensure good health and ward off sickness. The Eye of Horus is depicted as a human eye and eyebrow, decorated with the markings seen under the eyes of falcons. This was because Horus had the head of a falcon. The left eye is sometimes said to be the origin of the pharmacist's symbol for a prescription, 'Rx'.

Writing fractions today

It is likely that our method of writing common fractions today can be attributed to the Hindus, although they did not use the bar. Brahmagupta (c. 628) and Bhaskara (c. 1150) wrote fractions as we do but without the bar, i.e., they wrote

$\frac{1}{3}$ and not $\frac{1}{3}$

The **horizontal fraction bar** was introduced by the Arabs. The Arabs at first copied the Hindu notation, but later improved on it by inserting a horizontal bar between the two numbers.

Several sources attribute the horizontal fraction bar to al-Hassar around 1200 but Fibonacci (c.1175-1250) was the first European mathematician to use the fraction bar as it is used today. He followed the Arab practice of placing the fraction to the left of the integer, which is the opposite of what we do today.

There is another fraction bar that you may have seen; this is the **diagonal fraction bar**. It was introduced because the horizontal fraction bar was difficult to type with an old fashioned typewriter. An English mathematician, Augustus de Morgan (1806-1871), was credited to be the first to propose the use of an oblique stroke for printing fractions in the 19th century.

However, an earlier handwritten document, with forward slashes instead of fraction bars, has been found in Thomas Twining's Ledger of 1718, where a number of tea and coffee transactions are listed as '1/4 pound green tea', for example.

Nowadays we always write the fraction bar as horizontal.

In *So you really want to learn Maths* Books 1 and 2 we learnt about equivalent fractions, mixed numbers, cancelling down, and the link between fractions, decimals and percentages. Here's a reminder of the key facts.

Equivalent fractions have equal value. To find equivalent fractions we multiply or divide the numerator (top number) and the denominator (bottom number) by the same value:

Examples:

(i) $\dfrac{15}{24} = \dfrac{15}{24} \div \dfrac{3}{3}$

$= \dfrac{5}{8}$

(ii) $\dfrac{5}{6} = \dfrac{5}{6} \times \dfrac{4}{4}$

$= \dfrac{20}{24}$

A fraction is in its **lowest terms** when the numerator and denominator have no common factors (except for 1).

A **mixed number** is a mixture of a whole number and a fraction, and an **improper fraction** is top heavy:

Example:

Mixed number	Improper fraction
$1\dfrac{1}{6}$	$\dfrac{7}{6}$
$3\dfrac{4}{7}$	$\dfrac{25}{7}$

A mixed number

An improper fraction

Decimals are also known as **decimal fractions** because the number columns after the decimal point are: $\frac{1}{10}$, $\frac{1}{100}$, $\frac{1}{1000}$

Therefore, if we write 0.5, we are saying $\frac{5}{10}$ which is equivalent to $\frac{1}{2}$

If we write 0.75, we are saying $\frac{75}{100}$ which is equivalent to $\frac{3}{4}$

If we write 0.375, we are saying $\frac{375}{1000}$ which is equivalent to $\frac{1}{8}$

The word **percentage** means 'out of a hundred'. Therefore any fraction written out of 100 can also be written as a percentage:

So, if we write 0.5, we are saying $\frac{5}{10}$ which is equivalent to $\frac{50}{100}$ or 50%

If we write 0.25, we are saying $\frac{25}{100}$ which is equivalent to 25%

If we write 0.75, we are saying $\frac{75}{100}$ which is equivalent to 75%

You can **write a fraction as a decimal** either:

- by finding an equivalent fraction with a numerator that is a multiple of 10; or

- by dividing the top number by the bottom number.

Complete the next exercise to revise these methods.

Exercise 3.1

1. Replace the * to make these fractions equivalent:

   (a) $\frac{1}{4} = \frac{*}{8}$ (b) $\frac{12}{16} = \frac{*}{4}$ (c) $\frac{2}{5} = \frac{*}{10}$ (d) $\frac{9}{*} = \frac{3}{8}$

2. Write these improper fractions as mixed numbers:

   (a) $\frac{39}{4}$ (b) $\frac{12}{5}$ (c) $\frac{28}{8}$ (d) $\frac{32}{3}$

3. Write these mixed numbers as improper fractions:

   (a) $4\frac{1}{5}$ (b) $3\frac{3}{4}$ (c) $7\frac{4}{5}$ (d) $3\frac{1}{7}$

4. Cancel these fractions down to their lowest terms:

   (a) $\frac{15}{25}$ (b) $\frac{36}{54}$ (c) $\frac{14}{36}$ (d) $\frac{18}{42}$

5. Write each of these percentages as (i) a decimal (ii) a fraction (in its lowest terms):

   (a) 15% (b) 24% (c) 56% (d) 125%

6. Write these decimals as (i) fractions (ii) percentages:

   (a) 0.35 (b) 1.36 (c) 0.08 (d) 0.125

7. Write these fractions as (i) decimals (ii) percentages:

   (a) $\frac{2}{5}$ (b) $\frac{14}{25}$ (c) $\frac{13}{20}$ (d) $\frac{5}{8}$

8. Write:
   (a) 12 minutes as a fraction of an hour.
   (b) 300 g as a fraction of a kilogram.
   (c) 35p as a fraction of £2.00
   (d) 30 cm as a percentage of 4 metres.
   (e) 450 ml as a percentage of 5 litres.
   (f) 1.25 km as a percentage of 10 km.

Adding fractions

It is possible to compare fractions with different denominators. However we can only add fractions when they have the same denominator.

If we are asked $\frac{3}{8} + \frac{7}{12}$, we cannot directly add eighths to twelfths.

We have to write both fractions as **equivalent fractions**, with a **lowest common denominator**.

In this example the lowest common multiple of 8 and 12 is 24, so we multiply the top and the bottom of each fraction with a multiple that will make 8 up to 24 and 12 up to 24

i.e:

$$\frac{3}{8} = \frac{3 \times 3}{8 \times 3} = \frac{9}{24} \quad \text{and} \quad \frac{7}{12} = \frac{7 \times 2}{12 \times 2} = \frac{14}{24}$$

We can then write the fraction addition like this:

Example:

$$\frac{3}{8} + \frac{7}{12} = \frac{9+14}{24}$$

$$= \frac{23}{24}$$

With mixed numbers there is an extra stage in the calculation. The first step is to add the whole numbers and then to do the fraction bit as we saw above:

Example:

$$3\frac{3}{7} + 2\frac{8}{9} = 5\frac{27+56}{63} \qquad \left(\frac{3}{7} \times \frac{9}{9} = \frac{27}{63} \text{ and } \frac{8}{9} \times \frac{7}{7} = \frac{56}{63}\right)$$

$$= 5\frac{83}{63}$$

$$= 6\frac{20}{63}$$

Exercise 3.2

Add these fractions, remembering to put the answer in its simplest form. If the answer is an improper fraction, e.g. $\frac{13}{12}$, write it as a mixed number: $1\frac{1}{12}$

1. $\frac{2}{3} + \frac{1}{5}$

2. $\frac{1}{8} + \frac{3}{4}$

3. $\frac{2}{7} + \frac{3}{4}$

4. $\frac{2}{3} + \frac{4}{9}$

5. $\frac{5}{9} + \frac{3}{4}$

6. $\frac{5}{8} + \frac{3}{10}$

7. $1\frac{1}{4} + 3\frac{2}{3}$

8. $2\frac{2}{3} + 3\frac{3}{5}$

9. $2\frac{2}{7} + 3\frac{3}{5}$

10. $5\frac{2}{3} + 2\frac{2}{15}$

11. $4\frac{3}{4} + 3\frac{3}{16}$

12. $2\frac{1}{6} + 1\frac{2}{15}$

13. $4\frac{5}{9} + 3\frac{5}{8}$

14. $3\frac{5}{6} + 1\frac{7}{10}$

15. $4\frac{5}{6} + 3\frac{7}{9}$

16. $7\frac{5}{6} + 2\frac{3}{7}$

17. $5\frac{5}{6} + 3\frac{2}{7}$

18. $3\frac{3}{8} + 3\frac{2}{3}$

19. $1\frac{2}{3} + 2\frac{2}{15} + 2\frac{3}{5}$

20. $2\frac{1}{8} + 1\frac{3}{14} + 1\frac{5}{16}$

21. $3\frac{2}{3} + 1\frac{9}{14} + 2\frac{2}{7}$

22. $4\frac{7}{12} + 2\frac{1}{24} + 3\frac{1}{8}$

23. $1\frac{3}{7} + 3\frac{2}{3} + 2\frac{1}{2}$

24. $2\frac{3}{5} + 1\frac{1}{3} + 9\frac{3}{4}$

Subtracting fractions

Subtraction of fractions follows the same first steps as addition. First find the lowest common denominator, then work out the equivalent fractions and finally do the subtraction.

With mixed numbers you have to subtract the whole numbers first:

Example: $5\frac{4}{9} - 1\frac{1}{6} = 3\frac{8-3}{18}$

$= 3\frac{5}{18} = 4\frac{5}{18}$

First subtract the whole numbers. Then do the fraction subtraction just as before.

As in any other subtraction there will be times when the first subtraction is not possible such as (5 − 9); as usual you must then **change** a whole number from the next number on the left. Remember that you change 8 eighths, 12 twelfths, 16 sixteenths or whatever:

Example: $5\frac{4}{9} - 2\frac{5}{6} = 3\frac{8-15}{18}$

$= 2\frac{26-15}{18}$

$= 2\frac{11}{18}$

8 − 15 cannot be done, so we change one whole into 18 eighteenths from the whole number 3
18 + 8 = 26
The calculation is now 26 − 15

Exercise 3.3

1. $\dfrac{3}{4} - \dfrac{1}{3}$

2. $\dfrac{3}{4} - \dfrac{3}{5}$

3. $\dfrac{3}{8} - \dfrac{1}{6}$

4. $\dfrac{11}{12} - \dfrac{2}{3}$

5. $\dfrac{4}{7} - \dfrac{1}{2}$

6. $\dfrac{8}{15} - \dfrac{3}{10}$

7. $3\dfrac{3}{7} - 1\dfrac{1}{5}$

8. $5\dfrac{2}{3} - 2\dfrac{1}{5}$

9. $4\dfrac{4}{5} - 1\dfrac{3}{4}$

10. $2\dfrac{2}{7} - 1\dfrac{2}{9}$

11. $3\dfrac{3}{4} - 1\dfrac{2}{5}$

12. $4\dfrac{2}{5} - 2\dfrac{4}{9}$

13. $4\dfrac{1}{4} - 1\dfrac{2}{3}$

14. $3\dfrac{1}{7} - 2\dfrac{2}{3}$

15. $4\dfrac{3}{7} - 1\dfrac{4}{5}$

16. $3\dfrac{2}{5} - 2\dfrac{7}{10}$

17. $3\dfrac{2}{3} - 1\dfrac{8}{15}$

18. $4\dfrac{2}{9} - 3\dfrac{1}{3}$

19. $5\dfrac{5}{12} - 3\dfrac{1}{4}$

20. $3\dfrac{1}{4} - 1\dfrac{5}{12}$

21. $5\dfrac{13}{18} - 3\dfrac{7}{12}$

Mixed addition and subtraction

For questions with brackets remember to do the calculation in brackets first. Do write down your working out carefully, just like in these examples:

Example: (i) $\dfrac{3}{4} - \left(\dfrac{1}{5} + \dfrac{1}{6}\right) = \dfrac{3}{4} - \left(\dfrac{6+5}{30}\right)$

$$= \dfrac{3}{4} - \dfrac{11}{30}$$

$$= \dfrac{45 - 22}{60}$$

$$= \dfrac{23}{60}$$

Example: (ii) $1\frac{2}{3} + \left(3\frac{2}{5} - 1\frac{1}{4}\right) = 1\frac{2}{3} + \left(2\frac{8-5}{20}\right)$

$$= 1\frac{2}{3} + 2\frac{3}{20}$$

$$= 3\frac{40+9}{60}$$

$$= 3\frac{49}{60}$$

Exercise 3.4

1. $\frac{2}{3} + \frac{1}{4} - \frac{2}{5}$

2. $\frac{2}{5} + \left(\frac{1}{3} - \frac{2}{9}\right)$

3. $\frac{3}{4} - \frac{1}{5} + \frac{1}{2}$

4. $\frac{3}{4} - \left(\frac{1}{5} + \frac{1}{3}\right)$

5. $\frac{2}{5} + \frac{3}{4} - \frac{7}{10}$

6. $\frac{3}{7} + \left(\frac{2}{3} - \frac{1}{4}\right)$

7. $\frac{4}{5} - \frac{1}{3} + \frac{3}{4}$

8. $\frac{9}{10} - \left(\frac{3}{5} + \frac{1}{4}\right)$

9. $\left(\frac{2}{5} + \frac{1}{4}\right) - \left(\frac{2}{3} - \frac{1}{5}\right)$

10. $1\frac{4}{5} - \left(\frac{2}{3} + \frac{1}{4}\right)$

11. $1\frac{4}{5} - \frac{2}{3} + \frac{1}{4}$

12. $2\frac{1}{5} - 1\frac{7}{8} + \frac{3}{10}$

13. $2\frac{1}{5} - \left(1\frac{7}{8} + \frac{3}{10}\right)$

14. $2\frac{1}{5} + \left(1\frac{7}{8} - \frac{3}{10}\right)$

15. $4\frac{1}{6} + 7\frac{3}{8} - 1\frac{19}{24}$

16. $1\frac{1}{4} + 3\frac{2}{5} - 1\frac{7}{10}$

17. $3\frac{1}{5} - \left(2\frac{2}{3} - 1\frac{1}{4}\right)$

18. $4\frac{7}{10} - \left(2\frac{2}{5} + 1\frac{3}{4}\right)$

A fraction of an amount

One of the reasons why fractions are so useful is that we can use them to divide things into equal parts:

'Half an hour' is 30 minutes. We divide 60 minutes by 2

'Half a metre' is 50 cm. We divide 100 cm by 2

'Three quarters of an hour' is 45 minutes because 60 minutes is divided by 4, and then multiplied by 3

Exercise 3.5

Examples: (i) Find $\frac{1}{5}$ of 25

$$\frac{1}{5} \text{ of } 25 = 25 \div 5$$
$$= 5$$

(ii) Find $\frac{3}{4}$ of 1 kg. Give the answer in g.

$$\frac{3}{4} \text{ of } 1 \text{ kg} = 1000 \div 4 \times 3$$
$$= 250 \times 3$$
$$= 750 \text{ g}$$

1. Find $\frac{1}{4}$ of 20

2. Find $\frac{1}{7}$ of 42

3. Find $\frac{1}{8}$ of 96

4. Find $\frac{2}{3}$ of 45

5. Find $\frac{3}{4}$ of 72

6. Find $\frac{5}{8}$ of 104

7. Find $\frac{5}{6}$ of 138

8. Find $\frac{4}{5}$ of 72

9. Find $\frac{2}{5}$ of 3 m. Give the answer in cm.

10. Find $\frac{2}{3}$ of 2 hours. Give the answer in minutes.

11. Find $\frac{3}{4}$ of 3 kg. Give the answer in grams.

12. Find $\frac{7}{8}$ of 4 km. Give the answer in km and m.

For more complicated fractions of an amount we may need to write down the calculation.

Remember that 'of' can be written as × (multiply).

Example: $\frac{2}{5}$ of $240 = \frac{2}{5} \times 240$

These calculations are simplest if both terms are fractions, and so we can write the 240 as $\frac{240}{1}$

The multiplication becomes $\frac{2}{5} \times \frac{240}{1}$

We can simplify this in the same way that we simplify equivalent fractions, by dividing top and bottom by the same common factor:

Example: $\frac{2}{5}$ of $240 = \frac{2}{5_1} \times \frac{240^{48}}{1}$

$= 2 \times 48$

$= 96$

---

13. Find $\frac{5}{6}$ of 204

14. Find $\frac{7}{8}$ of 152

15. Find $\frac{15}{16}$ of 240

16. Find $\frac{15}{26}$ of 130

17. Find $\frac{11}{20}$ of 110

18. Find $\frac{4}{9}$ of 306

19. Find $\frac{7}{20}$ of 230

20. Find $\frac{11}{14}$ of 126

21. Find $\frac{5}{6}$ of 3 hours. Give the answer in hours and minutes.

22. Find $\frac{4}{5}$ of 6 m. Give the answer in mm.

23. Find $\frac{5}{12}$ of a minute. Give the answer in seconds.

Multiplying fractions

In the above examples we multiplied a whole number by a fraction. We use the same principle when we have to multiply a fraction by a fraction.

$$\frac{7}{15} \times \frac{9}{14} = \frac{\cancel{63}^9}{\cancel{210}_{30}}$$

Multiply the top numbers together and multiply the bottom numbers together. Then divide by a common factor: 7

$$= \frac{\cancel{9}^3}{\cancel{30}_{10}}$$

Are there any more common factors? Yes: 3

$$= \frac{3}{10}$$

In this example there was quite a complicated multiplication: 15×14

There is no reason why we cannot divide by the factors **before** the multiplication. This then allows us to do easier calculations:

Example:

$$\frac{7}{15} \times \frac{9}{14} = \frac{\cancel{7}^1}{\cancel{15}_5} \times \frac{\cancel{9}^3}{\cancel{14}_2}$$

Divide by common factors: 3 and 7

$$= \frac{3}{10}$$

Exercise 3.6

1. $\frac{2}{3} \times \frac{6}{7}$

2. $\frac{3}{5} \times \frac{10}{21}$

3. $\frac{3}{14} \times \frac{7}{9}$

4. $\frac{3}{5} \times \frac{3}{10}$

5. $\frac{5}{9} \times \frac{3}{10}$

6. $\frac{3}{8} \times \frac{16}{27}$

7. $\frac{3}{7} \times \frac{4}{9}$

8. $\frac{2}{7} \times \frac{3}{5}$

9. $\frac{5}{21} \times \frac{7}{15}$

These multiplications have all been with fractions of **less** than one. You will see that all the answers to these have also been less than one.

Sometimes we need to multiply numbers greater than one (mixed numbers). To do this we simply change the mixed numbers into improper fractions and then simplify the product and multiply as before.

Exercise 3.7

Example:

$$1\frac{2}{3} \times 2\frac{2}{5} = \frac{\cancel{5}^1}{\cancel{3}_1} \times \frac{\cancel{12}^4}{\cancel{5}_1}$$

$$= \frac{4}{1}$$

$$= 4$$

1. $1\frac{1}{4} \times \frac{2}{5}$ **5.** $\frac{7}{8} \times 2\frac{2}{7}$ **9.** $\frac{4}{5} \times 4\frac{2}{7}$

2. $\frac{1}{4} \times 2\frac{2}{5}$ **6.** $\frac{3}{4} \times 2\frac{1}{6}$ **10.** $5\frac{4}{5} \times \frac{5}{8}$

3. $\frac{2}{3} \times 1\frac{1}{5}$ **7.** $4\frac{2}{7} \times \frac{7}{10}$ **11.** $1\frac{1}{4} \times 2\frac{2}{5}$

4. $3\frac{1}{3} \times \frac{3}{5}$ **8.** $3\frac{1}{7} \times \frac{11}{7}$ **12.** $1\frac{1}{2} \times 5\frac{1}{2}$

We can use the same principle with three or more fractions multiplied together:

Example:

$$\frac{4}{5} \times \frac{10}{21} \times \frac{7}{8} = \frac{\cancel{4}^1}{\cancel{5}_1} \times \frac{\cancel{10}^2}{\cancel{21}_3} \times \frac{\cancel{7}^1}{\cancel{8}_2}$$

$$= \frac{1 \times \cancel{2}^1 \times 1}{1 \times 3 \times \cancel{2}_1}$$

$$= \frac{1}{3}$$

Here are some quite challenging calculations:

Exercise 3.8

1. $\frac{2}{5} \times \frac{10}{21} \times \frac{14}{15}$ **3.** $\frac{2}{3} \times \frac{6}{7} \times \frac{14}{35}$

2. $\frac{3}{8} \times \frac{16}{75} \times \frac{3}{4}$ **4.** $\frac{4}{9} \times \frac{1}{8} \times \frac{6}{7}$

5. $\frac{1}{12} \times \frac{6}{7} \times \frac{8}{15}$

6. $\frac{7}{15} \times \frac{11}{14} \times \frac{9}{22}$

7. $\frac{2}{5} \times \frac{4}{9} \times \frac{5}{8} \times \frac{3}{4}$

8. $\frac{7}{16} \times \frac{3}{5} \times \frac{8}{15} \times \frac{5}{14}$

9. $\frac{7}{20} \times \frac{11}{21} \times \frac{22}{25} \times \frac{5}{11}$

10. $\frac{3}{16} \times \frac{4}{5} \times \frac{7}{9} \times \frac{10}{21}$

11. $1\frac{1}{4} \times 2\frac{2}{3} \times 1\frac{2}{5}$

12. $2\frac{1}{2} \times 3\frac{1}{3} \times 1\frac{1}{4}$

13. $4\frac{2}{3} \times 3\frac{1}{7} \times 1\frac{1}{11}$

14. $3\frac{1}{3} \times 3\frac{1}{5} \times 1\frac{1}{8}$

15. $1\frac{1}{2} \times 2\frac{1}{6} \times \frac{2}{3} \times 5\frac{1}{7} \times \frac{7}{8}$

16. $1\frac{1}{2} \times 1\frac{1}{3} \times 1\frac{1}{4} \times 1\frac{1}{5} \times 1\frac{1}{6} \times 1\frac{1}{7}$

17. $\frac{1}{2} \times 1\frac{2}{3} \times 2\frac{3}{4} \times 3\frac{4}{5} \times 4\frac{5}{6}$

18. $1\frac{1}{2} \times 2\frac{2}{3} \times 3\frac{3}{4} \times 4\frac{4}{5} \times 5\frac{2}{5}$

Dividing with fractions

When we write $4 \times \frac{1}{2}$ we get the answer 2 because 4 halves are 2

This calculation could also be $\qquad 4 \div 2 = 2$

or $\qquad \frac{4}{2} = 2$

or $\qquad \frac{1}{2}$ of 4 is 2

We can see that $\div 2$ is the same as $\times \frac{1}{2}$ and similarly that $\div \frac{1}{2}$ is the same as $\times 2$

In other words, the $\div$ sign changes to $\times$ and the fraction turns upside down.

This works for all fractions, so $\div \frac{3}{4}$ is the same as $\times \frac{4}{3}$

Examples:

$$\text{(i)} \quad 4 \div \frac{4}{5} = \frac{\cancel{4}^{1}}{1} \times \frac{5}{\cancel{4}_{1}}$$

$$= 5$$

$$\text{(ii)} \quad \frac{2}{3} \div \frac{4}{5} = \frac{\cancel{2}^{1}}{3} \times \frac{5}{\cancel{4}_{2}}$$

$$= \frac{5}{6}$$

Exercise 3.9

Do these divisions. If your answer is an improper fraction, you should turn it into a mixed number:

1. $\dfrac{3}{4} \div \dfrac{6}{7}$

2. $\dfrac{1}{4} \div \dfrac{3}{8}$

3. $\dfrac{2}{3} \div \dfrac{3}{5}$

4. $\dfrac{7}{8} \div \dfrac{3}{10}$

5. $\dfrac{7}{18} \div \dfrac{5}{9}$

6. $\dfrac{9}{10} \div \dfrac{6}{25}$

7. $\dfrac{11}{12} \div \dfrac{33}{48}$

8. $\dfrac{5}{14} \div \dfrac{10}{21}$

9. $\dfrac{4}{5} \div \dfrac{1}{9}$

10. $\dfrac{5}{8} \div \dfrac{15}{64}$

11. $\dfrac{22}{35} \div \dfrac{4}{15}$

12. $\dfrac{14}{15} \div \dfrac{7}{10}$

The reciprocal

When we used the calculator in the first chapter of this book, we looked at the button marked: $\boxed{\dfrac{1}{x}}$ or sometimes $\boxed{x^{-1}}$

This is called the reciprocal button. If you push it repeatedly you get a recurring series:

Start with 2:   2, 0.5, 2, 0.5, 2, 0.5, ...

We know that $0.5 = \dfrac{1}{2}$

Therefore the series is: $2, \dfrac{1}{2}, 2, \dfrac{1}{2}, 2, \dfrac{1}{2}, \ldots$

If you start with 4 you will get:

$$4, 0.25, 4, 0.25, 4, 0.25, \ldots$$

or $$4, \frac{1}{4}, 4, \frac{1}{4}, 4, \frac{1}{4}, \ldots$$

We say that $\frac{1}{2}$ is the reciprocal of 2 and that 4 is the reciprocal of $\frac{1}{4}$

It follows therefore that: $\frac{2}{5}$ is the reciprocal of $\frac{5}{2}$ $(2\frac{1}{2})$

Exercise 3.10

Write down the reciprocals of the following:

1.	3	**5.**	$\frac{6}{7}$	**9.**	$\frac{1}{a}$
2.	$\frac{1}{5}$	**6.**	$\frac{4}{39}$	**10.**	$\frac{x}{y}$
3.	x	**7.**	$1\frac{1}{2}$	**11.**	$\frac{5}{x}$
4.	$\frac{3}{4}$	**8.**	$3\frac{1}{3}$	**12.**	$\frac{1}{x^2}$

We can now say that the rule for dividing by a fraction is:

To divide by a fraction, multiply by the reciprocal.

The rule works for mixed numbers as well. Just as we did with multiplication we must turn mixed numbers into improper fractions first.

Example:

$$1\frac{2}{3} \div 2\frac{1}{6} = \frac{5}{3} \div \frac{13}{6}$$

$$= \frac{5}{\cancel{3}_1} \times \frac{\cancel{6}^2}{13}$$

$$= \frac{10}{13}$$

Exercise 3.11

Calculate the answers to these:

1. $2\frac{1}{4} \div \frac{3}{8}$

2. $3\frac{2}{3} \div 4$

3. $4\frac{1}{5} \div 2$

4. $5\frac{3}{4} \div 3$

5. $3\frac{1}{4} \div \frac{1}{3}$

6. $2\frac{2}{5} \div 2\frac{4}{15}$

7. $2\frac{2}{3} \div \frac{1}{9}$

8. $2\frac{1}{4} \div 1\frac{7}{8}$

9. $4\frac{2}{5} \div 3\frac{2}{3}$

10. $2\frac{2}{3} \div 1\frac{1}{9}$

11. $3\frac{3}{4} \div 1\frac{3}{7}$

12. $4\frac{2}{7} \div 1\frac{1}{9}$

13. $4\frac{2}{5} \div 1\frac{7}{15}$

14. $3\frac{2}{3} \div 1\frac{2}{9}$

15. $4\frac{1}{5} \div 1\frac{2}{5}$

16. $5\frac{3}{4} \div 1\frac{7}{8}$

17. $4\frac{1}{6} \div 1\frac{7}{8}$

18. $1\frac{3}{5} \div 2\frac{3}{4}$

Exercise 3.12: Mixed operations

Remember the BIDMAS rule (**B**rackets, **I**ndices, **D**ivide, **M**ultiply, **A**dd, **S**ubtract) to calculate the answers to these:

1. $1\frac{1}{5} \times 2\frac{5}{6} - \frac{8}{15}$

2. $\left(\frac{2}{3} - \frac{4}{7}\right) \div \frac{2}{15}$

3. $3\frac{3}{4} - \frac{13}{18} \div \frac{2}{9}$

4. $\left(\frac{3}{4} + \frac{3}{7}\right) \div \frac{5}{18}$

5. $\left(3\frac{1}{3} - 1\frac{4}{9}\right) \div \frac{8}{9}$

6. $\frac{3}{14} \div \left(1\frac{4}{7} - \frac{7}{10}\right)$

7. $\dfrac{3\frac{3}{5}}{1\frac{2}{7}} - \dfrac{2\frac{1}{4}}{1\frac{1}{5}}$

8. $1 - \frac{1}{2}\left(1 - \frac{1}{3}\left(1 - \frac{1}{4}\right)\right)$

9. $9\left(1 - \frac{1}{2}\left(2 - \frac{2}{3}\left(3 + \frac{1}{4}\right)\right)\right)$

10. $\dfrac{1\frac{3}{5} + 2\frac{5}{7}}{3\frac{2}{7} - 1\frac{7}{10}}$

11. $1 - \frac{4}{5}\left(1 - \frac{3}{4}\left(1 - \frac{2}{3}\right)\right)$

12. $\dfrac{1 + \frac{1}{4}\left(1 + \frac{1}{2}\left(1 - \frac{3}{4}\right)\right)}{1 - \frac{3}{4}\left(1 - \frac{1}{4}\left(1 + \frac{3}{4}\right)\right)}$

Fractions on the calculator

Look for the fraction button on your calculator.

It usually looks like this: $\boxed{\textbf{a}^{b}/_{c}}$

To enter a mixed number, for example $1\frac{2}{5}$, you press the sequence:

$\boxed{1}\ \boxed{\textbf{a}^{b}/_{c}}\ \boxed{2}\ \boxed{\textbf{a}^{b}/_{c}}\ \boxed{5}$

The display should read $\boxed{\qquad\qquad\textbf{1 2 5}\quad}$

Now try adding $1\frac{2}{5}$ and you should get the answer $2\frac{4}{5}$

Exercise 3.13

Use your calculator to work out the answers to the first five questions in Exercises 3.1 – 3.10

Check you have the same answers as before.

Next work out the answers to Exercise 3.11 with your calculator. Remember to use the brackets and memory when you need to.

Exercise 3.14: Extension questions 1

Remember the special Egyptian fractions from the Eye of Horus:

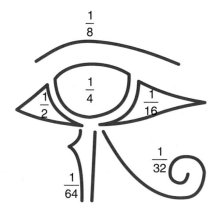

1. Add up the six fractions.

2. What fraction is the bit of magic needed to make the eye whole again?

3. Evaluate the following:

    (a) $\left(\dfrac{1}{2}\right)^2$　　(b) $\left(\dfrac{1}{2}\right)^3$　　(c) $\left(\dfrac{1}{2}\right)^4$　　(d) $\left(\dfrac{1}{2}\right)^5$

4. Evaluate the following:

    (a) $\left(\dfrac{1}{4}\right)^2$　　(b) $\sqrt{\left(\dfrac{1}{64}\right)}$　　(c) $\left(\dfrac{1}{8}\right)^2$　　(d) $\sqrt[3]{\left(\dfrac{1}{64}\right)}$

5. Write as many fraction equations as you can using the 6 fractions from the Eye of Horus. You can use +, −, × and ÷ but also use index numbers and roots. Apart from these you can use no other numbers.

    $\dfrac{1}{4} + \dfrac{1}{4} = \dfrac{1}{2}$ is allowed but $2 \times \dfrac{1}{4} = \dfrac{1}{2}$ is not.

We know that the Egyptians used to sum unit fractions to get non-unit fractions. So, to get $\dfrac{3}{8}$ they would add $\dfrac{1}{4}$ and $\dfrac{1}{8}$

6. Adding the minimum possible number of the 6 Eye of Horus fractions make fraction sums for the following:

    (a) $\dfrac{5}{8}$　　　(b) $\dfrac{9}{16}$　　　(c) $\dfrac{21}{32}$　　　(d) $\dfrac{25}{64}$

Consider this calculation:

$$\left(\dfrac{1}{2} + \dfrac{1}{4}\right) \div \left(\dfrac{1}{2} + \dfrac{1}{2} + \dfrac{1}{8}\right) = \dfrac{3}{4} \div \dfrac{9}{8}$$

$$= \dfrac{\cancel{3}^{1}}{\cancel{4}_{1}} \times \dfrac{\cancel{8}^{2}}{\cancel{9}_{3}}$$

$$= \dfrac{2}{3}$$

This time we have made a completely different fraction only by using the Eye of Horus fractions. The denominator is not a power of 2

We can do this only by combining two calculations with a division.

7. Using a similar method combine some of the Eye of Horus fractions to make the following:

    (a) $\dfrac{1}{3}$　　　(b) $\dfrac{3}{5}$　　　(c) $\dfrac{7}{9}$　　　(d) $\dfrac{11}{21}$

8. Now try to explain a general rule about how you can use the Eye of Horus fractions to make any fraction of the form $\frac{a}{b}$ where neither a nor b is greater than 63

   Remember the Egyptians used tables to help with their fraction calculations. Such a table might help you with your explanation.

Exercise 3.15: Extension questions 2 – Continued fractions

In **Maths Prep** Book 2 we looked at some fraction calculations that gave us an estimate of pi. One of them was in the form of a series of reciprocals:

$$\pi = 3 + \cfrac{1}{7 + \cfrac{1}{15 + \cfrac{1}{1 + \cfrac{1}{292 + \ldots}}}}$$

Fractions in this form are called 'continued' fractions and mathematicians have spent a lot of time exploring fraction sequences in this form.

We are going to try a few.

1. (a) Calculate the answer to the first five steps of this sequence:

   (i) $1 + \cfrac{1}{1 + 1}$

   (ii) $1 + \cfrac{1}{1 + \cfrac{1}{1 + 1}}$

   (iii) $1 + \cfrac{1}{1 + \cfrac{1}{1 + \cfrac{1}{1 + 1}}}$

   (iv) $1 + \cfrac{1}{1 + \cfrac{1}{1 + \cfrac{1}{1 + 1}}}$

   (v) $1 + \cfrac{1}{1 + \cfrac{1}{1 + \cfrac{1}{1 + \cfrac{1}{1 + 1}}}}$

   (b) Now work out your fraction answers as decimals. What do you notice? What do you think the final terms of the continued fraction sequence will approximate to?

2. Calculate the answer to the first five steps of this sequence:

(a) $1 + \dfrac{1}{2+1}$

(b) $1 + \dfrac{1}{2 + \dfrac{1}{3+1}}$

(c) $1 + \dfrac{1}{2 + \dfrac{1}{3 + \dfrac{1}{4+1}}}$

(d) $1 + \dfrac{1}{2 + \dfrac{1}{3 + \dfrac{1}{4 + \dfrac{1}{5+1}}}}$

(e) $1 + \dfrac{1}{2 + \dfrac{1}{3 + \dfrac{1}{4 + \dfrac{1}{5 + \dfrac{1}{6+1}}}}}$

(f) Do these fractions converge to a value?

3. Calculate the answer to the first five steps of this sequence:

(a) $1 + \dfrac{1}{1+1}$

(b) $1 + \dfrac{1}{1 + \dfrac{1}{2+1}}$

(c) $1 + \dfrac{1}{1 + \dfrac{1}{2 + \dfrac{1}{4+1}}}$

(d) $1 + \dfrac{1}{1 + \dfrac{1}{2 + \dfrac{1}{4 + \dfrac{1}{8+1}}}}$

(e) $1 + \dfrac{1}{1 + \dfrac{1}{2 + \dfrac{1}{4 + \dfrac{1}{8 + \dfrac{1}{16+1}}}}}$

(f) What does this sequence of continued fractions converge to?

4. By now you should have got the hang of how to calculate these, and you may decide that a good way to explore the rest of these series is by using a computer. See if you can use a spreadsheet programme to find the next five terms of the above three series.

5. Now is the time for you to design continued fraction series of your own. You need to decide on some basic rules, and then explore the fractions. Good luck!

Exercise 3.16: Summary exercise

Do not use a calculator for this exercise.

1. Write these decimals as (i) fractions and (ii) percentages:
   (a) 0.24   (b) 1.35   (c) 0.125

2. Write these fractions as (i) decimals and (ii) percentages:
   (a) $\frac{3}{5}$ (b) $\frac{2}{3}$ (c) $1\frac{17}{20}$

3. Evaluate:
   (a) $\frac{3}{5} + \frac{5}{6}$ (b) $2\frac{1}{8} + 1\frac{5}{12}$ (c) $4\frac{2}{3} + 5\frac{1}{12}$

4. Evaluate:
   (a) $\frac{5}{6} - \frac{1}{9}$ (b) $12\frac{5}{16} - 3\frac{1}{12}$ (c) $2\frac{1}{7} - 1\frac{3}{4}$

5. Now try these:

   (a) $\frac{3}{7} - \left(\frac{1}{5} - \frac{3}{14}\right)$ (b) $1\frac{2}{5} + \left(3\frac{1}{3} - 1\frac{7}{10}\right)$

6. Find $\frac{2}{7}$ of 413

7. Find $\frac{3}{8}$ of 7 km. Give your answer in metres.

8. (a) $\frac{12}{25} \times \frac{15}{16}$ (b) $\frac{7}{18} \times \frac{9}{20} \times \frac{8}{21}$ (c) $7\frac{2}{3} \times 2\frac{5}{8}$ (d) $4\frac{1}{3} \times 2\frac{1}{4}$

9. (a) $\frac{8}{15} \div \frac{2}{5}$ (b) $2\frac{5}{8} \div 1\frac{3}{4}$ (c) $6\frac{1}{2} \div \frac{2}{3}$ (d) $7\frac{1}{5} \div 3\frac{9}{10}$

10. (a) $12\frac{2}{5} - 3\frac{1}{5} \times 3\frac{3}{4}$ (b) $\dfrac{7\frac{31}{32} + 7\frac{7}{8}}{7\frac{1}{2} - 5\frac{7}{8}}$

11. (a) $\left(1 - \frac{1}{50}\right)\left(1 - \frac{1}{49}\right)\left(1 - \frac{1}{48}\right)$

    (b) What happens if you extend the multiplication pattern in part (a) until $\left(1 - \frac{1}{2}\right)$?

End of chapter 3 activity:

Fraction, decimal and percentage dominoes

On the worksheet you will find a set of dominoes. Cut these out and play!

The traditional game (for up to 4 players)

Turn all the pieces upside down and shuffle them around on the table. Each player takes one domino in turn until all players have seven.

The player with the highest double starts (i.e. the piece showing a double half). If no one has the double half, then find it from the remaining pieces and place it on the table. The player who picks up the last piece then starts.

The player places the double on the table (unless it is already there) and the other players have to add a matching domino to the first. For example:

$$\boxed{\frac{1}{2} \;\Big|\; \frac{1}{2}} \quad \boxed{0.5 \;\Big|\; 20\%}$$

The next player has to match one of his or her dominoes up to one of the ends of the chain. For example:

$$\boxed{\frac{1}{2} \;\Big|\; \frac{1}{2}} \quad \boxed{0.5 \;\Big|\; 20\%} \quad \boxed{\frac{1}{5} \;\Big|\; 0.7}$$

The next player then adds on to the end of the chain and so on. If the chain is getting too long then it can bend like this:

$$\boxed{\frac{1}{2} \;\Big|\; \frac{1}{2}} \quad \boxed{0.5 \;\Big|\; 20\%} \quad \boxed{\frac{1}{5} \;\Big|\; 0.7} \quad \boxed{}$$

If a player cannot go, he passes and forfeits his turn. The winner is the first player to put down all his pieces, and his score is the sum of all the numbers on the remaining players' dominoes.

The puzzle

The dominoes on the worksheet can be placed in a continuous rectangle with no pieces left out. The dominoes should be placed in such a way that the values of the touching ends are equal in value. Can you make this rectangle?

Chapter 4: Index numbers

When we worked out the prime factors of 375 (page 9) we wrote the numbers $5 \times 5 \times 5$ as 5^3

The little number 3 is known as the **index number** and tells us how many times 5 is multiplied by itself.

Here are some examples:

$5 \times 5 \times 5 \times 5 \times 5 = 5^5 = 3125$ (5^5 can be read as 'five to the power 5')
$5 \times 5 \times 5 \times 5 = 5^4 = 625$ (5^4 can be read as 'five to the power 4')
$5 \times 5 \times 5 = 5^3 = 125$ (5^3 can be read as 'five cubed')
$5 \times 5 = 5^2 = 25$ (5^2 can be read as 'five squared')
$5 = 5^1$ or $5 = 5$

The exact origin of the use of the index notation (which the Americans call 'exponent') is not clear. The Ancient Greeks knew about squares and how to use them. So did the Babylonians and the Egyptians. The Indians were solving quite complex equations using x^3 and x^2 in the 7th century but they did not record their numbers in the same way we do.

The first recorded use of index notation was in 1636, when James Hume, a Scotsman living in Paris, brought out a book describing the work of an earlier mathematician, Vièta, which he called: *Algebra: A New, Clear and Easy Method.*

In this book he used Roman numerals for the index numbers:

   x^{iii} instead of x^3

A year later in 1637 Rene Descartes wrote *Geometrie.* He was the first person to use numerical indices as we know them today.

Exercise 4.1

Use a calculator when necessary in this next exercise.

Examples:

(i) Write $5 \times 5 \times 5$ In index form: $5 \times 5 \times 5 = 5^3$

(ii) Work out the answer to 5^3: $5^3 = 125$

(iii) Write 125 in index form: $125 = 5 \times 5 \times 5$
$$= 5^3$$

---

1. Write these numbers in index form:
   (a) $2 \times 2 \times 2$ (c) $3 \times 3 \times 3$ (e) $2 \times 2 \times 2 \times 2 \times 2$
   (b) 9×9 (d) 8×8 (f) $4 \times 4 \times 4$

2. Work out the actual numbers in q.1

3. Write these numbers as products of primes in index form:
   (a) 9   (c) 49   (e) 243   (g) 1331
   (b) 16   (d) 144   (f) 343   (h) 169

Now let us look at what happens when we multiply and divide with indices:

When we multiply:
$$5^3 \times 5^2 = 5 \times 5 \times 5 \times 5 \times 5$$
$$= 5^5$$

N.B. $3 + 2 = 5$ we **add** the indices.

When we divide:
$$5^4 \div 5^2 = 5 \times 5 \times 5 \times 5 \ \div \ 5 \times 5$$
$$= 5^2$$

N.B. $4 - 2 = 2$ we **subtract** the indices.

As a general rule:

If numbers written in index form are **multiplied** together the resulting index is the **sum** of the indices:

$$5^3 \times 5^2 = 5^{3+2} = 5^5$$

If numbers written in index form are **divided** the resulting index number is the first index number **minus** the second:

$$5^4 \div 5^2 = 5^{4-2} = 5^2$$

Examples:

Simplify these numbers and if possible leave the answer in index form:

(i) $2^4 \times 2^6 = 2^{10}$ (as $^{4+6=10}$)

(ii) $6^7 \div 6^2 = 6^5$ (as $^{7-2=5}$)

(iii) $3^3 \times 3 = 3^4$ (as 3 is 3^1 so $^{3+1=4}$)

Exercise 4.2

Simplify these numbers leaving your answer in index form:

1.   (a) $3^3 \times 3^2$ (c) $6^7 \times 6^4$ (e) $4^3 \times 4^3 \times 4^3$
       (b) $7^2 \times 7^5$ (d) $3^2 \times 3^2 \times 3$ (f) $7^3 \times 7 \times 7$

2.   (a) $2^5 \div 2^2$ (c) $4^7 \div 4^3$ (e) $5^8 \div 5^7$
       (b) $7^5 \div 7$ (d) $3^5 \div 3^2$ (f) $7^3 \div 7$

3.   (a) $4^3 \times 4^3 \div 4^2$ (c) $5^7 \times 5^2 \div 5^4$ (e) $4^3 \times 4^3 \div 4^2$
       (b) $7^2 \times 7^4 \div 7^5$ (d) $3^2 \times 3^2 \div 3$ (f) $7^3 \times 7^2 \div 7$

4.   (a) $3^8 \times 3^3 \div 3$ (c) $7^3 \times 7^2 \div 7^4$ (e) $2^2 \times 2^3 \div 2^5$
       (b) $5 \times 5^3 \div 5^2$ (d) $3 \times 3 \div 3^2$ (f) $7 \times 7^4 \div 7^5$

Note that the adding and subtracting rules are **only** true when considering powers of the **same number**.

$$5^3 \times 2^3 \text{ does not equal either } 5^6 \text{ or } 2^6 \text{ (but does equal } 10^3\text{)}$$

5.   Simplify these numbers **if possible** and leave the answer in index form:
       (a) $3^3 \times 3^3$ (c) $6^7 \times 5^6$ (e) $6^7 \div 5^2$
       (b) $8^5 \div 8^2$ (d) $7^2 \div 2^2$ (f) $4^3 \times 4$

(g) $2^2 \times 2^3 \times 2^2$ (j) $3^2 \times 3^3 \div 3^2$ (m) $4^8 \times 3^3 \times 5^2$

(h) $3^2 \times 5^3 \times 2^2$ (k) $6^7 \times 5^5 \div 6^2$ (n) $6^7 \times 6^5 \div 6^2$

(i) $7^3 \times 7^3 \times 3^2$ (l) $5^5 \times 5^5 \div 5^3$ (o) $2^4 \times 3^4 \div 6^2$

Note that:

$$5^3 + 5^3 \text{ does not equal } 5^6 \text{ but equals } 2 \times 5^3$$

and that:

$$2 \times 5^3 \text{ does not equal } 10^3 \text{ !} \quad 2 \times 5^3 \text{ cannot be simplified to index form.}$$

---

6. Simplify these numbers leaving the answer in index form:

(a) $3^3 + 3^3$ (c) $4^2 + 4^2$ (e) $5^3 + 5^3$

(b) $7^2 + 7^2$ (d) $5^2 + 5^2$ (f) $7^3 + 7^3$

7. Simplify these numbers **if possible** and leave the answer in index form:

(a) $2^3 + 3^3$ (c) 3×4^2 (e) $4^5 + 4^5 + 4^5$

(b) $7^2 \div 7^2$ (d) 5×5^2 (f) 3×7^3

Negative indices

What happens when we divide 5^3 by 5^6?
We can look at this in two ways:

Either like this

$$5^3 \div 5^6 = 5^{3-6} \qquad \text{or} \qquad 5^3 \div 5^6 = \frac{5^3}{5^6}$$

$$= 5^{-3} \qquad\qquad\qquad = \frac{5^1 \times 5^1 \times 5^1}{5_1 \times 5_1 \times 5_1 \times 5 \times 5 \times 5}$$

$$= \frac{1}{5^3}$$

Therefore we can see that $5^{-3} = \frac{1}{5^3}$

Here is another interesting example

As $5^3 \div 5^3 = 5^{3-3}$ and also $5^3 \div 5^3 = 1$

$$= 5^0$$

It follows therefore that $5^0 = 1$

In fact any positive number to the power 0 is 1

The table of powers of 5 can be written like this:

$5^2 = 5 \times 5 = 25$

$5^1 = 5$

$5^0 = 1$

$5^{-1} = \dfrac{1}{5}$

$5^{-2} = \dfrac{1}{25}$

$5^{-3} = \dfrac{1}{125}$

and so on.

Exercise 4.3

Use a calculator when necessary with this exercise.

1. Write down the following in index form:

(a) $\dfrac{1}{2 \times 2 \times 2}$

(c) $\dfrac{1}{3 \times 3 \times 3}$

(e) $\dfrac{1}{2 \times 2 \times 2 \times 2 \times 2}$

(b) $\dfrac{1}{9 \times 9}$

(d) $\dfrac{1}{8 \times 8}$

(f) $\dfrac{1}{4 \times 4 \times 4}$

2. Work out the actual fractions in q.1

3. Write these in index form:

(a) $\dfrac{1}{9}$

(c) $\dfrac{1}{49}$

(e) $\dfrac{1}{128}$

(g) $\dfrac{1}{216}$

(b) $\dfrac{1}{16}$

(d) $\dfrac{1}{144}$

(f) $\dfrac{1}{27}$

(h) $\dfrac{1}{625}$

Simplify the following, leaving your answer in index form:

4. (a) $3^3 \div 3^6$ (c) $6 \div 6^4$ (e) $4^3 \div 4^7$
    (b) $7^3 \div 7^5$ (d) $3^2 \div 3^2$ (f) $7 \div 7^5$

5. (a) $2^5 \times 2^{-2}$ (c) $4^{-7} \times 4^3$ (e) $5^{-8} \times 5^7$
    (b) $7^5 \times 7^{-1}$ (d) $3^5 \times 3^{-2}$ (f) $7^{-3} \times 7$

6. (a) $4^3 \times 4^3 \times 4^{-2}$ (c) $5^7 \times 5^2 \times 5^{-4}$ (e) $2^3 \times 2^3 \times 2^{-2}$
    (b) $7^2 \times 7^4 \times 7^{-9}$ (d) $3^2 \times 3^2 \times 3^{-3}$ (f) $7^3 \times 7^2 \times 7^{-5}$

7. (a) $3^3 \times 3^{-3}$ (c) $6^3 \times 6^{-5}$ (e) $4^2 \times 4^{-3}$
    (b) $4^2 \div 4^{-2}$ (d) $3^2 \div 3^{-5}$ (f) $7^3 \div 7^{-7}$

Exercise 4.4: Solving equations with x^2

We know that $3 \times 3 = 9$ and also that $-3 \times -3 = 9$

Therefore we can see that equations with x^2 do in fact have **two** solutions.

Example: $x^2 = 9$

$x = 3$ or -3

Solve these equations:

1. $x^2 = 1$
2. $a^2 = 100$
3. $b^2 = 49$
4. $c^2 = 81$

5. $y^2 = 4$
6. $a^2 = 64$
7. $x^2 = 0.09$
8. $a^2 = 1600$

9. $b^2 = 0.16$
10. $y^2 = 400$
11. $x^2 = 0.0001$
12. $s^2 = 0.25$

Squares and square roots

If $x^2 = x \times x$, i.e. the square of x, we say that x is the **square root** of x^2

1 is the square of 1 and of −1
4 is the square of 2 and of −2
9 is the square of 3 and of −3
16 is the square of 4 and of −4

1 and −1 are the square roots of 1
2 and −2 are the square roots of 4
3 and −3 are the square roots of 9
4 and −4 are the square roots of 16

In reality we rarely need to use the negative square root and for the rest of this chapter we are only going to consider positive square roots.

The positive square root of 4 is written as: $\sqrt{4} = 2$

The little sign meaning 'square root' is an unusual one. There are no other mathematical symbols quite like it.

Where does it come from? One nice story is that it represents the root of a tree!

However it is more likely to have come from the Latin *radix* = root.

You can imagine that if you had to write the word *radix* out again and again you might develop some shorthand. A possible origin of the symbol ($\sqrt{}$) is that it therefore is simply an abbreviation (*r*) for *radix*:

$$radix9 = 3$$

$$r9 \quad = 3$$

$$\sqrt{9} \quad = 3$$

Although it had been used in this form in the 16th century, it was Rene Descartes who brought this sign into general use.

Exercise 4.5

Find these squares and square roots:

1. $\sqrt{16}$

2. $\sqrt{25}$

3. $\sqrt{10\ 000}$

4. 0.4^2

5. 1.2^2

6. $\sqrt{0.25}$

7. $\sqrt{144}$

8. 100^2

9. 0.1^2

10. 0.01^2

11. $\sqrt{0.0036}$

12. $\sqrt{1.21}$

13. $\left(\dfrac{0.3}{0.2}\right)^2$

14. $\sqrt{0.01}$

15. $\left(\dfrac{1}{10}\right)^2$

16. $\sqrt{\dfrac{1}{9}}$

17. $\sqrt{\dfrac{1}{25}}$

18. $\left(\dfrac{1}{2}\right)^2$

19. $\left(\dfrac{2}{3}\right)^2$

20. $\sqrt{\dfrac{4}{25}}$

21. $\sqrt{\dfrac{4^2}{2^2}}$

22. $\left(\dfrac{\sqrt{16}}{\sqrt{36}}\right)^2$

23. $\sqrt{\dfrac{1.6^2}{2^2}}$

24. $\left(\dfrac{\sqrt{0.04}}{0.2}\right)^2$

Using prime factors to find square roots

Consider the number: $2 \times 2 \times 2 \times 2 \times 3 \times 3 \times 3 \times 3$
this could be written as: $(2 \times 2 \times 3 \times 3) \times (2 \times 2 \times 3 \times 3)$

or like this:

$$2^4 \times 3^4 = (2^2 \times 3^2) \times (2^2 \times 3^2)$$
$$= (2^2 \times 3^2)^2$$

We can therefore say that $2^2 \times 3^2$ is the square root of $2^4 \times 3^4$

Exercise 4.6

Write these numbers as the products of their prime factors and so find their square root:

Example: Find the square root of 441

3	4	4	1	
3	1	4	7	
7		4	9	
7			7	
			1	

$\sqrt{441} = 3^2 \times 7^2$
$\quad\quad = (3 \times 7) \times (3 \times 7)$
$\sqrt{441} = 3 \times 7 = 21$

1. 144

2. 225

3. 576

4. 1521

5. 2025

6. 196

7. 324

8. 1225

9. 1089

10. 3969

11. 3136

12. 7056

Other roots

We can also use the same method to find other roots:

$2 \times 2 = 4$	and so 2 is the square root of 4
$2 \times 2 \times 2 = 8$	and so 2 is the cube root of 8 (because three 2s are multipled together to give 8) and this is written: $\sqrt[3]{8} = 2$
$2 \times 2 \times 2 \times 2 = 16$	and so 2 is the fourth root of 16 and this is written: $\sqrt[4]{16} = 2$

Exercise 4.7

Find these powers and roots:

1. 3^6
2. 6^4
3. $\sqrt[3]{125}$
4. 9^3

5. $\sqrt[3]{64}$
6. 2^8
7. $\sqrt[4]{81}$
8. 3^5

9. $\sqrt[6]{729}$
10. 4^4
11. $\sqrt[8]{256}$
12. $\sqrt[4]{625}$

13. Find these squares: (a) 5^2 (b) 6^2 (c) 25^2

Now look carefully at the answers. Notice that in each example the number being squared appears as the last figure, or figures, in the answer. There is only one number between 26 and 100 whose square has the number as the last two digits. Can you work out which number it is?

14. Here's a very interesting question for you to work through:
First, think of a number and square it.   (e.g. 42^2)
Now add 1 to the number and square that.   (e.g. 43^2)
Now take the original square away from the 2nd square (e.g. $43^2 - 42^2$)
Subtract 1 and divide your answer by 2. What do you have?

Try this with some other numbers and see if you always get the same result!

Using the index functions on the calculator

The square roots we have calculated so far have resulted in either a whole number or an exact decimal.

However most square roots do not work out so easily.

For example: We know that $2^2 = 4$ and so $\sqrt{4} = 2$

and that $20^2 = 400$ and so $\sqrt{400} = 20$

but what about $\sqrt{40}$?

It is very difficult to work this out just by looking at it. So let us look at how we can use a calculator to help.

Firstly find the index functions and the second function buttons on your calculator. Your calculator may look at little different from this one but you should still find all the buttons we are going to be talking about.

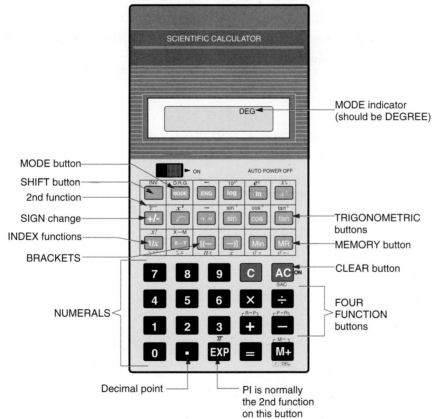

Firstly find the $\sqrt{}$ button, it may be a second function (see picture of the calculator above and the description of second functions below).

Depending on the type of calculator you have, follow one of these key sequences.

On older models enter $\boxed{4}$ $\boxed{0}$ then $\boxed{\sqrt{}}$; on newer models enter $\boxed{\sqrt{}}$ then $\boxed{4}$ $\boxed{0}$ and $\boxed{=}$.

Your calculator should read 6.3245553... . If you are not sure whether yours is old or new, try each of the routines and see which one gives the correct answer.

In this case, because $\sqrt{40}$ does not give an exact value, it is useful to round your answer to one or two decimal places:

6.3245553 = 6.3 (to 1 d.p.) or 6.32 (to 2 d.p.)

Second function

Second functions are the functions written above the function button on your calculator. Typically the cube root button: $\boxed{\sqrt[3]{}}$ is a second function. If this is the case, you have to push the second function button (often marked SHIFT or INV) and then the button marked below $\sqrt[3]{}$ (often the $\boxed{+/-}$ or $\boxed{x^3}$ button).

Index functions

Index functions refer to the functions that find the square, the cube, the square root, the cube root, the reciprocal and so on. The way they work depends on the type of calculator you have. It may be that many of the index functions are in fact second functions on your calculator.

Let us start by finding the cube root of 8

On most models:

Press 2nd function (or shift) then the cube root and then 8 and finally = Your answer should be 2
If you get no answer, 0 or 8 you have an older calculator.

Older calculators:

Try entering 8, second function (or shift) then cube root.
You should have the answer 2

If you cannot find this cube root then refer to your calculator manual.

Exercise 4.8

Use your calculator for this exercise.

1. Find these squares:

    (a) 5^2 (b) 15^2 (c) 23^2 (d) 125^2

2. Find these square roots:

    (a) $\sqrt{25}$ (b) $\sqrt{289}$ (c) $\sqrt{576}$ (d) $\sqrt{262\ 144}$

3. Calculate $\frac{1}{5}$ using the reciprocal button (i.e. $\boxed{\frac{1}{x}}$ or $\boxed{x^{-1}}$). Now push the reciprocal button again, then again and again. What do you notice? Try this with some other numbers.

4. Look for this button: $\boxed{x^y}$. This will calculate any power of any number.

    To find 3^5 you should enter 3 then the $\boxed{x^y}$ button (or $\boxed{y^x}$ or $\boxed{\wedge}$ buttons on some calculators), then 5, and then press enter or $\boxed{=}$
    You should get the number 243

    Now try these:

    (a) 2^7 (b) 5^7 (c) 7^4 (d) 2^{20}

5. Find the cube roots of the following:

    (a) 216   (b) 1728   (c) 8000   (d) 1 953 125

6. Look for this button: $\boxed{x^{\frac{1}{y}}}$ or $\boxed{\sqrt[x]{\ }}$. This is probably another second function and finds any root of any number. For example to find $\sqrt[4]{625}$ you should enter (depending on your calculator) 4 and then the second function followed by the $\boxed{\sqrt[x]{\ }}$ or $\boxed{\sqrt[x]{y}}$ button, then 625, and then $\boxed{=}$. You should get the answer 5. Use this button to find the cube roots of all the numbers in question 2 above.

    Now try these:

    (a) $\sqrt[4]{16}$ (b) $\sqrt[5]{243}$ (c) $\sqrt[6]{4096}$ (d) $\sqrt[7]{78125}$

Using the memory

For harder calculations you may need to use the memory. It is particularly useful when your answers are not whole numbers.

For example, let's try subtracting the square root of 37 from the square root of 56

You should get the answer 1.400 5522

On newer models the key sequence would be:

$\boxed{\sqrt{}}$ 56 $\boxed{M+}$ $\boxed{\sqrt{}}$ 37 $\boxed{M-}$ $\boxed{MR}$ $\boxed{=}$ Answer: 1.400 5522

For older models the key sequence to try is:

56 $\boxed{\sqrt{}}$ $\boxed{M+}$ 37 $\boxed{\sqrt{}}$ $\boxed{M-}$ $\boxed{MR}$ Answer: 1.400 5522

If neither of these work ask your teacher or refer to your calculator manual.

7.   Calculate $\sqrt[3]{39} - \sqrt{10}$

These are a little more complicated; see if you can get the correct answers:

8. $\sqrt{\dfrac{3.1 \times 0.9}{1.5 \times 2.1}}$

9. $\sqrt{(31^5 - 27^4}$

10. $\dfrac{\sqrt{704 \times 612}}{\sqrt{425 \times 176}}$

11. $\dfrac{\sqrt{423} + \sqrt{132}}{\sqrt{645} - \sqrt{312}}$

12. $\dfrac{\sqrt[3]{363 \times 792}}{\sqrt[4]{891 \times 1331}}$

13.   EARTH

$\dfrac{5^2(6284 - 4015)}{\sqrt[8]{390\,625}}$

Use the worksheet to help Captain H_2O on his second space adventure. This time there is an added catch. You have to work out the names of the planets written *upside-down.* The calculations all come out as an upside-down word so, if yours does not then you have gone wrong and you will need to try again!

Writing answers

In the above calculations, answers have been written to a full display of your calculator. Some problems require quite lengthy working out. It is important that each stage of your working is clearly shown and that **only** the final answer is rounded. Never calculate with rounded answers and always use the full display on your calculator.

Large and small numbers

Most problems that we have to solve have quite ordinary numbers, but, as we explore the world of science, geography and astronomy, we often come across very large numbers and very small numbers.

Consider these facts about the Universe:

A **light year** is a unit of distance in astronomy. It is the distance travelled by light in one year. Light moves at a velocity of about 300 000 000 metres (m) each second. In one year, it can travel about 10 trillion km. More precisely, light will travel around 9 461 000 000 000 kilometres in a year.

The distance to the nearest large galaxy, called Andromeda, is 21 quintillion km i.e. 21 000 000 000 000 000 000 km.

The **parsec** is equal to 3.3 light years. Using the light year, we can say that:

- The Crab supernova remnant is about 4000 light years away.
- The Milky Way galaxy is about 150 000 light years across.
- Andromeda is about 2.3 million light years away.

At the other end of the scale, the size of a typical human cell is 10^{-5} metres (10 microns).

10^{-7} seconds (100 nanoseconds) is the timing of a beam of the microwave laser used to calibrate the atomic clock in Boulder, Colorado. 100 nanoseconds is the exposure of the fastest stroboscopic camera.

Now look at your calculator. You will see that the display can only show 8 or 10 digits, so calculating with these very large and very small numbers is extremely difficult. The solution is to find a way of writing them in 'shorthand' so that we can use a calculator.

Writing these numbers in shorthand not only makes calculations easier but also makes it much easier to compare their relative sizes. It is also quicker to write shorthand.

The shorthand system we use is based on the fact that our number system is a decimal system and that the powers of ten can be written with indices:

For example: One thousand is 1000 or $10 \times 10 \times 10 = 10^3$

One hundredth is $\dfrac{1}{100} = \dfrac{1}{10 \times 10} = 10^{-2}$

Exercise 4.9

Write these numbers as powers of ten:

Examples:	(i) $100\ 000 = 10^5$
	(ii) $0.000\ 01 = 10^{-5}$

1. 10 000

2. 1000

3. 0.001

4. 0.000 001

5. 10 000 000 000

6. 0. 000 000 01

7. 10 000 000

8. 0.000 01

9. 1 000 000 000

10. 0.000 000 001

11. 0.01

12. 1

Exercise 4.10

Write these numbers as a single figure multiplied by a power of ten:

> Examples:
>
> (i) $5\ 000 = 5 \times 1000$
> $ = 5 \times 10^3$
>
> (ii) $0.006 = 6 \times 0.001$
> $ = 6 \times 10^{-3}$

1.	30 000	**7.**	0.000 06
2.	0.000 04	**8.**	0.000 008
3.	0.09	**9.**	7000
4.	0.0006	**10.**	0.000 000 000 000 006
5.	0.000 000 07	**11.**	700 000
6.	80 000 000	**12.**	30 000 000 000

Exercise 4.11

Write these numbers out in full. Remember to put the space in the correct position after each group of three numbers:

> Examples:
>
> (i) $3 \times 10^4 = 3 \times 10\ 000$
> $ = 30\ 000$
>
> (ii) $7 \times 10^{-5} = 7 \times 0.000\ 01$
> $\phantom{(ii)\ 7 \times 10^{-5}} = 0.000\ 07$

1.	2×10^2	**4.**	5×10^3
2.	6×10^{-6}	**5.**	7×10^{-7}
3.	7×10^8	**6.**	3×10^{-6}

7. 9×10^4

8. 3×10^{-2}

9. 6×10^6

10. 8×10^7

11. 9×10^{-4}

12. 7×10^{10}

Standard index form

Standard index form is a way of writing numbers where a number (between one and ten) is multiplied by a power of ten.

> The definition of standard index form is:
> A number between one and ten multiplied by a power of ten.

For example: 5×10^3

The numbers we have just looked at have all been single numbers but we can also write decimals in standard index form.

> Example:
>
> $$5.7 \times 10^3 = 5.7 \times 1000$$
> $$= 5700$$
>
> Note the 5 is × 1000 so the answer will be five thousand and something not fifty seven thousand. Remember to look carefully at the position of the decimal point.

Exercise 4.12

Write these numbers out in full:

1. 2.8×10^3

2. 4.9×10^2

3. 3.65×10^5

4. 9.36×10^6

5. 1.001×10^{-1}

6. 5.68×10^{-3}

7. 9.09×10^{-4}

8. 3.142×10^{-2}

9. 1.618×10^5

10. 7.205×10^{-3}

Exercise 4.13

Write these numbers in standard index form:

Examples: (i) 680 000 $= 6.8 \times 100\ 000$
$= 6.8 \times 10^5$

(ii) 0.000 207 $= 2.07 \times 0.000\ 1$
$= 2.07 \times 10^{-4}$

1. 3900

2. 11 500

3. 56 000 000

4. 405 000

5. 39 000

6. 77

7. 809 000 000 000

8. 20 050 000

9. 607 500

10. 9 080 000

11. 0.005

12. 0.006 84

13. 0.000 032

14. 0.000 000 809

15. 0.54

16. 0.008 004

17. 0.305 47

18. 609

19. 46 800 000

20. 0.000 019 09

Standard index form and the scientific calculator

Try this multiplication on your scientific calculator.

450 000 × 250 000

If you have an **older style** calculator the display showing the answer will look something like this:

$$1.125^{11}$$

This is the calculator's own shorthand for 1.125×10^{11} or 112 500 000 000

14. A newer unit of astronomical measurement is the parsec. One parsec is roughly 3.25 light years. How many kilometres is this?

15. An aeon is 10^9 years. The Sun was formed 4.5 aeons ago. How many years ago is that?

Roots as indices

We now know that $5^3 \times 5^2 = 5^5$

N.B. $3 + 2 = 5$

Remember that if numbers written in index form are multiplied together the resulting index is the sum of the indices (see page 67).

We also know that $5 \times 5 = 25$ and therefore we can see that 5 is the square root of 25

So now, what is the square root of 5?

Let's start by looking at the calculation $5^x \times 5^x$:

$$5^x \times 5^x = 5^{2x}$$

$$\text{If } x + x = 1$$

$$2x = 1$$

$$x = \frac{1}{2}$$

$$\text{and } 5^{\frac{1}{2}} \times 5^{\frac{1}{2}} = 5$$

Therefore $5^{\frac{1}{2}}$ is another way of writing $\sqrt{5}$

Calculating with roots and powers

Examples:

(i) $7^{\frac{1}{2}} \times 7^{\frac{1}{2}} \times 7^{\frac{1}{2}} \times 7^{\frac{1}{2}} = 7^{\frac{1}{2} + \frac{1}{2} + \frac{1}{2} + \frac{1}{2}}$

$$= 7^2$$

(ii) $\left(\sqrt{2}\right)^4 = \sqrt{2} \times \sqrt{2} \times \sqrt{2} \times \sqrt{2}$

$$= 2 \times 2$$

$$= 4$$

Exercise 4.15: Extension questions 1

1. $\sqrt{3} \times \sqrt{3}$

2. $7^{\frac{1}{2}} \times 7^{\frac{1}{2}}$

3. $\sqrt{4} \times \sqrt{4} \times \sqrt{4}$

4. $2^{\frac{1}{2}} \times 2^{\frac{1}{2}}$

5. $\sqrt{9} \times \sqrt{9} \times \sqrt{9}$

6. $\sqrt{7} \times \sqrt{7} \times \sqrt{7} \times \sqrt{7}$

7. $\left(\sqrt{7}\right)^2$

8. $5^{\frac{1}{2}} \times 5^{\frac{1}{2}} \times 5^{\frac{1}{2}} \times 5^{\frac{1}{2}}$

9. $\sqrt{11} \times \sqrt{11}$

10. $\left(5^{\frac{1}{2}}\right)^2$

11. $\left(3^{\frac{1}{2}}\right)^4$

12. $\left(9^{\frac{1}{2}}\right)^3$

More about square roots

Consider $\sqrt{4}$

What number multiplied by itself makes 4?

$2 \times 2 = 4$ but also $-2 \times -2 = 4$

and so we can say $\sqrt{4} = \pm 2$

Exercise 4.16: Extension questions 2

Find **both** square roots of these numbers:

1. 1

2. 9

3. 16

4. 81

5. 121

6. 289

7. 256

8. 144

9. 361

10. 625

11. 324

12. 225

Remember that whilst it is important to be aware that a number has a positive root and a negative square root, for the rest of this exercise we are going to consider the **positive** square root only.

Let us consider $\sqrt{3}$

Because there is no whole number answer to $\sqrt{3}$ (1.732) it is often easier to leave the number written as $\sqrt{3}$. This is particularly true if you are calculating with roots.

Consider the calculation $\sqrt{3} \times \sqrt{3}$

Because the numbers in the calculation are expressed as square roots it is easier keep the square roots and simply multiply $\sqrt{3} \times \sqrt{3}$ i.e.

$$\sqrt{3} \times \sqrt{3} = \sqrt{9} = 3$$

similarly $\qquad \sqrt{3} \times \sqrt{12} = \sqrt{36} = 6$

Exercise 4.17: Extension questions 3

Work out these products of square roots. Some will result in a whole number answer and some will not. If not, leave the answer in root form.

1. $\sqrt{3} \times \sqrt{48}$
5. $\sqrt{2} \times \sqrt{2} \times \sqrt{2}$
9. $\sqrt{3} \times \sqrt{18}$

2. $\sqrt{8} \times \sqrt{32}$
6. $\sqrt{5} \times \sqrt{25}$
10. $\sqrt{8} \times \sqrt{18}$

3. $\sqrt{3} \times \sqrt{7}$
7. $\sqrt{12} \times \sqrt{27}$
11. $\sqrt{3} \times \sqrt{27}$

4. $\sqrt{3} \times \sqrt{2} \times \sqrt{6}$
8. $\sqrt{7} \times \sqrt{28}$
12. $\sqrt{6} \times \sqrt{54}$

You should have found four numbers that you had to leave in root form:

$\qquad$ i.e. $\qquad \sqrt{8} \qquad \sqrt{125} \qquad \sqrt{48} \qquad \sqrt{54}$

Now although these are not whole number square roots they are multiples of square numbers. Here is what we mean:

Let's look at the first one:

$$\sqrt{8} = \sqrt{4 \times 2} \qquad \text{We know that } 4 \times 2 = 8$$

$$= \sqrt{4} \times \sqrt{2} \qquad \text{and that the square root of 4 is 2}$$

$$= 2\sqrt{2} \qquad \text{so we can write 2}$$

Hence: $\sqrt{125} = \sqrt{25 \times 5}$ and $\sqrt{48} = \sqrt{16 \times 3}$ and $\sqrt{54} = \sqrt{9 \times 6}$

$\qquad\qquad = \sqrt{25} \times \sqrt{5} \qquad\qquad = \sqrt{16} \times \sqrt{3} \qquad\qquad = \sqrt{9} \times \sqrt{6}$

$\qquad\qquad = 5\sqrt{5} \qquad\qquad\qquad\quad = 4\sqrt{3} \qquad\qquad\qquad = 3\sqrt{6}$

Using this method simplify these:

13. $\sqrt{75}$

14. $\sqrt{27}$

15. $\sqrt{162}$

16. $\sqrt{72}$

17. $\sqrt{2} \times \sqrt{3} \times \sqrt{10}$

18. $\sqrt{2} \times \sqrt{4} \times \sqrt{8}$

19. $\sqrt{3} \times \sqrt{5} \times \sqrt{15}$

20. $\sqrt{8} \times \sqrt{12}$

21. $\sqrt{21} \times \sqrt{14}$

22. $\sqrt{6} \times \sqrt{12}$

23. $\sqrt{8} \times \sqrt{24}$

24. $\sqrt{12} \times \sqrt{15}$

25. $\sqrt{2} \times \sqrt{18} \times \sqrt{4}$

26. $\sqrt{3} \times \sqrt{12} \times \sqrt{15}$

We now know that expressions with square roots can be factorised and simplified:

Examples

(i) $\sqrt{3} \times \sqrt{6} + \sqrt{72} = \sqrt{18} + \sqrt{72}$ Simplify

$\qquad\qquad\qquad\quad = \sqrt{2} \times \sqrt{9} \times \sqrt{2} \times \sqrt{36}$ Factorise 1

$\qquad\qquad\qquad\quad = \sqrt{2} \times \left(\sqrt{9} + \sqrt{36} \right)$ Factorise 2

$\qquad\qquad\qquad\quad = 3\sqrt{2} \times 6\sqrt{2}$ Extract squares

$\qquad\qquad\qquad\quad = 9\sqrt{2}$ Simplify

(ii) $\dfrac{1}{\sqrt{2}} + \sqrt{2} = \dfrac{1 + \sqrt{2} \times \sqrt{2}}{\sqrt{2}}$ First find a common denominator

$\qquad\qquad = \dfrac{1 + 2}{\sqrt{2}} = \dfrac{3}{\sqrt{2}} \times \dfrac{\sqrt{2}}{\sqrt{2}}$ Then make the denominator a whole number

$\qquad\qquad = \dfrac{3\sqrt{2}}{2}$ Simplify

Exercise 4.18: Extension questions 4

Simplify these:

1. $\sqrt{72} \times \sqrt{50}$

2. $\sqrt{12} \times \sqrt{27}$

3. $\sqrt{20} \times \sqrt{45}$

4. $\sqrt{20} \times \sqrt{10} + \sqrt{15} \times \sqrt{5}$

5. $\sqrt{8} \times \sqrt{10} + \sqrt{9} \times \sqrt{20}$

6. $\dfrac{\sqrt{3}}{3} + \sqrt{3}$

7. $\dfrac{1}{\sqrt{8}} + \dfrac{1}{\sqrt{12}}$

8. $\dfrac{1}{\sqrt{5}} + \sqrt{5}$

9. $\dfrac{7}{\sqrt{7}} - \sqrt{7}$

10. $\dfrac{1}{\sqrt{2}} - \sqrt{7}$

11. $\dfrac{\sqrt{3}}{\sqrt{2}} + \dfrac{\sqrt{2}}{\sqrt{3}}$

12. $\dfrac{\sqrt{6} + \sqrt{6}}{\sqrt{3}}$

Exercise 4.19: Summary exercise

1. Write these in index form:
   (a) $3 \times 3 \times 3$
   (b) $2 \times 2 \times 2 \times 2 \times 2 \times 2$
   (c) $4 \times 4 \times 4 \times 4 \times 4$
   (d) $7 \times 7 \times 7$

2. Now write down the answers to q.1

3. Write these numbers in index form:
   (a) 8   (b) 125   (c) 128   (d) 81

4. Write these as fractions:
   (a) 2^{-2} (b) 3^{-5} (c) 7^{-3}

5. Simplify these, if possible, leaving your answer in index form:
   (a) $3^2 \times 3^4$
   (b) $7^5 \div 7^2$
   (c) $3^2 \div 3^5$
   (d) $3^3 + 3^3$
   (e) $5^2 \div 3^3$
   (f) $3^3 \times 5^2$
   (g) $5^3 \times 5^7$
   (h) $5^4 \div 5$
   (i) $2^2 \div 2^8$
   (j) $3^3 + 2^3$
   (k) $6^4 \div 2^4$
   (l) $5^3 - 4^2$

6. Simplify these, leaving your answers in index form:

(a) $4^2 \times 4^{-3}$

(b) $3^{-2} \div 3^{-3}$

(c) $4^{-2} \times 4^{-2}$

(d) $2^7 \times 2^{-5}$

(e) $5^{-2} \div 5^2$

(f) $7^2 \times 7^{-2}$

7. Solve the following equations:

(a) $x^2 = 16$

(b) $a^2 = 100$

(c) $b^2 = \frac{1}{4}$

8. Find these squares and square roots:

(a) $\sqrt{16}$

(b) 1.1^2

(c) 0.3^2

(d) $\sqrt{0.04}$

9. Find the value of:

(a) 7×10^4

(b) 2.75×10^6

(c) 1.5×10^{-4}

(d) 9.702×10^{-3}

10. Write these in standard index form:

(a) 47 000

(b) 0.0081

(c) 506 000 000

(d) 0.000 402

11. Calculate the number of milligrams in 6.2 tonnes and give your answer in standard index form.

12. Evaluate:

(a) $\sqrt{5} \times \sqrt{5}$

(b) $\left(\sqrt{3}\right)^2$

(c) $\sqrt{3} \times \sqrt{48}$

(d) $\sqrt{5} \times \sqrt{28} \times \sqrt{35}$

End of chapter 4 activity: Chain letters

You may well have received a letter reading something like this:

'How do you like receiving letters? Most of us do, and this letter is to guarantee that you receive hundreds of letters. All you have to do is to send a letter to the person at the top of the list below. Then copy out this letter 5 times, take off the top person from the list and add your name at the bottom. Then send the five copies to five of your best friends.'

1. John Smith

2. Sara Ing

3. Pete Black

4. Imran Patel

5. Claire Jones

P.S. Don't break the chain and don't tell the post office.

Let us consider how true is the claim that you will receive hundreds of letters. This letter takes 5 stages to move you up to the top of the list.

Therefore your 5 friends will send letters to 5 friends who will send letters to 5 friends who will send letters to 5 friends who will send letters to 5 friends who will all send me a letter.

1.   How many letters will I receive if the chain has not been broken? (Not 25!)

2.   How many letters should I receive if there were 6 people on the list and I had sent letters to 6 friends?

3.   How many letters would I receive if there were 5 people on the list but everybody in the chain sent out 10 copies to friends?

4.   Investigate this for different numbers of people on the list and different numbers of copies. Can you find a rule for the number of letters that you receive in theory and the number of copies that you send out?

5.   One of the most famous chain letter 'scams' (and one of the reasons that they **are illegal**) asked you to send £10 to the person at the top of the list and then 'sell' your letters for £1 each to ten other people. This time there was a list of 10 people before you were sent the £10s. How many people should have been in the chain by then? How does this compare to the population of Britain?

A great many people lost their £10 because everybody else had heard of it first – and most people broke the chain!

Chapter 5: Percentages

The word 'percentage' has been used since the end of the fifteenth century. However, the idea started much earlier. When the Roman emperor Augustus levied a tax on goods he called it *centesima rerum venalium* and the rate was one hundredth. Other Roman taxes were one twentieth on every freed slave and one twenty-fifth on every slave sold. Without using a percentage as such, they used fractions easily reduced to hundredths.

In the fifteenth century Italian manuscripts contained expressions such as '20 p 100' and 'x p cento' to indicate 20 percent and 10 percent. By the sixteenth and seventeenth centuries percentages were commonly used for describing profit, loss and interest.

A form of the per cent sign is found in fifteenth century manuscripts on commercial arithmetic, where it appears as this symbol after the word 'per' or after the letter 'p' as the contraction for 'per cento'.

$$P \underset{\frown}{-} \overset{o}{}$$

The exact origin of the percent sign that we use today, %, is obscure but possibly evolved from a symbol introduced in an anonymous Italian manuscript of 1425. Instead of 'per 100', or 'P cento', which were common at that time, the author used this symbol:

$$\frac{o}{o}$$

You can see that there is an important connection between percentages and fractions and consequently with decimals. It is important therefore that you are fully confident in converting from one to another.

Here is a reminder:

Rules of conversion

- To turn a fraction into a decimal:
  Divide the top number (numerator)
  by the bottom number (denominator)

  $$\frac{3}{8} = 3 \div 8 = 0.375$$

- To turn a decimal or fraction into a percentage:

  Multiply by 100

  $$0.125 = 0.125 \times 100\%$$
  $$= 12.5\% \text{ or } 12\frac{1}{2}\%$$

- To turn a percentage into a decimal:
  Divide by 100

  $$85\% = 85 \div 100$$
  $$= 0.85$$

- To turn a percentage into a fraction:
  Write as a fraction with 100
  as the denominator
  and simplify if possible

  $$72\% = \frac{72}{100}$$
  $$= \frac{18}{25}$$

- To turn a decimal into a fraction:
  Write a fraction with the correct
  denominator (10, 100, 1000 ...)
  and simplify if possible

  $$0.64 = \frac{64}{100}$$
  $$= \frac{16}{25}$$

You should also know how to form a percentage and to find a percentage of an amount. Here are some examples to help you remind yourself.

Forming a percentage

Example:
My maths result was 24 out of 40
What is this as a percentage?

$$\text{Percentage} = \frac{24^{6}}{40_{1}} \times 100$$
$$= 60\%$$

Finding a fraction of an amount

Example:
Everything is marked down 20% in the sale.
What is the sale price of a discman previously marked at £88?

Discount $= \dfrac{2\cancel{0}}{10\cancel{0}} \times 88$

$= \dfrac{176}{10}$

$= £17.60$

Sale price $= £88.00 - £17.60$

$= £70.40$

The next exercise will help you to revise these concepts. In using the fraction method the numbers should cancel down and you should not need a calculator. You could check your answers with a calculator to verify your arithmetic.

Exercise 5.1

1. Write the following fractions as (i) percentages and then (ii) decimals:

    (a) $\frac{1}{5}$ (b) $\frac{3}{10}$ (c) $\frac{5}{8}$ (d) $\frac{4}{25}$

2. Write these percentages as (i) decimals and then (ii) fractions:

    (a) 14% (b) 65% (c) 33% (d) 44%

3. These percentages all contain a fraction, but you should recognise their fraction equivalents.
    Write them as (i) fractions and then (ii) decimals:

    (a) $12\frac{1}{2}\%$ (b) $66\frac{2}{3}\%$ (c) $16\frac{2}{3}\%$ (d) $37\frac{1}{2}\%$

4. Here are some recurring decimals.
    Write them as (i) fractions and then (ii) percentages:

    (a) $0.\dot{3}$ (b) $0.8\dot{3}$ (c) $0.\dot{2}$

5. 88% of my class had a BCG inoculation. What percentage did not?

6. 64% of people fail their driving test first time. What is the percentage pass rate?

7. What is 10% of £35?

8. What is 60% of 3 m?

9. What is 25% of two hours?

10. What is 35% of £5?

11. What is 63% of 500 km?

12. In my class of 25, 11 of us had flu. What percentage of the class has flu?

13. The cost of cat food has risen 5%. If the original price was 40p per can, what is it now?

14. In the sale prices are marked down 12%. What is the sale price of:
    (a) a pair of trainers normally costing £25
    (b) a jacket normally costing £35
    (c) a CD player normally costing £40?

15. We picked 65 apples but 26 of them had maggots in them.
    What percentage of apples did not contain maggots?

16. I have negotiated a rise of 15% in my pocket money. If it was £5 per week, what is it now?

17. If income tax is 25% how much tax do I pay on earnings of £2500?

18. Extra long jeans cost 5% more than standard length ones. If standard jeans are £25, how much are extra long jeans?

19. My friend and I were cleaning cars to raise money. When we had finished, we worked out our costs as £2 per car and realised we had made a 15% loss. What were we charging?

20. I cooked 144 mince pies for the Christmas Fayre, but 48 of them burnt. What percentage of them did not burn?

21. Service charge at our local Hamburger Restaurant is 15%. How much service was added on to our food bill of £25?

22. There is 10% discount from our computer suppliers for orders over £100 If boxes of 10 CDs usually cost £19, how many boxes must we buy before we qualify for the discount and how much will we save?

23. Write down the percentage of this pie chart that is:

(a) red   (b) blue   (c) yellow

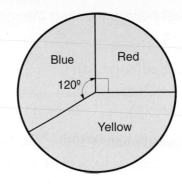

24. In a survey of 300 pupils in the school, 120 came to school by car, 50 walked, 70 came on a school bus and the rest came by public transport.
(a) What percentage came by public transport?
(b) Show this information on a pie chart.

Percentage as a decimal

The first exercise was done without a calculator and therefore used the fraction method. In this instance the numbers could be cancelled easily to make the arithmetic more straightforward. However, a lot of the time you will have to deal with more complicated numbers and use a calculator. Whilst you can use the fraction method when using a calculator, it is more efficient to convert the percentages to decimals.

Example:
Value Added Tax is currently $17\frac{1}{2}\%$
Find the VAT on a computer costing £599

VAT $= 17\frac{1}{2}\%$ of £599	$17\frac{1}{2}\% = 0.175$
$= 0.175 \times £599$	Write down the calculation you are entering.
$= £104.825$	Write the full answer from your calculator.
$= £104.83$ (to 2 d.p.)	Money is written to the nearest penny.

Note the way that the answer is structured. It is important that your calculations are clearly written. You need to write out the full answer given on the display before rounding it, just in case you need to use it in a subsequent calculation.

If you concentrate on getting into good habits you will not have to unlearn bad ones!

Finding a percentage using a calculator is done in the same way as before:

Example:

I started off with £120 in my building society account and a year later, after interest was added, I had £129

What rate of interest was applied?

Interest earned = 129 − 120 = £9   Calculate the difference between the two amounts.

Interest Rate $= \dfrac{9}{120} \times 100$

$= 7.5\%$

Then, because you want to know the % increase on the **original** amount, you divide the difference by this **original**.

Exercise 5.2

Use a calculator for this exercise. Write down all your working carefully.

1. VAT is currently $17\frac{1}{2}\%$. Write down the value of the VAT on these articles:
    (a) Teddy bear   £12
    (b) Fax machine   £279
    (c) Tennis racquet   £49
    (d) Bicycle   £150
    (e) Baseball cap   £2.50
    (f) Football   £16

2. Find the selling price of the articles in q.1

3. All prices are marked down 15% in a sale. What discount would be given on these articles?
    (a) Kite   £15   (d) Alarm clock   £12
    (b) Beach ball   £4   (e) Stereo system   £150
    (c) Walkman   £35   (f) Kettle   £25

4. What is the selling price of the articles in q.3 in the sale?

5.   My grandfather opened a building society account for me and put in £80
     If the interest rate is 6% how much interest did I earn in one year?

6.   A computer was marked at £699, but we bought it in the sale for £560
     By what percentage was the computer marked down?

7.   Tennis balls are normally sold for 99p each. In the sale there are two
     bargain packs. I can either buy 4 balls for £3.60 or 6 balls for £5.50
     Which pack gives the larger percentage discount?

8.   Theatre tickets are normally £12, but if you have a party of 10 or more
     people you save 15%. How many tickets do we have to buy to get two
     people in for free?

Percentage increase and decrease

In the above exercises there have been several examples of amounts rising or
falling through a percentage increase or decrease. It can be quite confusing to
work out whether some changes result in a rise or fall. These are the ones that
you are most likely to meet:

Decrease	Increase
Discount	Premium
Sale Price	Surcharge
Income Tax	Value Added Tax (V.A.T.)
Devaluation	Service Charge
No Claims Bonus	Commission
Loss	Profit

When we talk about percentage problems it is often in relation to money. Some
decreases are good things in that we save money, for example discounts, sale
prices and no-claims bonuses; whilst others mean that we have less money or
need to spend more, for example income tax and service charge.

Most increases cost us money. If we are **buying** services. commission, VAT,
and service charges are all added to the bill and therefore increase the cost.
However if we are **selling** services then these percentages make up our
earnings. Some workers rely entirely on percentage commissions for their
income.

Calculating percentage increase and decrease

In the last exercise you calculated VAT as a percentage and then added it to the original price to find the selling price.

This can be done in one calculation. Consider the original price as being 100% of itself, you then add VAT as $17\frac{1}{2}\%$ of the original price and that gives you $117\frac{1}{2}\%$:

Original price		VAT		New price
100%	+	$17\frac{1}{2}\%$	=	$117\frac{1}{2}\%$ or 1.175

The number 1.175 is known as the **multiplying factor**. If you multiply all the prices in q.1 of the last exercise by 1.175 you should get the prices in q.2

A sale price involves a percentage decrease and so the percentage calculation looks like this:

Original price		Discount		New price
100%	−	15%	=	85% or 0.85

The number 0.85 is known as the **multiplying factor**. If you multiply all the prices in q.3 of the last exercise by 0.85 you should get the prices in q.4

Examples:

(i) A service charge of 12% is added to my restaurant bill of £52.50 What is the total amount of my bill?

Total amount = 1.12 × 52.50
            = £58.80

(ii) The value of my car has fallen by 12% over the last year. If it was worth £5000 last year, what is its current value?

New value = 0.88 × 5000
          = £4400

Exercise 5.3

1. **Calculator maze**

   Work through the worksheet using your calculator. You will find it helpful to record your routes and the values calculated on the way to your targets.

2. Multiply all the prices in q.1 of the previous exercise by 1.175 and check that you get the answers in q.2

3. Multiply all the prices in q.3 of the previous exercise by 0.85 and check that you get the answers in q.4

4. Write down the **multiplying factor** to get the final price in the following examples:

   (a) an increase of 4%

   (b) a surcharge of 5%

   (c) a discount of 8%

   (d) income tax at 20%

   (e) a saving of 18%

   (f) a no claims bonus of 15%

   (g) commission at 8%

   (h) a service charge of $12\frac{1}{2}$%

   (i) a premium of 10%

   (j) a devaluation of 16%

   (k) a decrease of 32%

   (l) supertax at 40%

5. Trainers are normally sold at £49 a pair. In the sale they are marked down by 12%. What is the sale price of the trainers?

6. A service charge of 12% is added to my bill. If the bill was £25 before the service charge was added, what is the total amount (including the service charge) I have to pay?

7. My local pizza take away is offering 10% off all orders over £15 this week. If I order two pizzas at £8.25 each, what will I have to pay?

8. We are trying to sell our house for £150 000

   The estate agent's commission will be 2%. How much money would we receive from the sale?

9. A new car is said to devalue 15% in its first year and 10% in its second year. If my mother bought a new car costing £8500 two years ago, what was its value at the end of one year? What was its value at the end of two years?

10. A length of bungy jumping elastic is said to stretch up to 22% of its original length. If its original length is 20 m, what is its maximum stretched length?

11. The instructions for cooking roast lamb tell me to roast it for 40 minutes per kg, but to reduce the time by 15% if the joint is boned. How long should I roast a 4 kg leg of lamb with a bone in?

12. Water increases in volume by 4% when it freezes and becomes ice. What is the frozen volume of 4 litres of water? Give your answer in cubic cm (1 litre = 1000 cm³).

Income tax

Income tax is worked out as a percentage of your earnings, although you are allowed to earn a certain amount without having to pay tax at all.

Tax is paid to the government and different governments change the rate of tax depending on how much revenue they wish to raise. This is not a new practice. Your study of history should have shown many occasions when rulers, kings and governments have raised taxes to pay for a variety of expenses – most notably to pay for wars and for the repairs caused by war. A large part of present government expenditure goes on the National Health, Defence and Social Services.

At present (2005), income tax is charged at 10% of the first £2000 of your taxable earnings and then at 22% of all higher earnings until a threshold of £30 000. Earnings above £30 000 are taxed at 40%. All these amounts are per year. However the Chancellor of the Exchequer frequently changes tax rates in the Budget, so you should always check the latest rate before you work out your own tax.

The fact that this is so complicated means that many people employ an accountant to work out their tax for them. Accountants have to be good at working with figures but in return they earn a lot of money themselves. In this next exercise you can see how good an accountant you might be.

Example:

A single man earning £16 000 p.a. has a tax free allowance of £4700
What does he earn per year after paying tax?

Taxable earnings	= 16 000 – 4700
	= £11 300
	= £2000 + £9300
10% of £2000	= 0.1 × 2000
	= £200
22% of £9300	= 0.22 × 9300
	= £2046
Therefore the tax paid	= £200 + £2046
	= £2246
Earnings after tax	= £16 000 – £2246
	= £13 754

Here we have split the total taxable earnings into two amounts so that we can apply 10% to the first £2000 and 22% to higher earnings up to the £30 000 threshold.

Exercise 5.4

1. A single person's allowance is £4700
   Work out the annual income after tax for these single people:
   (a) A shop assistant earning £12 000 per year.
   (b) A teacher earning £20 000 per year.
   (c) A nurse earning £15 000 per year.
   (d) A solicitor earning £50 000 per year.

2. Work out the total income for these couples. Each person has a single person's allowance of £4700:

   (a) A mechanic earning £16 000 per year and a nurse earning £15 000 a year.

   (b) A manager earning £32 000 per year and a teacher earning £26 000 a year.

   (c) A salesman who earned £20 000 in the first six months and £8000 in the second six months, and his wife who is a temporary secretary and earns £10 000 a year.

   (d) A model earning £120 000 per year married to a singer who has only managed to earn £5000 this year.

3. Which person in q.2 paid the smallest percentage of tax, and which person the highest percentage?

Percentage change

In the examples we have just seen, the percentage has meant a change of value. Sometimes the change has been **caused** by a percentage such as tax, or commission or a bonus, at other times the percentage **records** the change in values.

A percentage is a useful way of recording change because it does not look at the actual values themselves but at the **proportion that has changed**.

The percentage change can be seen from the multiplying factor:

> **1.20** means a percentage **increase** of **20%**   (1 + 0.2 = 1.20)
> **0.72** means a percentage **decrease** of **28%**   (1 − 0.28 = 0.72)

Remember how we found new values by using the calculation:

---

new amount = original amount × multiplying factor

This can be rearranged such that:

multiplying factor = $\dfrac{\text{new amount}}{\text{original amount}}$

Example:

A car dealer buys in a car for £1250   He spends £200 on repairs
and then sells the car for £2750

What is his percentage profit?

$$\text{multiplying factor} = \frac{\text{new amount}}{\text{original amount}}$$

$$= \frac{2750}{1250 + 200}$$

$$= 1.896 \ldots$$

$$= 1.90 \text{ (to 3 s.f.)} \qquad \text{Now write this as a percentage.}$$

The dealer made a 90% profit.

Exercise 5.5

In each of the following questions write down the **original value** and the **new value** and thus whether there has been an **increase** or a **decrease**:

1.   The shirt cost £15 before the sale and £12 in the sale.

2.   The bill was £52.50
     After VAT and service were added it was £67.86

3.   I bought a car for £2500 and sold it for £1750

4.   There were 416 pupils in the school last year. This year there are 395

5.   The account was £300; with commission and tax we paid £423

6.   I earn £18 000 per year. I take home £1200 per month.

7.   A wholesaler buys 100 discs for £50
     He sells five discs for £8

8.   We paid premiums of £220 last year. We pay premiums of £190 this year.

9.   The tickets cost £15 each. We paid £240 for 20 of us.

10. Now work out the percentage change in each of the above.

Finding the original amount

Many of the prices that we see around us are the result of tax being added. During the sales, prices are often reduced, so it is useful to be able to find the original cost of the item.

Prices you see in most shops already have VAT added and during the sales you see the sale price. If you are running your own business it is important to know how much money you will need to give to the government (i.e. the VAT element of a price) and how much money you will actually get for the goods you sell.

Again, remember how we found new values by using the calculation:

new value = original value × multiplying factor

When we know the value after a percentage increase or decrease, we can find the original value by substituting into this formula.

Example:
Find the original price of an article to which VAT at $17\frac{1}{2}$% has been added and is now marked at £23.50

$$\text{new value} = \text{original value} \times \text{multiplying factor}$$
$$£23.50 = \text{original value} \times 1.175$$
$$\text{original value} = 23.50 \div 1.175$$
$$= £20$$

Exercise 5.6

In this exercise find the original amount. Give answers to 2 d.p. if they are not whole numbers.

1. A second hand car dealer makes 20% profit when he sells a car for £2640   How much did he pay for the car?

2. A stereo being sold for £58.75 includes VAT at $17\frac{1}{2}$%. What is the price without VAT?

3. The value of our house has dropped 8% in the last year. It is now worth £147 000
   What was it worth last year?

4. Our local MP won 42% fewer votes in this election than in the last election. If he won 14 500 votes this time how many did he win the time before?

5. A music shop is selling off last month's Top 10 CDs to make room for this month's new Top 10
   By selling each CD at £9.85 the shop is giving an 18% discount. What was the price of a CD last month?

6. The volume of water increases by 4% when it freezes and becomes ice. What volume of water in litres is equivalent to a block of ice 10 cm × 10 cm × 25 cm?

7. My height has increased by 5% this year and I now measure 1.60 m. What was my height last year?

8. The number of pupils boarding at my school has dropped by 8% in the last five years. If there are 142 pupils boarding now, how many were boarding five years ago?

9. A wholesaler buys in 25 kg bags of potatoes and sells the potatoes to the public in bags of 10 kg to make 25% profit. If he sells the 10 kg bags at £1.20 each, what did he pay for the 25 kg bags?

10. A car is said to devalue 15% in its first year and then 10% in its second. If our two-year-old car is worth £6120 now what was it worth last year? What did we pay for it when it was new?

Exercise 5.7

In this exercise you must decide if you are required to find the original amount or the new amount. Give answers to 2 d.p. if they are not whole numbers.

1. I pay £300 premium for my car insurance after a no claims bonus of 20% What is my premium without the no claims bonus?

2. An art dealer paid £4000 for a painting and sold it at a 15% loss. What was the selling price?

3. Tax at 25% is paid on our company's profits of £90 000
   How much tax do we pay?

4. My accountant charges me 45% of the amount that he saves my company over the year. If I paid him £675 this year how much has he saved my company?

5. The bill including service at 15% came to £48.30
    What would the bill have been without the service added?

6. The number of Labour councillors in our local council has risen by 5% at the last local election. There were 60 Labour councillors, how many are there now?

7. The library charges have risen by 11%. The charge is now 12p per book per day. What was the charge before the rise?

8. In hot weather the volume of air can expand by up to 10%. If I need a maximum of 16 litres of air in my tyres when they are hot, how many cubic cm of cold air should I put in?

9. My building society paid 8% interest in 2004 and 6% interest in 2005. If I had £237.60 in my account in January 1995, what did I have in my account in January 1996? What did I have in January 1994?

10. VAT increased from 15% to $17\frac{1}{2}$%. The VAT on a television set thus increased by £10
    What was the original selling price (including VAT) of the television?

11. (a) I found out that £100 was put into a building society account for me when I was born. Everyone then forgot about it. The money has been earning 6% interest per year. How much money do I have in my account on my thirteenth birthday?

    (b) However, I discovered that because I am under 18 and not earning a salary, I am entitled to extra interest of 2% per annum. What is the amount that I now receive on my thirteenth birthday?

Exercise 5.8: Extension questions – Compound interest

Think back to the last question (q.11) and let us look at the situation in more detail.

If I invest £100 for a year at 6% at the end of the year I will have £100 x 1.06 in my account.

If I keep that amount in my account for another year at the same interest rate I will have [(£100 × 1.06) × 1.06] in my account.

This amount can be re-written as £100 × 1.06^2

If I keep this amount in my account for a third year at the same interest rate I will then have [(£100 × 1.06^2) × 1.06] in the account.

This amount can be re-written as £100 × 1.06^3

If this then continues for 13 years then the amount in the account will total:

£100 × 1.06^{13}

We can work this out using our calculators in the following way.

Find the $\boxed{x^y}$ button on your calculator. (It may be $\boxed{y^x}$ or $\boxed{\wedge}$ – it may be a second function.)

1.06^{13} is found by entering 1.06 then pressing the $\boxed{y^x}$ or $\boxed{\wedge}$ button, then entering 13 and finally $\boxed{=}$ to get the answer. (If this does not work ask your maths teacher or refer to the calculator manual.) You should get the answer 2.13 292 83

You then multiply by 100 to get the final amount £213.29 (to 2 d.p.)

You could do the whole calculation in one go by entering 100 then x and then open brackets, followed by 1.06 then the $\boxed{y^x}$ or $\boxed{\wedge}$ button and 13, then close the brackets. Finally press $\boxed{=}$ and you should get the answer 213.29 283

In q.11 (b) the interest rate has increased by 2% and is now 8%. So you do the calculation this time using 1.08 instead of 1.06   This time your answer should be 271.96 237

Warning: A common mistake is to increase the first answer 213.29 283 by 2%, but, as you should be able to see, this does not give the correct answer. **It is always important to work out percentage problems from first principles**.

The calculation of the interest gained over several years is called **compound interest**. If C is the capital invested, at x% for n years then the formula for the amount received at the end of that period is:

new amount $= C \times \left(1 + \dfrac{x}{100}\right)^n$

Example:
If £150 is invested for 10 years at 5%, how much is in the bank after 10 years?

$$\text{new amount} = C \times \left(1 + \frac{x}{100}\right)^n$$

$$= 150 \times 1.05^{10}$$

$$= £244.33\ 419$$

$$= £244.33 \text{ (to 2 d.p.)}$$

1. £50 is invested at birth for a baby. The interest rate is fixed at 8%. Calculate how much will be in the bank when the baby becomes:
   (a) five years old.   (c) 18 years old.
   (b) ten years old.   (d) 21 years old.

2. Banks pay higher interest for larger deposits. If I invest £5000 in a bank at a fixed interest rate of 12%, calculate the amount that will be in the bank after:
   (a) one year.   (b) three years.   (c) five years.

3. A car reduces in value by 12% each year. If a car cost £12 000 when it was new, write down what it will be worth when it is:
   (a) two years old.   (b) five years old.   (c) ten years old.
   (d) What does the car actually lose in value in its first year?
   (e) What does the car actually lose in value in its tenth year?

4. I receive an annual salary of £20 000
   (a) If my pay increases at a steady rate of 5% per annum, what should I be earning in 5 year's time?
   (b) How many years will it take for my salary to double to £40 000 per annum?
   (c) If I am 30 years old now and my salary continues to increase at the same rate, will I ever receive £60 000 before I retire at 65 years old?
   (d) What salary will I be receiving before I retire?

5. (a) The population of China was expanding at 10% per annum. How many years did it take for the population to double?
   (b) After strict population controls the population of China has started to fall by 2% per annum. How many years will it take to halve the size of the population?

6. Assuming an average inflation rate of 5%, write down the probable cost in ten year's time of:
   (a) a family car (now £6500)
   (b) a television (now £350)
   (c) a kg of best rump steak (now £10)

   Assuming the same rate of inflation, what would the cost of these items have been ten years ago?

7. Draw the graph of $y = 1.05^x$, taking values of x from 0 to 10
   With an average interest rate of 5%, use your graph to find how many years it will be for a price rise by:
   (a) a quarter.
   (b) a half.
   (c) a third.
   (d) Will the answer depend on the original price of the goods? Explain your answer.

Exercise 5.9: Summary exercise

1. I scored 63 marks out of 80 for my maths test. What is this as a percentage?

2. Last year I spent 1 hour and 30 minutes on my homework each night. This year I have to spend 25% longer. How much time do I now spend on homework?

3. We collected 12% fewer apples from our garden this year. Last year we collected 308 kg. How many apples did we collect this year?

4. Fred estimated that there were 500 words in his English essay. He then counted and found there were 524 words. What was the percentage error of his estimate?

5. In a sale, all items are reduced by 25%.
   (a) If the price of a leather jacket was normally £175, what would the price be in the sale?
   (b) The price of a jumper in the sale was £11.80, what was its original price?

6. (a) The value of the Boshida laptop has dropped by 25%. If the old price was £630, what is the new price?

> SALE!!!
> 25% off all
> marked prices

(b) When the Boshida laptop first came out VAT was 15%. It is now 17.5%. If the price before VAT was £500 what difference did the change in VAT make to the price?

(c) The new model Boshida laptop version 2 is sold for £999.99 How much of this is VAT at 17.5%. Give your answer to the nearest penny.

7. My monthly allowance has risen by 40%. If it is now £28 per month, what was it before?

8. The value of my house has dropped 12% in the last year. I am told that it is worth £340 800 now. What was my house worth a year ago?

9. My journey to work at my usual speed takes 20 minutes. How long will my journey take if I increase my speed by 25%?

10. I have £2000 in the bank. Last year the interest rate was 8% and this year it has dropped to 6%. How much money will I have in the bank at the end of this year?

End of chapter 5 activity: The trading game

On the worksheet you will find the nets of two dice, the money cards, the goods cards and the playing board you will need to play this game. You will probably need at least two copies of the money worksheet so that you have lots of money! First start by making up the two trading dice. You will also need a normal die.

Object
The objective of this game is to be the player with the most money at the end of the time allowed for the game.

The rules of the game
This game is for two players.

The banker and the bank

The players take it in turn to run the bank. The older player starts by being the banker but any player who changes from being a customer to being a shopkeeper or vice versa takes over the running of the bank. This will make more sense when you see how the game is played.

To start the game

1. Place the goods cards on the corresponding squares on the board.
2. The banker gives each player £500
3. The playing board is in two sections. Both players start at the top left hand corner of the outer board (Budget Day) and play the game as customers.
4. The players roll the normal die. The player with the higher score goes first. On your turn, roll the normal die and move clockwise around the outer board. The space you land on will determine what you have to do (see Playing the game).
5. Any player landing on a special 'Become a shopkeeper' square transfers to the inner board. Remember that this player, if she or he is not already the banker, now becomes the banker (see The banker and the bank). Shopkeepers move anticlockwise round the inner board.

Playing the game as a customer

A customer moves clockwise round the outer board by rolling the normal die. Every time you pass a budget square, you are paid £50 by the bank.

Landing on a goods square

If a customer lands on a goods square, with a goods card on it, he is obliged to purchase the goods, if he has enough money. To work out what price you pay, throw the two trading dice.

The trading dice will tell you how you should increase or decrease the 'marked price' and by how much. The answer will be the price you need to pay for the goods. You pay the money and hand over the relevant goods card to the bank. (All prices are worked out to the nearest £1)

Landing on a sales square

If you land on a sales square, throw again and move as before. If you then land on a goods square, you only roll the percentage die and pay the 'marked price' minus **double** that percentage (because the sales square says 'Double the discount').

Landing on a Budget Day square

If you land on a Budget Day square, throw again and move as before. If you then land on a goods square, you only roll the percentage die and pay the 'marked price' plus **double** that percentage.

Landing on a Lottery win, Share dividend or Fined square

If you land on one of these squares, then you pay or receive money from the bank accordingly.

Playing as a shopkeeper

As a shopkeeper you move around the inner board in an anti-clockwise direction.

Landing on a goods square

When you land on a goods square with a goods card, you are obliged to sell those goods. To work out what price you sell at, throw the two trading dice.

The trading dice will tell you how you should increase or decrease the 'marked price' and by how much. Calculate your cost price and thus your actual profit or loss. This represents the profit or loss that you have made.

If you have made a profit, you receive that amount from the bank. If you have made a loss you pay that amount to the bank.

Landing on a Become a customer square

If you land on a 'Become a customer' square you cross to the outer board and play as a customer as before.

The winner

The winner is the player with the most money at the end of the time allowed for the game. If either player runs out of money, then he (or she) is the loser.

Happy trading!

Chapter 6: Equations and inequations

In *So you really want to learn Maths* Books 1 and 2 we learnt to solve equations. Remember that equations are solved by doing the same thing to both sides. This keeps them balanced. Remember also that it is very useful to show what you are doing in brackets down the right hand side of your calculation. This helps you to work out each stage and explains your thinking, which is very important for harder equations.

Exercise 6.1

Here's a warm up exercise. These are one-stage equations:

Examples:

(i) $x - 5 = 3$

$\qquad$ (+ 5)

$x = 8$

(ii) $\frac{x}{3} = 2$

$\qquad$ (× 3)

$x = 6$

1. $3 + x = 11$

2. $2 = x - 5$

3. $9x = 15$

4. $\frac{x}{4} = 8$

These are two-stage equations. As you may recall there is no reason why your answer cannot be negative or a fraction:

Examples:

(i) $\frac{x}{3} + 5 = 2$

$\qquad$ (− 5)

$\frac{x}{3} = -3$

$\qquad$ (× 3)

$x = -9$

(ii) $4x - 5 = 6$

$\qquad$ (+ 5)

$4x = 11$

$\qquad$ (÷ 4)

$x = \frac{11}{4}$

$x = 2\frac{3}{4}$

5. $5x + 1 = 7$

7. $7 = 2x - 8$

6. $9 + \dfrac{x}{4} = 3$

8. $11 = 7 - x$

These next few questions require three or even more stages. The x term should be kept positive:

Example:

$$4 - 5x = 7 - x$$
$$(+ 5x)$$
$$4 = 7 + 4x$$
$$(- 7)$$
$$-3 = 4x$$
$$(\div 4)$$
$$-\frac{3}{4} = x$$
$$x = -\frac{3}{4}$$

9. $5x + 4 = 2x + 7$

11. $2x + 4 = 6 - x$

10. $3 - 2x = 9 + x$

12. $5 - 7x = 10 - 2x$

Remember that if the equation has **brackets,** multiply the brackets out first, then **simplify** and finally **solve** the equation.

Example:

$$4 - (5 - 2x) = 3(5 + 2x) - x$$
$$(B)$$
$$4 - 5 + 2x = 15 + 6x - x$$
$$(S)$$
$$-1 + 2x = 15 + 5x$$
$$(- 2x)$$
$$-1 = 15 + 3x$$
$$(- 15)$$
$$-16 = 3x$$
$$(\div 3)$$
$$-\frac{16}{3} = x$$
$$x = -5\frac{1}{3}$$

13. $3(x + 4) = 2(x - 1)$ **15.** $3 - (x + 4) = 4x - 1$

14. $5x + (4 - x) = 3(x - 1)$ **16.** $5x - 3(3 - 2x) = 2(x + 1)$

And finally a few more with brackets and fractions:

Example:

$$\frac{2(2 - x)}{3} = 7$$

$$2(2 - x) = 21 \qquad (\times 3)$$

$$4 - 2x = 21 \qquad (B)$$

$$4 = 21 + 2x \qquad (+ 2x)$$

$$-17 = 2x \qquad (- 21)$$

$$-\frac{17}{2} = x \qquad (\div 2)$$

$$x = -8\frac{1}{2}$$

17. $\frac{1}{3}(x - 5) = 3$ **19.** $\frac{3}{5}(x - 2) = 4$

18. $8 = \dfrac{3x - 5}{2}$ **20.** $\dfrac{5x}{4} - 4 = 2x$

Using algebra to solve problems

You should by now be quite proficient in solving equations in various forms. Being able to solve equations is a very useful skill to have. We often have to solve problems that involve an unknown quantity. The neatest way to do this is to let the unknown quantity be x and then to form an equation around it.

Make sure that you define x carefully at the beginning of your solution and then, when you have your answer, check it by putting the value back into the original problem. Remember always to answer the question and to put the answers in the correct units if required.

Often questions that you meet in examinations are to do with ages. Look carefully at the example on page 118 and see how the solution is constructed.

The first stage is to write the two ages in terms of x
Then the ages in ten years time are written in terms of x
Finally the equation is written and then solved.

It often helps to write down a few simple expressions before writing the equation.

Exercise 6.2

Example:

My mother is three times my age. In ten years time I will be half my mother's age. How old am I?

Let my age be x years.
Now I am x my mother is $3x$
In ten years time I will be $x + 10$, my mother will be $3x + 10$

$$3x + 10 = 2(x + 10)$$
(B)
$$3x + 10 = 2x + 20$$
$(- 2x)$
$$x + 10 = 20$$
$(- 10)$
$$x = 10$$

I am ten years old

1. If my age is x, write an expression in x for the following:
   (a) My brother's age when my brother is ten years younger.
   (b) My sister's age when my sister is four years older.
   (c) My age five years ago.
   (d) My age in nine years time.
   (e) My brother's age in nine years time.
   (f) My sister's age five years ago.

2. In nine years time I will be twice as old as my brother. Using two of your answers above, form an equation in x and solve it to find my age.

3. If my age is x, write an expression in x for the following:
   (a) My father's age if my father is four times my age.
   (b) My age in six years time.
   (c) My father's age in six years time.

4. In six years time my father will be three times as old as I am. Form an equation in x and solve it to find my father's age.

5. My sister is 2 years older than me, and my father is four times as old as my sister. If I am x years old find in terms of x:
   (a) My sister's age.
   (b) My father's age.
   (c) My father is five times as old as I am. Form an equation in x and solve it to find my age.

6. My mother is three times as old as I am and my father is four times as old as I am.
   (a) If I am x years old find, in terms of x:
      (i) My mother's age.
      (ii) My father's age.
   (b) My father is 9 years older than my mother. Form an equation in x and solve it to find my age.

7. My brother is four years younger than I am. Four years ago I was twice his age.
   (a) If my age now is x years find, in terms of x:
      (i) My brother's age now.
      (ii) My age 4 years ago.
      (iii) My brother's age 4 years ago.
   (b) Form an equation in x and solve it to find my brother's age now.

8. In 12 years time I will be twice as old as I am now. How old am I now?

9. Eight years ago I was half as old as I am now. How old am I now?

10. I will be three times as old as I am now in 24 years time. How old am I?

The questions in the next exercise are nothing to do with ages but use the same method.

Exercise 6.3

1. A farmer goes to market and buys some chickens. The following week he goes to market again and buys four more chickens than he bought in the previous week. He also buys lots of ducklings; in fact he bought twice as many ducklings as chickens.
   (a) If the number of chickens that he bought the first week is x, find in terms of x:
      (i) The number of chickens he bought the second week.
      (ii) The number of ducklings he bought the second week.
   (b) If the total number of chickens and ducklings he bought the second week is four times the total number of chickens he bought the first week, form an equation in x and solve it.
   (c) How many ducklings did he buy?

2. In a bag of marbles there are four times as many red marbles as yellow marbles, and three times as many green marbles as red marbles.
   (a) If the number of yellow marbles is x find, in terms of x:
      (i) The number of red marbles.
      (ii) The number of green marbles.
   (b) If there are 34 marbles in the bag, form an equation in x and solve it to find the number of yellow marbles.

3. My brother and sister and I were picking strawberries. I picked 3 kg more than my sister, but my brother picked twice as many kg as I did.
   (a) If the number of kg that I picked was x find, in terms of x:
      (i) The number of kg my sister picked.
      (ii) The number of kg my brother picked.
   (b) If we picked 21 kg altogether, form an equation in x and solve it to find how many kg of strawberries my sister picked.

4. A company makes Widgets and Wotsits. They make 4p more profit on Widgets than they do on Wotsits.
   (a) If the profit on a Wotsit is x pence find, in terms of x:
      (i) The profit on one Widget.
      (ii) The profit on 100 Wotsits.
      (iii) The profit on 200 Widgets.
   (b) For every batch of 100 Wotsits and 200 Widgets the company makes £23 Form an equation in x and solve it to find the profit on each Widget and Wotsit.

5. I have dripped cola over my maths prep and cannot read the questions clearly. They now say:

    (a) A plant was ✳ cm high. It has grown 10%. What is its new height?

    (b) My pocket money was ✳ p and has risen by 20%. What is it now?

    (c) After a 10% rise I now earn £✳ for my paper round. What did I earn before?

    (d) My puppy eats more and more each week. This week he ate ✳ kg of 'Doggyo' which is 25% more than last week. What did he eat last week?

    I called my friend Freda for help. Freda says the answers are:

    (a) 35.2 cm   (b) £6   (c) £15   (d) 4 kg

    It was helpful to have the answers but my teacher expects me to show all my working. Write down how you replace each ✳ by x and work out the exact question.

For each of the next questions, form an equation in x and solve it to find the answer to the question:

6. The number of boys in the school this year is 5 more than the number of girls. Altogether there are 195 children in the school. How many are girls?

7. In any one day I spend a third of it asleep, I spend four times as much time at school as I spend on my homework, one hour watching television and three hours doing everything else. How much time do I spend on my homework?

8. My class want to raise £250 for charity. We are going to do this by washing cars. The cost of materials is £15 for all the cloths and brushes, then 75p per car for shampoo. The headmaster says we can only charge £5 per car. How many cars do we have to wash to raise £250?

9. In science we are using a balance to weigh chemicals. If 5 mg and 3 measures of chemical A have the same mass as 2 mg and 8 measures of chemical A, what is the mass of 1 measure of chemical A?

10. The average height of the 18 boys in my class is 10 cm more than the average height of the 20 boys in the class below. The total of all the heights of the 18 boys in my class is 100 cm less than the total height of the 20 boys in the class below. What is the average height of my class?

Equations with fractions

We are familiar with the rule 'multiply out brackets first' when solving equations, but now let us look at what happens when the bracket is multiplied by a fraction.

For example: $\frac{1}{3}(2x + 1) = 5$

The brackets could be multiplied by the fraction but that would give:

$$\frac{2x}{3} + \frac{1}{3} = 5$$

which is not a terribly inviting calculation. It is actually much better to **multiply both sides** of the equation by the denominator ($\times$ 3) first, giving:

$$2x + 1 = 15$$

This is now a much simpler equation to solve.

Exercise 6.4

Solve these equations involving fractions. Remember to multiply **both sides of the equation** by the denominator first:

1. $\frac{x}{3} = 4$

2. $\frac{1}{4}x = 3$

3. $\frac{2x}{5} = 4$

4. $\frac{3}{4}x = 6$

5. $\frac{(x + 2)}{3} = 4$

6. $\frac{(2x - 3)}{5} = 2$

7. $\frac{1}{5}(4 - 3x) = 4$

8. $\frac{(3 - 4x)}{2} = x$

9. $\frac{1}{4}(2 - x) = x$

10. $\frac{2(2x + 1)}{3} = x$

The equations above have had only one term on each side of the equals sign. Let us see what happens where there is more than one term.

For example: $\dfrac{x}{4} + 3 = 2x$

The general rule, multiply both sides by the denominator, is still the correct rule to follow, but be careful to multiply **every term** on each side of the equals sign by the denominator.

Example:

$$\frac{x}{4} + 3 = 2x$$

$$\frac{\cancel{4} \times x}{\cancel{4}} + 4 \times 3 = 4 \times 2x \qquad (\times 4)$$

$$\text{(cancel)}$$

$$x + 12 = 8x$$

$$(-x)$$

$$12 = 7x$$

$$(\div 7)$$

$$\frac{12}{7} = x$$

$$x = 1\frac{5}{7}$$

Exercise 6.5

1. $\dfrac{x}{3} + 1 = 4$

2. $\dfrac{x}{5} - 3 = 1$

3. $\dfrac{x}{2} + 3 = x$

4. $\dfrac{x}{7} - 3 = x$

5. $4 + \dfrac{x}{2} = 3$

6. $4 - \dfrac{x}{5} = x$

7. $\dfrac{x}{3} = 14 + x$

8. $\dfrac{1}{3}x = 4 - 2x$

9. $\dfrac{2x}{5} + 3 = 2$

10. $4 - \dfrac{3x}{5} = 2x$

Some equations with fractions may need brackets:

Example:

$$\frac{2}{3}(x+4) = 3x - 4$$

$$(\times\ 3)$$

$$2(x+4) = 3(3x-4)$$

$$(B)$$

$$2x + 8 = 9x - 12$$

$$(-2x)$$

$$8 = 7x - 12$$

$$(+12)$$

$$20 = 7x$$

$$(\div 7)$$

$$\frac{20}{7} = x$$

$$x = 2\frac{6}{7}$$

11. $\dfrac{2x}{5} = x + 2$

12. $\dfrac{3}{4} = 3x - 5$

13. $\dfrac{1}{3}(x+3) = x + 2$

14. $\dfrac{3}{5}(2x+3) = 2 - 3x$

15. $2x + 1 = \dfrac{2x}{7} - 2$

16. $\dfrac{2(3+2x)}{5} = 3x - 2$

Equations with two fractions

The equations so far have had only one fraction and thus only one denominator, but there will often be occasions when there are two fractions.

Example: $\quad \dfrac{3x}{4} = \dfrac{2}{5}$

We only need to get rid of the fraction on the same side as the x term, so we multiply both sides of the equation by 4:

$$\frac{4 \times 3x}{4} = \frac{2 \times 4}{5}$$

$$3x = \frac{8}{5} \qquad \text{(simplify)}$$

$$x = \frac{8}{15} \qquad (\div 3)$$

Exercise 6.6

1. $\dfrac{2x}{3} = \dfrac{1}{4}$

4. $\dfrac{2}{3} = \dfrac{3x}{5}$

2. $\dfrac{3x}{4} = \dfrac{2}{5}$

5. $\dfrac{3}{4} = \dfrac{4x}{9}$

3. $\dfrac{3}{7}x = \dfrac{2}{5}$

6. $\dfrac{x}{3} = \dfrac{5}{6}$

When there are two fractions in an equation and other terms then you need to multiply **every term** by both denominators, and then cancel:

Example:

$$\frac{x}{4} + 3 = \frac{2}{3}$$

$$(\times\ 4 \times 3 = \times\ 12)$$

$$\frac{3 \times 4 \times x}{4} + 3 \times 12 = \frac{3 \times 4 \times 2}{3}$$

(simplify)

$$3x + 36 = 8$$

$$(-\ 36)$$

$$3x = -28$$

$$(\div\ 3)$$

$$x = -\frac{28}{3} = -9\frac{1}{3}$$

Now that the equations are more complex, it is particularly helpful to write down exactly what you are doing at each stage, in the brackets to the right.

7. $\dfrac{x}{4} + 2 = \dfrac{x}{3}$

11. $\dfrac{x}{4} = 2x + \dfrac{1}{3}$

8. $5 + \dfrac{2x}{3} = \dfrac{1}{5}$

12. $\dfrac{x}{4} + 2 = \dfrac{1}{3}$

9. $\dfrac{3x}{4} - 2 = \dfrac{2}{3}$

13. $\dfrac{3}{4} - 2x = \dfrac{x}{5}$

10. $5 - \dfrac{x}{2} = \dfrac{3}{5}$

14. $\dfrac{3x}{5} = \dfrac{1}{3} - 4x$

Inexact answers

Most problems in mathematics have an exact answer such as 4 x 7 = 28, but some problems give a range.

For example:

'It takes me between 10 and 15 minutes to get to school.'

     I could write this as: $10 \le$ time ≤ 15

Remember that > means 'greater than', and < means 'less than',
     and that $\ge$ means 'greater than or equal to',
       and $\le$ means 'less than or equal to'.

Consider this inequality: $2 < x < 5$

This is mathematical shorthand for: x is greater than 2 and less than 5

This can be shown on the number line:

The integer values of x that satisfy this inequality are 3 and 4

Consider this pair of inequalities: $x < -1$ $x \ge 4$

     x is less than −1, and x is greater than or equal to 4

This can be shown on the number line; note the hollow circle for < or > and the solid circle for $\le$ or $\ge$:

Note that there are **no values** of x that satisfy this pair of inequalities.

Exercise 6.7

Give all the possible whole numbers of x for these inequalities; show the range on a number line:

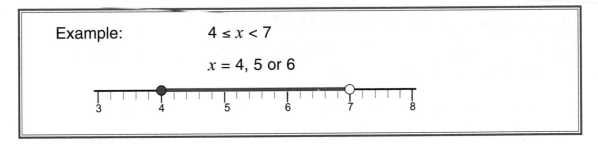

Example: $4 \leq x < 7$

$x = 4, 5$ or 6

1. $3 \leq x < 6$
2. $1 \leq x \leq 4$
3. $5 < x \leq 8$
4. $0 < x < 5$
5. $-2 \leq x < 3$

6. $-5 > x \geq -7$
7. $3 \geq x > -1$
8. $2 \geq x > -2$
9. $x \geq 4$ and $x < 8$
10. $x < 10$ and $x \geq 5$

Solving inequalities

An inequality, or an inequation, is written like an equation, but using a greater than or less than sign instead of an equals sign. It is then solved using the same steps that you have learnt to use when solving equations.

Example:

(a) $4x > 24$
$\qquad$ $(\div 4)$
$\quad x > 6$

(b) $x - 4 > 6$
$\qquad$ $(+ 4)$
$\quad x > 10$

Exercise 6.8

Solve these inequalities:

1. $3x < 6$
2. $5x \geq 15$
3. $7x \geq 21$

4. $14 < \dfrac{x}{2}$
5. $21 \geq 3x$
6. $x + 4 < 6$

7. $4 + x < 5$

8. $3x + 7 > 9$

9. $3 + 2x \geq 5$

10. $7 < x - 4$

11. $\frac{x}{3} - 2 \leq 7$

12. $3 + \frac{x}{4} > 3$

13. $14 \geq 6 + \frac{x}{3}$

14. $5 \leq \frac{x}{5} + 3$

The inequalities above have been solved by adding, subtracting, dividing or multiplying positive numbers of x.

Now consider the inequality: $4 > 1$

What happens when we add, subtract, multiply or divide the inequality using the constant 2?

$4 > 1$ $(+ 2)$ $6 > 3$	$4 > 1$ $(- 2)$ $2 > -1$	$4 > 1$ $(\times 2)$ $8 > 2$	$4 > 1$ $(\div 2)$ $2 > \frac{1}{2}$

In this instance **all** the new inequalities are **true**.

Now do the same again but with the negative constant −2:

$4 > 1$ $(+ (-2))$ $2 > -1$	$4 > 1$ $(- (-2))$ $6 > 3$	$4 > 1$ $(\times (-2))$ $-8 > -2$	$4 > 1$ $(\div (-2))$ $-2 > -\frac{1}{2}$

This time the resulting inequalities are **not** all true.

−8 is **not greater** but less than −2, and −2 is **not greater** but less than $-\frac{1}{2}$

Multiplying or dividing an inequality by a negative constant **reverses** the inequality:

      If $-x > 4$ then $x < -4$

As we have already seen it is better to keep the x term positive when solving equations. This is particularly true when solving inequalities. By keeping the x term positive we do not have to worry about reversing the inequality.

Example: Solve these inequalities:

(i) $7 - 2x > 6$

$(+ 2x)$

$7 > 6 + 2x$

$(- 6)$

$1 > 2x$

$(\div 2)$

$\dfrac{1}{2} > x$

$x < \dfrac{1}{2}$

(ii) $3 - \dfrac{x}{4} \leq 4$

$(\times 4)$

$12 - x \leq 16$

$(+ x)$

$12 \leq 16 + x$

$(- 16)$

$-4 \leq x$

$x \geq -4$

However, it is worth noting that if the x term had not been positive, the last line of each inequation would have been:

$-x > -\dfrac{1}{2}$ and $-x \geq 4$

When multiplied by -1 these become:

$x < \dfrac{1}{2}$ and $x \geq -4$

Exercise 6.9

Solve these inequalities:

1. $3 + 2x < 4$

2. $5 > 3 - 4x$

3. $3 - 2x \leq 7 + 3x$

4. $3 + 4x > 7x - 5$

5. $16 \geq 4 - \dfrac{x}{3}$

6. $4 + \dfrac{3x}{4} > 9$

7. $7 - 3x \leq 5x - 1$

8. $\dfrac{x}{4} - 1 > 6$

9. $8 - \dfrac{x}{3} \geq 5$

10. $5 < 6 - \dfrac{x}{2}$

11. $\dfrac{2x}{3} + 5 \leq 2$

12. $7 - \dfrac{3x}{5} < 3$

13. $4 + 2x < 9 - 2x$

14. $3 + 4(x - 3) > x$

15. $5 - 2(x + 5) \leq 3x$

16. $3(x - 4) > 5(4 - 2x)$

Exercise 6.10: Extension questions

Sometimes the inequation is written with two inequalities:

$$3 < 3x - 2 \leq 5$$

In this case you should solve each part separately:

Example: $3 < 3x - 2 \leq 5$

$3 < 3x - 2$		$3x - 2 \leq 5$	
	$(+\,2)$		$(+\,2)$
$5 < 3x$		$3x \leq 7$	
	$(\div\,3)$		$(\div\,3)$
$\dfrac{5}{3} < x$		$x \leq \dfrac{7}{3}$	

$$1\tfrac{2}{3} < x \leq 2\tfrac{1}{3}$$

1. Solve these inequalities and give all the integers that satisfy each one:

   (a) $3 + x < 2 - x < 5$

   (b) $7 \leq 3x + 4 < 13$

   (c) $6 \leq \dfrac{x}{2} + 1 < 8$

   (d) $5 > 6 - \dfrac{2x}{3} \geq \dfrac{1}{2}$

2. If $x > -5$:
   (a) What is the smallest perfect square that x could be?
   (b) What is the smallest prime number that x could be?

3. Consider $10 \leq x < 26$, give the value of x if:
   (a) x is odd and square.
   (b) x is even and a triangle number.
   (c) x is a factor of 90 and a multiple of 9
   (d) x is prime and a factor of 299

4. (a) Solve this inequality: $9 - 3x > 2 - x$
   (b) Give two prime numbers that satisfy this inequality.

5. (a) Solve this inequality $2(3x + 2) < 4 - 3(2 - x)$
   (b) Write down which of these numbers satisfies the inequality:

-3	-2	2	4

6. (a) Solve the inequality $\dfrac{x}{3} - \dfrac{2(x-2)}{4} \geq \dfrac{1}{6}$

(b) What is the highest prime number that satisfies the inequality?

7. (a) Solve the inequality $4 - \dfrac{x}{3} > 2x + 1 > 3$

(b) Give all the whole number values of x that satisfy the inequality.

8. Find all the whole number values of x that satisfy the inequality:

$$\frac{x}{2} + 1 < 6 - x \leq 2x - 3$$

9. Find all the whole number values of x that satisfy the inequality:

$$3 + \frac{x}{4} < \frac{2x}{3} < \frac{x+3}{2}$$

10. Why do no values of x satisfy the inequality: $\dfrac{1}{2} > \dfrac{x}{3} - 4 > \dfrac{3}{4}$?

11. If the symbol Δ between two numbers means 'greater than half of' then:

5 Δ 8 is true, because 5 is more than 4, half of 8
5 Δ 10 is not true, because 5 is equal to 5, half of 10
5 Δ 12 is not true, because 5 is less than 6, half of 12

(a) State which of the following statements are true, explaining each of your answers with a brief statement:

(i) 2 Δ 3   (iv) 3 Δ 7
(ii) 2 Δ 4   (v) 101 Δ 200
(iii) 19 Δ 10   (vi) 3 Δ 3²

(b) Now state which of the following statements are always true, explaining each answer with a brief statement:

(i) $x \, \Delta \, x + 1$ (iv) $x \, \Delta \, 2x - 1$
(ii) $x \, \Delta \, 2x$ (v) $x \, \Delta \, 2(x + 1)$
(iii) $x \, \Delta \, 2x + 1$ (vi) $x \, \Delta \, x^2$

(c) In part (b) there were some statements which were not always true but could sometimes be true. Give the range of values for x that would make these statements true.

12. If the symbol ¥ between two numbers means 'less than one more than half of' then:

    4 ¥ 8 is true, because 4 is less than 1 plus 4, (half of 8)

    4 ¥ 6 is not true, because 4 is equal to 1 plus 3, (half of 6)

    4 ¥ 4 is not true, because 4 is more than 1 plus 2, (half of 4)

    (a) State which of the following statements are true, explaining each answer with a brief statement:

    (i)   4 ¥ 7   (iv) 50 ¥ 51
    (ii) 3 ¥ 5   (v) 101 ¥ 200
    (iii) 7 ¥ 11   (vi) 5 ¥ 5^2

    (b) Now state which of the following statements are always true, explaining each answer with a brief statement:

    (i) x ¥ $x + 1$ (iv) x ¥ $2x - 1$
    (ii) x ¥ $2x$ (v) x ¥ $2(x + 1)$
    (iii) x ¥ $2x + 1$ (vi) x ¥ x^2

    (c) In part (b) there were some statements which were not always true but could sometimes be true. Give the range of values for x that would make these statements true.

Exercise 6.11: Summary exercise

1. Solve these equations:
   (a) $3x + 2 = 5$ (d) $4x + 1 = 4 - 2x$
   (b) $6 - 2x = 3$ (e) $3x - 1 = x + 9$
   (c) $3(2x - 1) = 7$ (f) $\frac{1}{3}(2 - 3x) = 4$

2. My sister is three times as old as I am. Four years ago my sister was four times as old as I was. If my age is x years now, find in terms of x:
   (a) My sister's age now.
   (b) My age 4 years ago.
   (c) My sister's age 4 years ago.
   (d) Now form an equation in x and solve it to find my sister's age now.

3. For the same amount of money I can buy either 5 sticks of liquorice and 8 penny sweets or 4 sticks of liquorice and 12 penny sweets.
   (a) If the cost of a stick of liquorice is x pence what is the cost, in terms of x, of 5 sticks of liquorice and 8 penny sweets?
   (b) What is the cost, in terms of x, of 4 sticks of liquorice and 12 penny sweets?
   (c) Write an equation in x and solve it to find the cost of a stick of liquorice.

4. Solve these equations:

   (a) $\frac{x}{3} + 5 = 2$

   (b) $4 - \frac{2x}{3} = 1$

   (c) $\frac{x}{4} = \frac{2}{3}$

   (d) $\frac{1}{3}(2x + 4) = 3$

   (e) $\frac{2x}{5} + 4 = x$

   (f) $\frac{3}{4} = 3 - \frac{2x}{5}$

5. Find all the whole number values of x that fit these inequalities. In each case show the range on a number line:
   (a) $1 \leq x < 5$ (b) $-3 < x \leq 1$

6. Solve these inequalities:
   (a) $2x - 7 < 1$ (b) $\frac{x}{5} \geq 3 - x$ (c) $3(2 - 3x) \geq 2 - (3x + 1)$

7. Find all the whole number values of x that satisfy this inequality:

   $\frac{x}{4} + 1 > \frac{2x}{3} > 1 - x$

End of chapter 6 activity: Polyhedral numbers

A tetrahedron is a triangular based pyramid and a regular tetrahedron has a net of four equilateral triangles:

 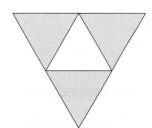

Tetrahedral numbers are made up from forming tetrahedrons from triangles:

1   4   1 + 3 = 4   10   1 + 3 + 6 = 10

1. What are the above set of numbers being added together called?

2. Copy this table and extend it by another three rows:

n		Tetra no:
1	1	1
2	1 + 3	4
3	1 + 3 + 6	10
4	1 + 3 + 6 + 10	
5	1 +	
6		
7		
8		

3. (a) What is the 10th tetrahedral number?
(b) The 100th?

4. By considering the formula for the nth triangle number, or otherwise, find a formula for the nth tetrahedral number.

The next set of polyhedral numbers are those formed by square based pyramids, the 1st such number will be 1, the second 1 + 4 = 5, the third 1 + 4 + 9 = etc.

The next set will be those formed by the sum of the pentagonal numbers.

5. Investigate sets of polyhedral numbers and see what rules you can find. You might find it interesting to include Pascal's trinagle as part of your investigation.

Chapter 7: Indices and algebra

In chapter 3 we looked at numerical indices. In this chapter we are going to look at using algebra with indices.

Multiplying

Consider: $2^3 \times 2^2 = (2 \times 2 \times 2) \times (2 \times 2)$
$= 2^5$
$= 32$

Similarly: $x^3 \times x^2 = (x \times x \times x) \times (x \times x)$
$= x^5$

| Can you remember the general rule? | $x^a \times x^b = x^{a+b}$ |

Exercise 7.1

Calculate these, leaving your answers in index form:

1. $x^2 \times x^5$

2. $b^3 \times b^3$

3. $a^4 \times a^3$

4. $2^3 \times 2^2 \times 2^4$

5. $2^a \times 2^b$

6. $3^2 \times 3^3$

7. $a^3 \times a^2 \times a^4$

8. $3^a \times 3^b$

9. $x^2 \times x^2 \times x^2$

10. $3^2 \times 3^2 \times 3^2$

11. $x^2 \times x^3 \times x$

12. $b^2 \times b^4 \times b$

13. $a \times a^5 \times a^2$

14. $2^x \times 2^y \times 2$

15. $a^x \times a^y$

16. $2^a \times 3^b$

17. $a \times a^y \times a^y \times a$

18. $x^a \times y^a$

19. $x \times x^x \times x^y$

20. $a^y \times b^y \times b^y$

Division

Consider

$$16 \div 4 = 4 \qquad\qquad 81 \div 3 = 27$$

or

$$2^4 \div 2^2 = 2^2 \qquad\qquad 3^4 \div 3^1 = 3^3$$

The general rule is:

$$x^a \div x^b = x^{a-b}$$

Exercise 7.2

Calculate these, giving your answers in index form:

1. $a^6 \div a^5$

2. $b^7 \div b^3$

3. $x^6 \div x^3$

4. $2^6 \div 2^3$

5. $3^x \div 3^y$

6. $a^5 \div a^4$

7. $x^5 \div x$

8. $5^3 \div 5^3$

9. $x^7 \div x^2$

10. $a^x \div a^x$

11. $4y^5 \div y$

12. $x^x \div x$

13. $4x^a \div 2x^3$

14. $3a^b \div 6a^c$

The power 0

Remember the case $5^3 \div 5^3$

Using the above rule gives us: $5^3 \div 5^3 = 5^0$

We know that if we divide a number by itself the answer is always 1

Thus: $\qquad\qquad 5^0 = 1$

In general terms: $\begin{aligned} x^a \div x^a &= x^{a-a} \\ &= x^0 \\ &= 1 \end{aligned}$

Negative index numbers

Remember that index numbers can be negative:

$$10^{-2} = \frac{1}{10^2} = \frac{1}{100} \quad \text{similarly} \quad x^{-3} = \frac{1}{x^3}$$

Exercise 7.3

Calculate these, giving your answers in index form:

1. $2^4 \div 2^7$

2. $a^3 \div a^6$

3. $x^2 \div x^5$

4. $x^7 \div x^7$

5. $7^a \div 7^b$

6. $x^4 \div x^5$

7. $b \div b^5$

8. $a^2 \div a^2$

9. $x^4 \div x^2$

10. $a^2 \div b^2$

11. $2x^2 \div x^3$

12. $a^3 \div 5a^6$

13. $y^6 \div 3y^3$

14. $4x^2 \div 16x^5$

Powers

An expression containing an index number may itself be raised to a power.

(i) $(2^4)^2 = 2^4 \times 2^4$
$= (2 \times 2 \times 2 \times 2) \times (2 \times 2 \times 2 \times 2)$
$= 2^8$
$= 256$

(ii) $(x^4)^2 = x^4 \times x^4$
$= (x \times x \times x \times x) \times (x \times x \times x \times x)$
$= x^8$

In general terms: $(x^a)^b = x^{ab}$

Exercise 7.4

Express in index form:

1. $(3^4)^2$

2. $(2^3)^2$

3. $(x^3)^2$

4. $(a^3)^5$

5. $(2b^3)^2$

6. $(3a^3)^5$

7. $(4^a)^b$

8. $(x^m)^m$

9. $(3a^m)^2$

10. $(2x^m)^m$

Example:
$$(2^3)^2 \div (2^2)^2 = 2^6 \div 2^4$$
$$= 2^2$$
$$= 4$$

11. $(3^2)^3 \div (3^2)^4$

12. $(4^4)^3 \div (4^2)^2$

13. $(2^2)^2 \div (2^2)^3$

14. $(x^3)^4 \div (3x^2)^3$

15. $(a^2)^4 \div (a^2)^2$

16. $(x^2)^2 \div (3x^3)^3$

17. $(2a^4)^3 \div (a^2)^3$

18. $(4x^2)^2 \div (x^2)^2$

19. $(3a^3)^3 \div (9a^2)^2$

20. $(3b^2)^3 \div (9b^2)^3$

Index numbers as fractions

- Remember that $x^a \times x^a = x^{2a}$

- Then the square root of x^{2a} is x^a

Therefore to find the square root we halve the index number:

- the square root of x^{4a} is x^{2a}

- the square root of x^a is $x^{\frac{a}{2}}$

- the square root of x is $x^{\frac{1}{2}}$

Exercise 7.5

Express these either as whole numbers or in index form:

1. $9^{\frac{1}{2}}$

2. $16^{\frac{1}{4}}$

3. $25^{\frac{1}{2}}$

4. $27^{\frac{1}{3}}$

5. $16^{\frac{1}{2}}$

6. $125^{\frac{1}{3}}$

7. $8^{\frac{1}{3}}$

8. $(x^2)^{\frac{1}{2}}$

9. $(4x^2)^{\frac{1}{2}}$

10. $(9x^2)^{\frac{1}{2}}$

11. $(x^2)^{\frac{1}{2}} \times (x^3)^{\frac{1}{3}}$

12. $(4x^2)^{\frac{1}{2}} \div (2x)^2$

Combining multiplication and division

We may need to combine expressions in algebra, for example:

(i) $2x^2 \times 3x^3 = 2 \times x \times x \times 3 \times x \times x \times x$

$$= 6x^5$$

(ii) $3ab^3 \times 4a^2 = 12a^3b^3$

It is important **not to confuse adding** and **multiplying**:

You can **add** (or **subtract**) 'like terms':

$a^2b + a^2b + a^2b = 3a^2b$ or $a^2b + 3a^2b + a^2b = 5a^2b$

but **not** 'unlike terms':

$ab + a^2b + ab^2 = ab + a^2b + ab^2$ This expression **cannot** be simplified.

You can **multiply** together any terms:

$a^2b \times a^2b \times a^2b = a^6b^3$

$ab \times a^2b \times ab^2 = a^4b^4$

Exercise 7.6

Simplify these expressions, if possible:

1. $a \times a^2 \times a^3$

2. $3a \times 2a^2 \times a^3$

3. $3b + b^2 + 2b^3$

4. $2b^2 + b^2 + 3b^2$

5. $2ab \times a^2b \times 3ab^2$

6. $4x^2y + x^2y + 3x^2y$

7. $4xy + x^2y - xy$

8. $4xy + x^2y - xy^2$

9. $3ac \times a^2b \times 4bc$

10. $2bc + a^2b + 4ac$

A fraction in algebra may be cancelled down in the same way as a numerical fraction. These algebraic fractions may have common factors in the same way as ordinary fractions:

Example:

$$3x^3y^2 \div 6xy = \frac{3x^3y^2}{6xy}$$

$$= \frac{3 \times x \times x \times x \times x \times y \times y}{6_2 \times x \times y} \qquad 3, x \text{ and } y \text{ are all common factors}$$

$$= \frac{x^2 y}{2}$$

Exercise 7.7

Simplify these if possible. Check that each answer is in the simplest form possible:

1. $\dfrac{3a^2 b}{a}$

2. $\dfrac{3a^2 b}{b}$

3. $\dfrac{6a^2 b}{2b}$

4. $\dfrac{8xy^2}{2xy}$

5. $\dfrac{15xy}{3xy}$

6. $\dfrac{3a^2 b}{5b}$

7. $\dfrac{3a^2 b}{24b^3}$

8. $\dfrac{2mn}{8m^2 n}$

9. $\dfrac{24x^2 y^3}{15x^3 y}$

10. $\dfrac{6b^5 c^2}{9bc^3}$

11. $\dfrac{12x^3 y^2}{4x^2 y}$

12. $\dfrac{18a^3 b^2}{6ab^3}$

13. $\dfrac{6x^2 y^2}{4x^3 y^2}$

14. $\dfrac{15a^2 bc^3}{10ab^2 c}$

15. $\dfrac{18x^3 y^2 z}{12x^2 yz^2}$

Indices and brackets

When there is a number outside a bracket, we know that we multiply everything inside the bracket by the number:

Example: $2(3x + 4) = 6x + 8$

When there is an x outside the brackets, then you multiply through by x in the same way:

Examples:

(i) $x(x + 2) = x^2 + 2x$
(ii) $x(x^2 + 2x) = x^3 + 2x^2$
(iii) $x^2(x^2 + 2x) = x^4 + 2x^3$

Exercise 7.8

Multiply out these brackets:

1. $x(2x + 1)$

2. $x(3x - 1)$

3. $x(4 - 3x)$

4. $2x(x + 4)$

5. $3x(2x - 5)$

6. $x^2(x + 1)$

7. $x(x^2 + x - 1)$

8. $x^2(4 - 3x)$

9. $2x^2(3x - 2)$

10. $x^2(2x^2 + 3x + 4)$

11. $x^3(x^2 + 1)$

12. $3x^3(2x^2 - 4x + 3)$

Now try the next set of questions, multiplying out the brackets and simplifying.

Remember that multiplying by a negative number changes the sign.

So, if there is a minus outside the brackets, when you multiply out, the sign of the numbers in the brackets will change.

Example:

$$x(3x + 2) - 2x(x - 4) = 3x^2 + 2x - 2x^2 + 8x$$

$$= x^2 + 10x$$

13. $x(2x + 1) + 2x(x - 3)$

14. $x(2x + 5) - x(x - 3)$

15. $x(3x - 1) + x(3 - x)$

16. $x(2 - x) - 2x(x + 1)$

17. $x(2x - 5) - 2x(4 - x)$

18. $3x(2x + 1) - 2x(x + 3)$

19. $2x(3x - 1) + 3x(x - 3)$

20. $2x(x - 3) - x(3x + 1)$

21. $x(3x + 4) - 2x(3 - 2x)$

22. $4x(3x - 1) - 2x(4 + 6x)$

Now try these with both x and y:

Example:

$$2x(3x + y) - y(2x + y) = 6x^2 + 2xy - 2xy - y^2$$

$$= 6x^2 - y^2$$

23. $x(x + y) + y(x + y)$

24. $2x(3x + y) - 2y(x + 2y)$

25. $x(2x - y) + y(3x + 2y)$

26. $xy(2x + y) - y(3x^2 + xy)$

27. $x(3y - x) + 2x(3x + y)$

28. $xy^2(3x + 2) - x^2y(4 - 2y)$

29. $x^2(4 + 3y) - 4x(2x + 2xy)$

30. $xy(3y - 2x) - x^2(4y + y^2)$

31. $3x^3(2x - 3y + 1) - 2y(3x^3 + 4)$

32. $2x^2y(3x + 4y) - 3xy^2(2x + 3y)$

Factorising

In the last exercise we multiplied brackets by a number or letter outside the brackets.

Factorising is the reverse process. In this instance a common factor is taken out of each term and then written outside the brackets:

Example:

(i) $6x^2 + 2y = 2(3x^2 + y)$ 2 is the common factor

(ii) $6x^2 + 5xy = x(6x + 5y)$ x is the common factor

(iii) $6x^2y + 3xy = 3xy(2x + 1)$ $3xy$ is the common factor

(iv) $6x^2 + 5y$ Does not factorise

Exercise 7.9

Factorise these expressions where possible. Some of these six questions have a number as a common factor:

1. $3x + 6$

2. $8y - 4$

3. $6 + 9x$

4. $18 - 4y$

5. $24x + 16$

6. $7x - 6$

Some of the following questions have a letter as a common factor:

7. $x^2 + 5x$

8. $y^2 - 7y$

9. $3x + x^2$

10. $5x - y^2$

11. $x^3 + 2x$

12. $x^3 - 3x^2$

Some of the following questions have both a number and a letter as common factors:

13. $2x^2 + 4x$

14. $6a - 9a^2$

15. $9xy + 6y^2 - 3y$

16. $9a^2 - 8b$

17. $12x^2 - 9xy + 6x$

18. $8ab - 4a^2$

Now try these. Remember some may not factorise:

19. $3xy + 16x^2 + 4x$

20. $8a^2b + 14ab$

21. $8x^2 + 5y^2$

22. $12y^2 - 9y + 3x$

23. $12y + 8x^2y - 16y^2$

24. $3a^2 + 6b^2 - 2ab$

25. $12xy + 16x^2y - 4xy^2$

26. $14x^2 + 8xy + 3y^2$

27. $10xy + 14y^2 - 4$

28. $16x^2 - 12xy - 9$

29. $16x^2 - 14xy - 6x$

30. $20a^2b - 4ab^2 - 2b$

31. $20a^2b - 4ab^2 + 8ab$

32. $16xy^2 + 8x^2 - 2xy$

Trial and improvement

In the early calculations of the last chapter we were able to make an equation in x and then solve it.

Sometimes however the equation may not be very simple to solve.

Example:

My garden is rectangular. The length is 5 m longer than the width and the area is 130 m². Find the length and the width of the garden to the nearest 10 cm.

If the width is x then the length will be $x + 5$,

and an expression for the area would be $x(x + 5)$

and the equation : $x(x + 5) = 130$

$$x^2 + 5x = 130$$

Because there is an x^2 in the equation, it cannot be solved in the usual way and a different method is needed.

Trial and improvement methods work in the opposite way to normal equation solving. First we make an estimate of the answer, then substitute that answer into the equation, and see how accurate it is. Then we make a better estimate and try again.

We continue doing this until we have the correct answer, or close to the correct answer. It is very important that all the results are recorded so that earlier results can be used to help us to find the correct answer more quickly.

The best way to record our results is in a table. For the example above the table would look like this:

Width	Length	Area	Note
8	13	104	too small
9	14	126	too small
10	15	150	too big

Now that we know that x lies between 9 and 10 m, and appears closer to 9 m, we have to look at decimals. Start with one decimal place:

Width	Length	Area	Note
9.1	14.1	128.31	too small
9.2	14.2	130.64	too big

We can now see that x lies between 9.1 and 9.2 m, and appears closer to 9.2 m. However we have been asked to give an answer to one decimal place and because we can only approximate to one decimal place from an answer written to two decimal places, we need to continue the table with two decimal places:

Width	Length	Area	Note
9.15	14.15	129.4725	too small
9.16	14.16	129.7056	too small
9.17	14.17	129.9389	too small
9.18	14.18	130.1724	too big

The width is between 9.17 m and 9.18 m and so to the nearest 10 cm the garden is 9.2 m by 14.2 m.

However we could have stopped our table at 9.15 because we know that the width is between 9.15 m and 9.20 m and so to the nearest 10 cm the width must equal 9.2 m.

Exercise 7.10

> **Example:**
>
> I have a box with a square base and a height 5 cm longer than the width.
>
> (i) Show that the volume of the box can be written as the expression $x^2(x + 5)$
>
> (ii) If the volume of the box is 90 cm³, find x by trial and improvement correct to one decimal place.
>
> (i) If the width $= x$ cm
>   the length $= x$ cm
>   the height $= x + 5$ cm
>   the volume $= x \times x \times (x + 5)$
> $= x^2(x + 5)$
>
> (ii)
>
> | x | x^2 | $(x + 5)$ | Volume | Notes |
> |------|--------|-----------|---------|-----------|
> | 3 | 9 | 8 | 72 | too small |
> | 4 | 16 | 9 | 144 | too big |
> | 3.5 | 12.25 | 8.5 | 104.125 | too big |
> | 3.4 | 11.56 | 8.4 | 97.104 | too big |
> | 3.3 | 10.89 | 8.3 | 90.387 | too big |
> | 3.2 | 10.24 | 8.2 | 83.968 | too small |
> | 3.25 | 10.562 | 8.25 | 87.140 | too small |
>
> Therefore x lies between 3.25 and 3.30 cm, and so:
> $x = 3.3$ cm (to 1 decimal place)

1. Solve these equations by trial and improvement, giving your answers correct to (i) 1 decimal place, (ii) 2 decimal places:
   (a) $x(x - 3) = 25$
   (b) $x^2 + 5x = 60$
   (c) $(x - 3)(x + 5) = 100$

2. (a) A rectangle has its base 6 cm longer than its height. If the height is
h cm, draw a sketch of the rectangle and write an expression for the
length of the base.

(b) Write an expression for the area of the rectangle.

(c) The area of the rectangle is 118 cm². Copy and continue the table
below and, using trial and improvement methods, find the height and
the base length of the rectangle correct to 1 decimal place.

Height	Length	Area	Note
8	14	112	Too small
9	15		

3. The height of a parallelogram is 5 cm less than the length of its base:

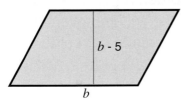

(a) Write an expression in b for the area of the parallelogram.

(b) The area of the parallelogram is 40 cm² . Copy and continue the table
below to find the value of b to 2 decimal places using trial and
improvement.

b	$b - 5$	Area	Note
10	5		

4. The length of my bedroom is 2 m longer than the width, and the floor
area is 70 m². Find the length and width of the room by trial and
improvement. Give your answer to the nearest 10 cm.

5. The height of a rectangle is 5 cm more than the length of its base. If the
perimeter of the rectangle is 23 cm what is its height, to the nearest
millimetre?

6. The area of my garden is 120 m². Its length is one and a half times the
width. How long is my garden? Give your answer to the nearest 10 cm.

7. The height of a triangle is 3 cm more than the length of the base. The area of the triangle is 60 cm². Find the base length and height of the triangle using trial and improvement methods. Give your answer correct to one decimal place.

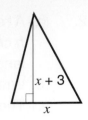

8. The height of this triangle is two-thirds the length of its base and its area is 31 m². Find the length of the base correct to the nearest 10 cm.

9. A square photograph is surrounded by a border that is 5 cm wide.
(a) If the length of a side of the photograph is x cm, write an expression for the length of a side of the border.
(b) Write an expression for the area of the border.
(c) If the area of the border is 182 cm², use trial and improvement methods to find the dimensions of the photograph correct to the nearest millimetre.

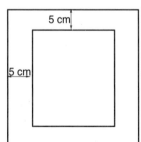

10. (a) Given that the formula for the area of a trapezium is:

$$\text{Area} = \frac{h(a+b)}{2} \quad \text{(where } a \text{ is the top and } b \text{ the bottom)}$$

write an expression for the area of this trapezium:

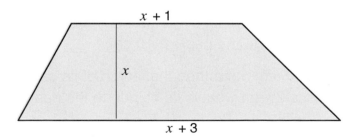

(b) The area of the trapezium is 20 cm². Copy and complete this table and continue it to find, by trial and improvement, the value of x correct to 2 decimal places:

x	$x + 2$	area	note
3	5	15	
4			

Exercise 7.11: Extension questions – More about square roots

Before the advent of the modern electronic calculator it was quite a lengthy process to find a square root.

Heron of Alexandria, who lived around 10-70 AD, was a Greek mathematician and engineer. As an engineer he frequently needed to find square roots and his method for finding square roots was used for many centuries. It is surprisingly accurate, especially when you consider the Greek system for recording numbers made it difficult even to multiply.

Heron's method works on a system of repetitive calculations and is accurate after 5 approximations to 17 decimal places. Computers and calculators frequently use this method to calculate square roots.

Heron's method

1. Find the approximate square root of a number x and call it y_1

2. Calculate $\frac{x}{y_1}$

3. Find the average of y_1 and $\frac{x}{y_1}$ Call this answer y_2

4. Find the average of y_2 and $\frac{x}{y_2}$ Call this answer y_3

5. Continue in this way until you have the accuracy that you need.

Example:

Find the square root of 10 without a calculator:

Step 1: Let y_1 be 3 (as $\sqrt{10} \approx 3$)

Step 2: $\dfrac{x}{y_1} = \dfrac{10}{3}$

Step 3: The average of $\quad 3 + \dfrac{10}{3} = \dfrac{1}{2}\left(3 + 3\dfrac{1}{3}\right)$

$$= \dfrac{1}{2} \times 6\dfrac{1}{3}$$

$$y_2 = 3\dfrac{1}{6}$$

$$= 3.16666 \ldots$$

$$= 3.17 \text{ (to 2 d.p.)}$$

Use fraction arithmetic to find the square root in the next few questions, using Heron's approximation. In each case calculate y_2 and write the answer as a decimal.

1. 8

2. 17

3. 23

4. 15

5. 27

6. 105

7. 13

8. 22

9. 85

10. 21

11. 55

12. 72

Now check your answers with a calculator.

Exercise 7.12: Summary exercise

1. Simplify these expressions, leaving your answers in index form:
    (a) $a^3 \times a^2$ (b) $b^4 \times b$ (c) $c^3 \times d^2$

2. Simplify these expressions, leaving your answers in index form:
    (a) $a^4 \div a^2$ (b) $b^6 \div b^3$ (c) $c^4 \div c$

3. Simplify these expressions, leaving your answers in index form:
    (a) $a^2 \div a^4$ (b) $b^3 \div b^3$ (c) $c \div c^5$

4. Simplify these expressions, if possible:
   (a) $a^4 \times a^2 + a^5$
   (b) $3b^3 + 2b^3 - b^3$
   (c) $c^4 + c + c^2$

5. Simplify these expressions, if possible:
   (a) $\dfrac{3 \times a^2 \times b^3}{6 \times a \times b}$
   (b) $\dfrac{15ab^2c}{3bc^2}$
   (c) $\dfrac{18a^2b}{4b}$

6. Multiply out these brackets:
   (a) $x(x + 3)$
   (b) $2x(3x - 5)$
   (c) $x^2(6 - x)$

7. Multiply out these brackets and simplify:
   (a) $x(x + 3) + x(3x - 2)$
   (b) $3x(2x - 6) - 2x(5 - 2x)$

8. Factorise the following expressions, if possible:
   (a) $3x + 9$
   (b) $12x - 7$
   (c) $4xy + 2y^2$
   (d) $3x^2 - 12y$
   (e) $3x^2 - 12x + 3$
   (f) $4x^2y - 8y^2 + 6x$
   (g) $12x^2y + 5y^2 - 8y$
   (h) $9x^3 - 6x^2y + 15x^2$

9. This rectangle has a width 7 cm less than its length and an area of 55 cm²:

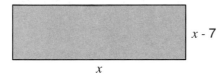

$x - 7$

x

Copy and complete this table to find the length and width of the rectangle, to 2 decimal places, by trial and improvement:

x	$x - 7$	Area	Note
12	5	60	too big
11			

End of chapter 7 activity: My Great Uncle's bequest (or heir today – gone tomorrow)

I was very surprised to get this letter from my rich Great Uncle, Ben:

'Sumalot'
Times Square,
Percentchester
Sumerset
PC7 1AB

Dear Great Nephew,

Thank you very much for the birthday card. I really liked the bright red 75 you drew on the front. I do hope you are well and behaving yourself. I was very pleased to hear from Mum and Dad that you are working hard at school. Your maths test result was excellent.

It made me think. I believe that you deserve some of my fortune for working so hard. I want to give you some money now and some more each year. All you have to do is choose one of these schemes:

a) £100 now, then £90 next year, then £80 the year after and so on.

b) £10 now, then £20 the year after, £30 the year after and so on..

c) £10 now, one and half that amount the year after, one and a half times THAT amount the following year and so on..

d) £1 now, £2 the year after, £4 the year after that, £ 8 the year after that and so on.

Of course these schemes can only operate while I am still alive.

I look forward to hearing which of these you choose and exactly why you chose it!!

Lots of love,
Great Uncle Ben

You have to write a reply to this letter and include the mathematical reasons for your choice.

A spreadsheet programme is a useful tool to analyse the 4 schemes.

Using the spreadsheet programme

1. Log on to the computer. Open your Spreadsheet programme. Then open a New document and Save it as Great Uncle.

2. In cell A1 type 'year', in cell A2 type 1 and in cell A3 type the correct formula to add one to the value in cell A2. When your formula produces the value 2 in cell A2 click on the cell, keep the mouse button down and drag down 10 cells to A11. From the Calculate menu select Fill down. You should now have the numbers 1 to 10 in the year column.

3. In cell B1 type 'scheme A'. In this scheme you can see that you are given £100 in the first year, and then £10 less each year. Type 100 in cell B2, and then type the correct formula in cell B3 to deduct £10. When your formula produces 90 in cell B3, then fill down the formula to cell B11 as before. In B11 you will have 0. (Let us assume that Uncle Ben does not expect **you** to pay **him** £10 in year 12)

4. The important part of Uncle Ben's bequest is to work out the total amount that he is giving you. In cell C1 type 'total A'. Cell C2 will need the formula = B2 but cell C3 will need the formula = B2 + B3
    Fill down this formula in column C.

5. Cells D1 and E1 will need 'scheme B' and 'total B'. You should be able to write the correct formulae for these, you may like to fill down the D and E columns until D11 and E11 to see what happens if Uncle Ben lives for 10 years.

6. Cells F1 and G1 will need 'scheme C' and 'total C'. The formulae in the F columns are interesting as having started with £10 you are going to the multiply each preceding cell by 1.5. Remember that 'multiply' is shown by the asterix above 8

7. Cells H1 and I1 are for 'scheme D' and 'total D'. Again you are going to multiply the preceding cell by a number.

Saving and Printing

8. Save your work. Highlight all cells from A1 to I11 and pull down the Options menu to select Print area, then press return for OK.

9. From the view menu select Page view.

10. From the File menu select Page set up and select Landscape.

11. From the Format menu select Insert footer and type your name and form. Now print your document.

12. Go back to the View menu and select Display. Click in the Display formula box and then Print again. Then go back to Display and de-select Display Formula.

Drawing graphs

One really useful facility of the spreadsheet package is its ability to draw graphs from the data. We do not need graphs of all the columns above but only the data in columns A, C, E, G and I.

13. De-select Page View from the View menu. In cell A15 type = A1. Now highlight click highlight and fill down the next 10 cells.

14. In cell B15 type = C1, and fill down, in cell C15 type = E1 and fill down, in cell D15 type = G1 and fill down and finally in cell E15 type = I1 and fill down. You now have a new table containing the relevant data only.

15. Highlight cells from A15 to E25. From the options menu select 'make chart'. Select line graph.

16. Follow the instructions on the next few screens.

17. You should now have a chart showing the information that you calculated earlier.

Printing the chart

18. Your chart should have little black squares on each corner. Click on the chart and move it to a blank area of the spreadsheet. Highlight all the cells surrounding your chart.

19. From the Options menu select Print area and press return.

20. Now select Print from the File menu. Before pressing return de-select print row headings, print columns headings and print cell grid.

Finally

21. Select New from the File menu. Select Word-processing and answer Uncle Ben's letter.

Chapter 8: Sequences

In *So you really want to learn Maths* Book 2 (chapter 21) we looked at sequences. A sequence is a succession of terms with some rule connecting them.

For example:

2, 4, 6, 8, 10, ...　　　is the sequence of even numbers. Each term is found by adding 2 to the previous term.

Some sequences follow numerical rules, while others, such as prime numbers, do not.

Exercise 8.1

Write down the next three numbers in these sequences. If you can find a numerical rule write that down:

1.　　1, 3, 5, 7, 9, ..., ..., ...

2.　　1, 4, 9, 16, 25, ..., ..., ...

3.　　3, 6, 9, 12, 15, ..., ..., ...

4.　　1, 3, 6, 10, 15, ..., ..., ...

5.　　1, 4, 7, 10, 13, ..., ..., ...

6.　　0, 3, 8, 15, 24, ..., ..., ...

7.　　1, 1, 2, 3, 5, 8, 13, ..., ..., ...

8.　　1, 2, 4, 7, 11, ..., ..., ...

9.　　2, 6, 10, 14, 18, ..., ..., ...

10.　1, 6, 11, 16, 21, ..., ..., ...

You probably found the missing terms in the above sequences by looking at the previous two terms and working out a rule. Using this method is not so helpful when trying to find, for example, the 100th term in a sequence.

In question 4 above we had:

1, 3, 6, 10, 15, 21, 28, 36, 45, 55, ... the sequence of triangle numbers.

To find the 100th term we have to look at the pattern of the numbers and try to find a rule that works for all the terms in that sequence.

Before we do that let us remind ourselves of the four types of sequences that we studied in *So you really want to learn Maths* Book 2:

1. Sequences based on a times table:

Sequences based on a times tables go up by the same number each time.
For example:
6, 12, 18, 24, 30, 36, ... goes up by 6 each time

The hundredth term would be $100 \times 6 = 600$

$$\text{The } n^{th} \text{ term} = n \times 6 = 6n$$

Other sequences that go up by the same number each time can be compared to a times table:

5, 11, 17, 23, 29, 35, goes up by 6 each time. Each term is 1 less than the 6 times table.

The hundredth term would be $100 \times 6 - 1 = 600 - 1$

$$\text{The } n^{th} \text{ term} = n \times 6 - 1 = 6n - 1$$

2. Sequences based on square numbers:

Sequences based on square numbers go up by increasing consecutive odd numbers.
For example:
1, 4, 9, 16, 25, 36, ... goes up by the sequence 3, 5, 7, 9, 11, ...

The hundredth term would be $100^2 = 100 \times 100$
$$= 10\ 000$$
$$\text{The } n^{th} \text{ term} = n^2$$

Other sequences that go up by a succession of increasing consecutive odd numbers can be compared to the sequence of square numbers:

3, 6, 11, 18, 27, 38, ... goes up by the sequence 3, 5, 7, 9, 11, ... and, as you can see, each term is 2 more than a square number.

The hundredth term would be $100^2 + 2 = 100 \times 100 + 2$
$$= 10\ 002$$
$$\text{The } n^{th} \text{ term} = n^2 + 2$$

3. Sequences based on triangle numbers:

Sequences based on triangle numbers go up by one number more each time.

For example:
1, 3, 6, 10, 15, 21, ... goes up by the sequence 2, 3, 4, 5, 6, ...
The hundredth term would be $\frac{1}{2} \times 100 \times 101 \quad = 50 \times 101$
$$= 5050$$

$$\text{The } n^{\text{th}} \text{ term} = \frac{1}{2}n(n + 1)$$

Other sequences that go up by one number more each time can be compared to the triangle numbers:

4, 6, 9, 13, 18, 24, ... goes up by the sequence 2, 3, 4, 5, 6, ... and, as you can see each term is 3 more than a triangle number.

The hundredth term would be $\frac{1}{2} \times 100 \times 101 + 3 = 50 \times 101 + 3$
$$= 5053$$

$$\text{The } n^{\text{th}} \text{ term} = \frac{1}{2}n(n + 1) + 3$$

N.B. Sometimes the triangle number sequence starts with 0:
0, 1, 3, 6, 10, 15, ... etc.

For this sequence the nth term $= \frac{1}{2}n(n - 1)$

4. Sequences based on a Fibonacci type number pattern:

Each term in the Fibonacci sequence is formed by adding the previous two terms together:

For example:
1, 1, 2, 3, 5, 8, 13, 21, ... goes up by the sequence 0, 1, 1, 2, 3, 5, 8, ...

or:

1, 3, 4, 7, 11, 18, 29, ... goes up by the sequence 2, 1, 3, 4, 7, 11, ...

When the sequence of differences is the same as the original sequence then you have a Fibonacci style pattern.

Exercise 8.2

1. (a) Using the information you have just been given, state whether each sequence in Exercise 8.1 was:
   (i) a table based sequence.
   (ii) a square number type sequence.
   (iii) a triangle number type sequence.
   (iv) a Fibonacci style sequence.

   (b) Write down the nth term of each of the sequences, unless it was a Fibonacci style sequence.

2. Find the next three terms and the nth term of each of these sequences:
   (a) 2, 5, 8, 11, 14, ..., ..., ...
   (b) 2, 5, 10, 17, 26, ..., ..., ...
   (c) 2, 4, 7, 11, 16, 22, ..., ..., ...
   (d) 2, 7, 12, 17, 22, 27, ..., ..., ...

3. We have looked at sequences that increase, now write the next three terms and the nth term of each of these decreasing sequences:
   (a) −5, −10, −15, −20, −25, ..., ..., ...
   (b) −3, −6, −9, −12, −15, ..., ..., ...
   (c) −7, −14, −21, −28, −35, ..., ..., ...
   (d) −4, −8, −12, −16, −20, ..., ..., ...

4. Using your answers to q.3, write the next three terms and the nth term of each of these decreasing sequences:
   (a) 30, 25, 20, 15, 10, ..., ..., ...
   (b) 9, 6, 3, 0, −3, ..., ..., ...
   (c) 100, 93, 86, 79, 72, ..., ..., ...
   (d) 20, 16, 12, 8, 4, ..., ..., ...

5. Write the next three terms and the nth term of each of these decreasing sequences:
   (a) 15, 12, 9, 6, 3, 0, ..., ..., ...
   (b) 99, 88, 77, 66, 55, 44, ..., ..., ...
   (c) 51, 49, 47, 45, 43, ..., ..., ...
   (d) 5, 2, −1, −4, ..., ..., ...

So far we have looked at sequences where the next term is found by adding or subtracting a number, or by multiplying or dividing by a number. We have also looked at sequences of square numbers. Remember also cube numbers, numbers to the power 4, etc.

Exercise 8.3

1. Write down the next three terms in these sequences:
    (a) 1, 2, 4, 8, 16, ..., ..., ...
    (b) 8, 4, 2, 1, ..., ..., ...
    (c) 0.1, 0.5, 0.25, 0.125, ..., ..., ...
    (d) 100, 10, 1, 0.1, ..., ..., ...
    (e) 25, 5, 1, 0.2, ..., ..., ...

2. (a) Write down the next three terms in these sequences:
    (i) 1, 8, 27, 64, ..., ..., ...
    (ii) 1, 16, 81, 256, ..., ..., ...

    (b) Deduce the nth term of the sequences.

3. Here are some sequences you might just be able to recognise. Write down the next three terms of these sequences:
    (a) 2, 3, 5, 7, 11, ..., ..., ...
    (b) M, T, W, T, ..., ..., ...
    (c) J, F, M, A, M, J, J, ..., ..., ...
    (d) O, T, T, F, F, ..., ..., ...

4. Some sequences combine rules and so the terms have to be deduced from more than one pattern. Write down the next three terms of these sequences:
    (a) 1, 3, 2, 4, 3, ..., ..., ...
    (b) 1, 1, 3, 2, 5, 3, ..., ..., ...
    (c) 1, 2, 3, 2, 5, 2, ..., ..., ...
    (d) 1, 2, 3, 4, 5, 8, 7, ..., ..., ...

5. Fill in the missing terms in these sequences:
    (a) 5, 8, ..., 14, 17, ...
    (b) 0, 3, ..., 15, ..., 35, ...
    (c) 4, ..., 1, 0.5, ...
    (d) 2, 3, 5, ..., 8, 9, ...
    (e) 2, 5, ..., 12, ..., 31, ...

Sequence notation

Instead of writing out in full the terms of a sequence, it can be useful to use a shorthand method.

So if we want to discuss a sequence we could describe each one by a capital letter:

$$S = 1, 3, 5, 7, 9, ...$$
$$T = 1, 4, 7, 10, 13, ...$$
$$U = 1, 5, 9, 13, 17, ...$$
$$V = 1, 6, 11, 16, 21, ...$$

We can now describe each term by a number:

$S_3 = 5$ means the third term of sequence S is 5
$V_5 = 21$ means the fifth term of sequence V is 21

We can then describe the nth term of sequence S as S_n
This gives us the rule for the sequence:

$$S_n = 2n - 1$$

Exercise 8.4

1. From the four sequences above find the value of:
    (a) S_2 (b) T_4 (c) U_5 (d) V_3

2. In sequence notation write a term that equals:
    (a) 3   (b) 11   (c) 17   (d) 10

3. If the sequences were to be extended give the value of:
    (a) S_7 (b) T_9 (c) U_7 (d) V_8

4. Write down the next three terms of each sequence. Use the correct notation:
    (a) $S_6 = ..., S_7 = ..., S_8 = ...,$
    (b) $T_6 = ..., T_7 = ..., T_8 = ...,$
    (c) $U_6 = ..., U_7 = ..., U_8 = ...,$
    (d) $V_6 = ..., V_7 = ..., V_8 = ...,$

5. Consider the next few terms of each sequence and write in sequence notation a term that equals:
    (a) 20   (b) 21   (c) 22   (d) 23

6. Consider further terms of each sequence and write in sequence notation a term that equals:
   (a) 100   (b) 101   (c) 102   (d) 103

7. Write down the rule for each sequence:
   (a) T_n (b) U_n (c) V_n

Working to a rule

Sometimes we are given the nth term, or rule, for a sequence and from that we have to find the actual terms.

Example:

If $S_n = 3n + 1$, find the 1st, 2nd and 10th terms of the sequence.

$$S_1 = 3 \times 1 + 1$$
$$= 4$$

$$S_2 = 3 \times 2 + 1$$
$$= 7$$

$$S_{10} = 3 \times 10 + 1$$
$$= 31$$

Exercise 8.5

1. If $S_n = 5n - 2$, find:
   (a) S_1 (b) S_2 (c) S_5 (d) S_{10}
   (e) What is the first term where $S_n > 100$?

2. (a) If $T_n = 6n + 3$, find the 1st, 2nd 3rd and 10th terms of the sequence.
   (b) What is the first term where $T_n > 100$?

3. If the nth term of a sequence is given by the rule $V_n = 20 - 3n$, write down:
   (a) V_1 (b) V_2 (c) V_3 (d) V_{10}
   (e) What is the first term where $V_n < 0$?

4. If the nth term of a sequence is given by the rule $W_n = n^2 + 3$, write down:
   (a) W_1 (b) W_5 (c) W_{10} (d) W_{20}
   (e) What is the first term where $W_n > 200$?

5. If the nth term of a sequence is given by the rule $S_n = 2^n$, write down:
   (a) S_1 (b) S_2 (c) S_3 (d) S_5
   (e) What is the first term where $S_n > 100$?

6. If the nth term of a sequence is given by the rule $T_n = 100 - 2n^2$, write down:
   (a) T_1 (b) T_2 (c) T_4 (d) T_{10}
   (e) What is the first term where $T_n < 0$?

7. If $U_n = n(n - 2)$, find:
   (a) U_1 (b) U_2 (c) U_5 (d) U_{10}
   (e) What is the first term where $U_n > 100$?

8. If $W_n = (n - 1)(n + 2)$, find:
   (a) W_1 (b) W_2 (c) W_5 (d) W_{10}
   (e) What is the first term where $W_n > 200$?

More about quadratic sequences

Consider this sequence:

$$T_1 = 1$$
$$T_2 = 1 + 3$$
$$T_3 = 1 + 3 + 5$$
$$T_4 = 1 + 3 + 5 + 7$$

If you add up the numbers you should find that $T_1 = 1$, $T_2 = 4$, $T_3 = 9$, $T_4 = 16$

And so the sequence $T_n = 1, 4, 9, 16, 25, ...$

This is the sequence of square numbers and so we can say $T_n = n^2$

Sometimes it is easier to think about sequences if we have a series of drawings or patterns to help us.

Exercise 8.6

1. (a) Draw the next two patterns in this sequence:

    (b) Explain why the pattern of adding odd numbers gives the sequence of square numbers.

2. Look at these rectangle numbers.
    In each rectangle the length is always one more than the width:

    (a) Draw the next two rectangle numbers.
    (b) Copy and complete this table, and hence find the rule for R_n:

Rectangle number	Dots up	Dots along	Number of dots
R_1	1	2	$1 \times 2 = 2$
R_2	2	3	$2 \times 3 = 6$
R_3			
R_4			
R_5			
R_6			
R_n			

3. Here are the first four triangle numbers:

    (a) Draw the next two triangle numbers.

(b) Copy and complete this table:

Triangle number	Number of dots
T_1	1
T_2	3
T_3	
T_4	
T_5	
T_6	

(c) Compare the number of dots in the rectangle numbers with the number of dots in the triangle numbers. What do you notice?

(d) Now write the rule for T_n

Use the results for square, rectangle and triangle numbers to find the rule for the nth term of the following sequences:

4. A square with a bite out of it:

5. A rectangle with width 2 units less than the length:

6. A truncated triangle:

7. Two truncated squares:

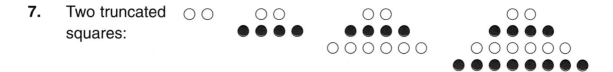

Exercise 8.7

The following patterns and sequences may need a little more thought:

1.

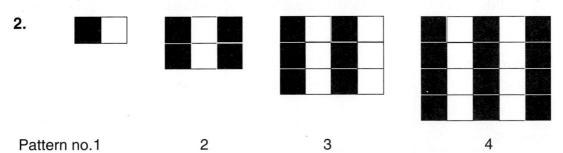

| Pattern no. | 1 | 2 | 3 | 4 | 5 |

(a) Copy and complete this table:

Pattern no:	White balls	Black balls	Total balls
1	1	0	1
2	2	2	4
3	5		
4	8		
5			
6			

(b) How many balls in total will there be in pattern number 10?
(c) How many black balls will there be in pattern number 10?
(d) How many white balls will there be in pattern number 10?
(e) Write down the total number of balls in the nth pattern.
(f) Write down the total numbers of black balls and white balls in the nth pattern.

2.

| Pattern no.1 | 2 | 3 | 4 |

(a) Copy and complete this table:

Pattern no.:	Black squares	White squares	Total squares
1	1	1	2
2	4	2	6
3	6		
4			
5			
6			

(b) How many squares in total will there be in pattern number 10?
(c) How many white squares will there be in pattern number 10?
(d) How many black squares will there be in pattern number 10?
(e) Write down the total number of squares in the nth pattern.

3.
   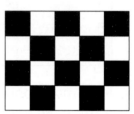

Pattern no.1   2   3   4

(a) Copy and complete this table:

Pattern no:	Black squares	White squares	Total squares
1	1	1	
2	3		
3			
4			
5			
6			

(b) How many black squares will there be in pattern number 20?
(c) How many white squares will there be in pattern number 50?
(d) How many squares in total will there be in pattern number 100?
(e) Write down the total number of black squares in the nth pattern.

4.

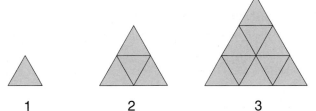

Pattern no. 1   2   3   4   5

(a) Copy and complete this table:

Pattern no:	White balls	Black balls	Total balls
1	1	0	1
2	2	1	3
3	4	2	
4	6		
5			
6			

(b) How many balls in total will there be in pattern number 10?
(c) How many black balls will there be in pattern number 10?
(d) How many white balls will there be in pattern number 10?
(e) Write down the total number of balls in the nth pattern.
(f) Write down the total numbers of black balls and white balls in the nth pattern.

5.

Pattern no.   1   2   3

(a) Copy and complete this table:

Pattern no:	Lines	Triangles
1	3	1
2	9	4
3		
4		
5		
6		

(b) How many lines in total will there be in pattern number 10?

(c) How many triangles will there be in pattern number 10?

(d) How many lines will there be in pattern number 100?

(e) Write down the total number of lines in the nth pattern.

(f) Write down the total number of triangles in the nth pattern.

Geometric sequences: An introduction to fractals

When using numbers or algebra to generate a sequence we apply the same operation over and over again.

For example:

2, 5, 8, 11, 14, 17, ... we add 3 to each previous term

2, $x + 2$, $2x + 2$, $3x + 2$, $4x + 2$, ... we add x to each term

The same can be done in geometry. If we apply the same rule over and over again we can make a **repeating pattern within a pattern**. This is called a **fractal**.

In 1975 Polish mathematician Benoit Mandelbrot published his work introducing fractal geometry. He invented the word fractal to signify certain complex geometric shapes. The word is derived from the Latin *fractus*, meaning 'fragmented' or 'broken' and refers to the fact that these objects are self-similar – that is, their component parts are similar to the whole shape. These forms repeat themselves on an increasingly smaller scale, so that if each component is magnified it will look basically like the object as a whole.

Here is an example of what we mean:

Step 1: Divide a line into three equal parts:

Step 2: Replace the central section with two sides of an equilateral triangle:

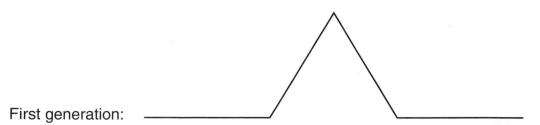

First generation:

Step 3: Divide the lines into three equal parts:

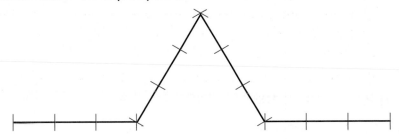

Step 4: Replace each central section with two sides of an equilateral triangle:

Second generation:

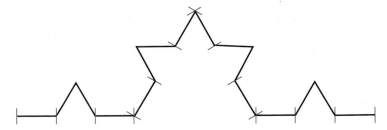

Exercise 8.8

You will need the worksheet for this exercise.

1. The first pattern on the worksheet is a triangle with sides of 9 units. What is its perimeter? What is its area in triangular units?

2. To produce the second generation of this fractal you have to divide each side of the triangle into three parts and then build an equilateral triangle on the central part.
   (a) Do this to each side of the triangle on the worksheet. This is your second generation fractal.
   (b What is the perimeter of this pattern? What is its area?

3. (a) Copy your second generation fractal into the third box on the worksheet and repeat the divide and build process to each side of the pattern as described in q.2 (that will be 12 times in total). This is your third generation fractal.
   (b) What is the area of this pattern?
   (c) What is the perimeter of this pattern? (Hint: It is now easier to find the perimeter by counting the number of sides and then to multiply this by the length of one side.)

4. Now fill in this table at the bottom of the worksheet:

Generation number	Area	No of sides	Length of each side	Perimeter
1	81	3	9	27
2	108	12	3	36
3	...	...	...	...
4	...	...	...	...

5. Now draw a ×3 enlargement of your first triangle on the worksheet. The sides will be of length 27 units. This time you can draw a fourth generation fractal.

6. Write down the number of sides for the fourth generation in the table. Can you find a rule for the number of sides in the nth generation?

7. The fourth generation fractal is a ×3 enlargement and so you must divide the length of each side by 3, before filling in the length and thus going on to find the perimeter. Can you find a rule for the perimeter of the nth pattern?

8. As the number of sides becomes larger and larger what can you say about the area? What can you say about the perimeter?

Geometric sequences and numbers

Exercise 8.9

You will need the worksheet for this exercise:

1. Sierpinski's gasket

You are going to shade and then rub out in this sequence, so do the first shading very lightly.

(a) Look at the equilateral triangle of side 16 units on the worksheet. Divide it into 4 equal triangles. Do not shade in the central triangle:

(b) Divide each remaining triangle into four and remove (rub out) the central one – this is the second generation gasket.

(c) Repeat this procedure as many times as you can. Shade the final result carefully.

(d) Complete this table:

Generation number	1	2	3	4	5
No. of triangles (including the unshaded ones)	4	13			
Fraction of whole triangle unshaded	$\frac{1}{4}$				

(e) How many triangles (including the unshaded ones) will there be in the nth generation?

2. Now let's look at another equilateral triangle with sides of 16 units.

(a) Pascal's triangle has been started for you. Note that the numbers are formed by adding the number above on the left to the number above on the right ($3 + 3 = 6$, $4 + 6 = 10$, $5 + 10 = ?$). Finish it so that all the 16 rows are completed. (Use a calculator if you need to!)

(b) Shade all the odd numbers.

(c) Compare your two triangles (the ones from q.1 and q.2). What do you notice? Can you explain your answer?

Exercise 8.10: Extension questions

Now try to write the rule for these sequences. Look at the patterns and see if the terms go up in a fixed number, or if they compare to square numbers, triangle numbers, rectangle numbers, or if the terms are formed by a pattern of products (e.g. 1×2, 2×3, 3×4).

Example:

Find the next three terms and the rule for the nth term of this sequence: 2, 5, 10, 17, ..., ..., ...

Look at the pattern of differences:

$2 + 3 = 5$ $5 + 5 = 10$ $10 + 7 = 17$

The pattern +3, +5, +7 is the same as the one for the square numbers: 1, 4, 9, 16, ...

Therefore the sequence is the same as the one for square numbers plus 1

The next three terms are 26, 37, 50
The nth term is $n^2 + 1$

Write down the nth term for each of the following:

1. 2, 4, 7, 11, ...

2. 3, 9, 18, 30, ...

3. 2, 6, 10, 14, ...

4. 4, 10, 18, 28, ...

5. 2, 7, 14, 23, ...

6. What sequence do you get if you add a square number to the pattern number (e.g. $1 + 1$, $4 + 2$, $9 + 3$)? What is the rule?

7. What sequence do you get if you multiply each triangle number by 8, and then add 1? What is the rule for this sequence?

8. What sequence do you get if you multiply each triangle number by 2 and subtract the pattern number? What is the rule for this sequence?

9. What sequence do you get if you multiply each triangle number by 3 and subtract the pattern number? What is the rule for this sequence?

10. What sequence do you get if you multiply each triangle number by 2 and subtract the corresponding square number? What is the rule for this sequence? Can you explain it with algebra?

Exercise 8.11: Summary exercise

1. Write down the next three terms of these sequences:
   (a) 2, 7, 12, 17, ..., ..., ...
   (b) 16, 4, 1, $\frac{1}{4}$, ..., ..., ...
   (c) 4, 2, 0, −2, ..., ..., ...

2. Look at these patterns of matches:

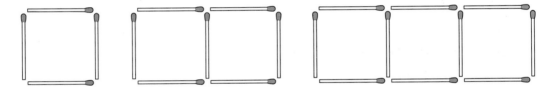

   (a) How many matches will be needed in the fourth pattern?
   (b) How many matches will be needed in the tenth pattern?
   (c) What is the rule for the number of matches that will be needed for the nth pattern?

3. (a) Draw the next two patterns in this sequence:

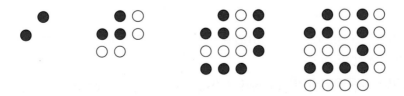

(b) Copy and complete this table:

Pattern no:	White balls	Red balls	Total balls
1	0	2	2
2	4	3	7
3	5		
4			
5			
6			

(c) Add a final row to the table and work out the numbers of white balls and red balls and hence the total number of balls, in the nth row.

4. If the nth term in a series is $S_n = 20 - 3n$, find:
   (a) S_1 (b) S_4 (c) S_6 (d) S_{10}

5. Find the next three terms in the series and hence the rules for the sequences:
   (a) $S_1 = 4$ $S_2 = 7$ $S_3 = 10$ $S_4 = 13$ $S_5 = 16$
   (b) $T_1 = 2$ $T_2 = 7$ $T_3 = 14$ $T_4 = 23$ $T_5 = 34$
   (c) $W_1 = 5$ $W_2 = 3$ $W_3 = 1$ $W_4 = -1$ $W_5 = -3$

6. Pascal's triangle contains several of the sequences that you have studied in this chapter. Try adding up each row of the triangle like this:

```
            1                    1
         1 + 1                   2
      1 + 2 + 1                  4
   1 + 3 + ... + 1              ...
1 + ... + 6 + ... + 1          ...
```

(a) Can you find a rule for the sum of the nth row?
(b) Can you find the pattern of triangle numbers? (Hint: It is a sloping diagonal not a row or column.)
(c) What pattern is there in the next diagonal?
(d) Can you find a rule for the fourth term in the nth row?

7. You may have noticed that English people are very reserved. If they enter a room and have to sit down, they choose a chair that is not next to anyone else. When the next person comes in, he or she too will choose a chair with no neighbours.

We can explore this mathematically like this:

1 chair: There are **2 ways** to fill the seats
○ unoccupied (where no-one is sitting down)
☺ occupied

2 chairs: There are **3 ways** to fill the seats
○ ○
☺ ○
○ ☺

3 chairs: There are **5 ways** to fill the seats
○ ○ ○
○ ☺ ○
○ ○ ☺
☺ ○ ○
☺ ○ ☺

(a) Work out the number of ways you can fill a row of chairs (note one way of 'filling' a row is where no-one is sitting down) when the row has:
(i) 4 chairs   (ii)   5 chairs   (iii)   6 chairs

You should have started to generate the Fibonacci sequence.
(b) Without drawing, write down the number of ways you can fill 10 chairs.

End of chapter 8 activity: 3D fractals

We can see fractals in 3D by repeating a pattern of cuts. This pattern is a bit like a snowflake except that we are going to turn the middle thirds into 3D squares:

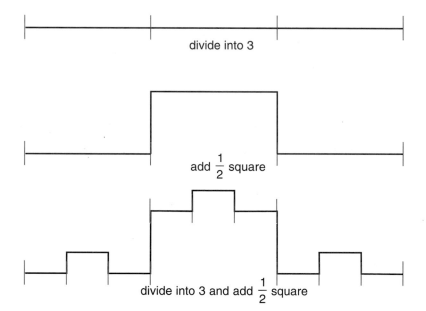

divide into 3

add $\frac{1}{2}$ square

divide into 3 and add $\frac{1}{2}$ square

Take a piece of paper 18 cm by 18 cm.

Step 1.   (a) Fold it in half.

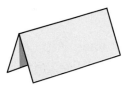

(b) Divide the fold line into 3   Make the central part into a square:

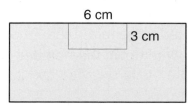

6 cm

3 cm

(c) Score the lines as shown ---------- .

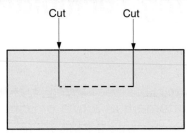

(d) Cut the solid lines and fold out your first generation pattern along the score lines.

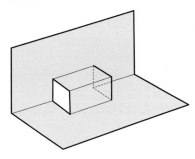

Step 2. (a) Flatten the sheet again and divide all the lines that have been folded inwards into three parts. Make the central parts into squares as you did in step 1(b).

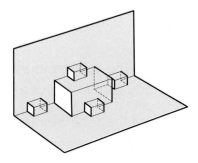

(b) Fold and cut as shown in the diagram below. Now fold out your second generation pattern.

Step 3. Flatten the sheet again, divide, square, score and cut to produce your third generation pattern.

If you stick your 3D fractal on to folded coloured card it really shows up the repeating pattern.

Now design some 3D fractals of your own, or look at Tarquin Publications' book *Fractal Cuts* and make some of those described.

Chapter 9: Using formulae

What is a formula?

A formula is a mathematical statement of a rule or principle written in the form of an equation. When you found the rule for the nth term of a sequence in the last chapter, you were finding the formula for that sequence.

Formulae are written using symbols and without any units (i.e. kg, cm etc.) in them. As algebraic equations they should not contain any x or ÷ signs but should use brackets and fractions.

> Example: Write a formula for A, where A is the average, in kg,
>
> of three masses, x kg, y kg, and z kg.
>
> $$A = \frac{x + y + z}{3}$$

Exercise 9.1

1.   Write a formula for N, where N is the total amount of money that I have in pounds, when I start with £x and I am then given £y more.

2.   Write a formula for N, where N is the total amount of money that I have left, in pounds, when I start with £a and spend £b.

3.   Write a formula for A, where A is the average of four lengths, w metres, x metres, y metres and z metres.

4.   Write a formula for P, where P is the perimeter of this rectangle:

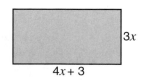

$3x$

$4x + 3$

5.   Write a formula for A, where A is the area of the rectangle in q.4

6. Write a formula for *P*, where *P* is the perimeter of this triangle:

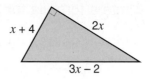

7. Write a formula for *A*, where *A* is the area of the above triangle.

8. Write a formula for *N*, where *N* is the total amount of money that I have, in pence, when I start with £*x* and am then given £*y* more.

9. Write a formula for *N*, where *N* is the total amount of money that I have, in pounds, when I start with *x* pence and am then given *y* pence more.

10. Write a formula for *N*, where *N* is the cost, in pounds, of buying 10 articles at £*y* each.

11. Write a formula for *N*, where *N* is the cost in pounds, of buying *n* articles at £*y* each.

12. Write a formula for *N*, where *N* is the cost, in pounds, of buying *n* articles at *x* pence each.

13. Write a formula for *P*, where *P* is the perimeter of this shape:

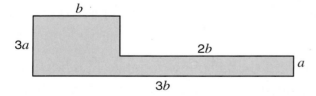

14. Write a formula for *A*, where *A* is the area of the above shape.

15. Write a formula for *P*, where *P* is the perimeter of this shape:

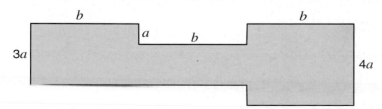

16. Write a formula for *A*, where *A* is the area of the above shape.

17. Write a formula for *A*, where *A* is the shaded area of this shape:

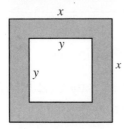

18. Write a formula for *A*, where *A* cm² is the area of a frame where the outside of the frame is *x* cm by *y* cm and the frame is 5 cm wide.

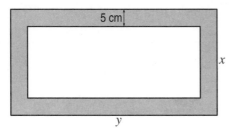

Substituting into formulae

When using a formula to calculate an answer, we must first substitute the numbers into the formula and then work out the answer. While this can often appear simple, particularly if you use a calculator, it is very important that certain rules are followed. Following the rules will help you to avoid making careless mistakes and will allow someone else to follow your working out.

Particular care needs to be taken when substituting negative numbers into a formula. It is very easy to make a mistake with the signs, which can then lead to a wrong answer.

Example: If $a = -2$, $b = -3$ and $c = 2$ calculate *N* where $N = ab^2 - bc$

$$N = ab^2 - bc \qquad \text{Formula}$$
$$= (-2) \times (-3)^2 - (-3) \times 2 \qquad \text{Substitute}$$
$$= (-2) \times 9 - (-6) \qquad \text{Calculate}$$
$$= -18 + 6$$
$$= -12 \qquad \text{Answer}$$

The steps: 1. Formula
               2. Substitute
               3. Calculate
               4. Answer
               5. Units

All of these steps need to be conscientiously performed and written down. The calculation may be done using a calculator but it is important that the calculation being performed is written down.

Most mistakes using formulae are made through careless substitution. **Do not try to combine substitution and calculation**.

One common mistake is to confuse ab^2 with $(ab)^2$

$$ab^2 = a \times b \times b \qquad \text{whilst} \qquad (ab)^2 = a \times b \times a \times b$$

and $\qquad 2a^2 = 2 \times a \times a \qquad$ whilst $\qquad (2a)^2 = 2 \times a \times 2 \times a$

also note $\quad -a^2 = -a \times a = -a^2 \qquad$ but $\qquad (-a)^2 = (-a) \times (-a) = a^2$

Exercise 9.2

1. If $a = -2$, $b = -1$ find N when:
    (a) $N = a + b$ (c) $N = a - b$ (e) $N = b - a$
    (b) $N = ab$ (d) $N = 3a + 2b$ (f) $N = 3a - 2b$

2. If $a = -3$, $b = 2$ and $c = -4$ find N when:
    (a) $N = a^2$ (c) $N = a^2 + b^2$ (e) $N = 3a^2 - 2c^2$
    (b) $N = ab - bc$ (d) $N = a(b - c)$ (f) $N = a^2(2b - 3c)$

3. If $a = -0.5$, $b = -2$ and $c = -0.2$ find N when:
    (a) $N = ac$ (c) $N = ab + c^2$ (e) $N = abc$
    (b) $N = ab - bc$ (d) $N = a(b - c)$ (f) $N = b(b^2 - c^2)$

4. If $x = -3$, $y = 4$ and $z = -1$ find M when:

(a) $M = \dfrac{x}{y}$ (c) $M = \dfrac{xy}{z}$ (e) $M = \dfrac{xyz}{4}$

(b) $M = \dfrac{(x+y)}{(y-z)}$ (d) $M = \dfrac{(x^2 - z^2)}{(x+y)}$ (f) $M = \dfrac{(3x^2 - 2y^2)}{(3y - 2z)}$

5. If $a = -1$, $b = -2$ and $c = 3$ find N when:

(a) $N = ab^2$ (c) $N = (ab)^2$ (e) $N = abc$

(b) $N = ab - bc$ (d) $N = a^2b - b^2c$ (f) $N = a^2(4b^2 - 3bc^2)$

6. If $a = 0.24$, $b = 2.1$ and $c = 0.3$ find N when:

(a) $N = ab^2$ (c) $N = (ab)^2$ (e) $N = abc$

(b) $N = ab - bc$ (d) $N = a^2b - b^2c$ (f) $N = a^2(4b^2 - 3bc^2)$

7. If $a = -3$, $b = 2$ and $c = -2$ find N when:

(a) $N = ab^2$ (c) $N = (ab)^2$ (e) $N = abc$

(b) $N = \dfrac{a^2}{c}$ (d) $N = \dfrac{a(c - b)}{2b}$ (f) $N = b^2 - 4ac$

8. If $x = 3.1$, $y = -0.07$ and $z = -1.25$ find A when:

(a) $A = x^2 + y^2$ (c) $A = x(y + z)$ (e) $A = x^2 - yz$

(b) $A = \dfrac{xy - z^2}{4}$ (d) $A = \dfrac{2(x - 2z)}{y}$ (f) $A = \dfrac{(x - 2y)}{1 - 4z}$

9. If $x = -0.5$, $y = 2.5$ and $z = -1.2$ find V when:

(a) $V = x^2y$ (c) $V = x(y^2 + z^2)$ (e) $V = x^2 - y^2z$

(b) $N = \dfrac{x(y - z)^2}{5}$ (d) $N = \dfrac{2xy^2 - 3yz^2}{2}$

10. If $a = -0.25$, $b = 2.1$ and $c = -0.8$ find N when:

(a) $N = ab^2 - bc^2$ (c) $N = (ab - bc)^2$ (e) $N = \sqrt{b^2 - 4ac}$

(b) $N = \dfrac{b^2 - a^2}{1 + c}$ (d) $N = \dfrac{a(c - b)}{2}$

Area and volume formulae

Here are some familiar formulae for length, area and volume.

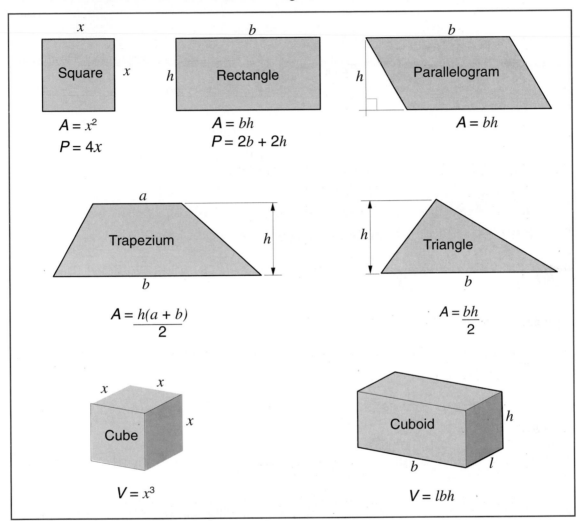

When using these formulae it is a good idea not just to write $A =$, but say exactly what A stands for. This stops you from getting the formulae confused.

In the next exercises you should set your working out as follows:

Start each question with a sketch, making sure you choose the correct formula. You may use a calculator but write down the **four stages** of working, and remember the units. Give non-exact answers to 3 s.f.

Example: Find the area of a trapezium with parallel
sides of 4 cm and 7 cm and height 6 cm.

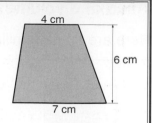

Area of trapezium $= \dfrac{h(a+b)}{2}$ Step 1: Formula

$= \dfrac{^3\cancel{6}(4+7)}{\cancel{2}_1}$ Step 2: Substitution

$= 3 \times 11$ Step 3: Calculation

$= 33$ cm²   Step 4: Answer and Units

Exercise 9.3

1. Find the area of a triangle of base 5.6 cm and height 2.8 cm.

2. Find the perimeter of a rectangle of base 45 cm and height 1.4 m. Give your answer in metres.

3. Find the volume of a cube of edge 1.2 m.

4. Find the area of a parallelogram of base 1.3 m and height 55 cm. Give your answer in m².

5. Find in m³ the volume of a cuboid of length 5.2 m, breadth 45 cm and height 45 cm.

6. Find in litres the volume of a cuboid with width 55 cm, height 90 cm and length 1.2 m.

7. Find in m² the area of a trapezium with parallel sides of lengths 55 cm and 1.4 m and height 65 cm.

8. Using the formula for the area of a triangle, find the formula for the area of a kite in terms of its diagonals. Then find the area of a kite with diagonals of 12 cm and 15 cm.

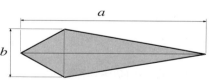

9. Using the formula for the area of a square derive a formula for the surface area of a cube. Then find the surface area of a cube of side 12 cm.

10. Using the formula for the area of a rectangle derive a formula for the surface area of a cuboid. Then find the surface area of a cuboid of length 14 cm, breadth 20 cm and height 12 cm.

Finding an unknown quantity

In the above examples you were given the lengths of various shapes and then asked to find the area, perimeter or volume. However, there are times when you know the volume, area or perimeter and you are asked to find the length.

Finding the missing lengths follows exactly the same steps as before. First of all you substitute into the formula and then treat it just like an equation to find the unknown.

Example: The area of a triangle is 24 cm² and its base is 12.4 cm. Find the height of the triangle.

$$\text{Area of triangle} = \frac{bh}{2} \qquad \text{Step 1: Formula}$$

$$24 = \frac{12.4 \times b}{2} \qquad \text{Step 2: Substitute}$$

$$24 = 6.2 \times b \qquad \text{Step 3: Calculate}$$

$$\frac{24}{6.2} = b \qquad (\div 6.2)$$

$$b = 3.870 \dots$$

$$= 3.87 \text{ cm (to 3 s.f.)} \quad \text{Steps 4 and 5:}$$
Answer and units

Exercise 9.4

Using the formulae given earlier, answer these questions, giving non-exact answers to 3 s.f.

1. Find the side of a square of area 289 cm².

2. Find the height of a rectangle of base 12 cm and area 228 cm².

3. Find the base of a parallelogram of height 14 cm and area 238 cm².

4. Find the base of a triangle of height 5.5 cm and area 132 cm².

5. Find the length of an edge of a cube of volume 343 cm³.

6. Find the height of a trapezium with parallel sides of 10 cm and 12 cm and area 132 cm².

7. Find the height of a trapezium with parallel sides of 55 cm and 1.2 m and area of 4 m².

8. A trapezium has one parallel side twice as long as the other and a height of 5 cm. If the area is 12 cm², find the lengths of the parallel sides.

9. Find one parallel side of a trapezium if the other is 20 cm, the height is 12 cm and the area is 264 cm².

10. Find one parallel side of a trapezium if the other is 1.4 m, the height is 60 cm and the area is 1.5 m².

These last few questions are a little more challenging:

11. A parallelogram has a base twice as long as its height and an area of 30 cm². How long is the base?

12. The height of a triangle is three times the length of its base and it has an area of 25 cm². What is the height?

13. The sides of a rectangle are in the ratio 3:4 and the area of the rectangle is 100 cm². What are the lengths of the sides?

14. The base and height of a triangle are in the ratio 3:5 and the triangle has an area of 150 cm². What are the lengths of the base and the height?

15. A cuboid has edges in the ratio 5:7:8 and a volume of 1 m³. What are the lengths of the sides?

Polygon formulae

Here are some familiar formulae for finding the interior and exterior angles of polygons:

For all polygons with n sides:

Sum of exterior angles = 360°

Sum of interior angles = $180(n - 2)°$

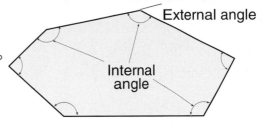

External angle

Internal angle

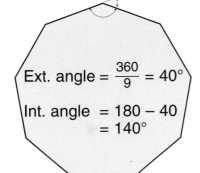

Ext. angle = $\frac{360}{9}$ = 40°

Int. angle = 180 − 40
= 140°

For regular polygons with n sides:

Ext. angle = $\frac{360°}{n}$ and $n = \frac{360°}{\text{ext. angle}}$

Int. angle = 180 − ext. angle or = $\frac{180(n-2)°}{n}$

Exercise 9.5

1. Find the sum of the interior angles of a pentagon.

2. Find the sum of the interior angles of a nonagon.

3. Find the sum of the interior angles of an octagon.

4. Find the exterior angle of a regular hexagon.

5. Find the exterior angle of a regular heptagon.

6. Find the exterior angle of a regular decagon.

7. Find the interior angle of a regular pentagon.

8. Find the interior angle of a regular octagon.

9. How many sides has a regular polygon whose exterior angles are all 18°?

10. How many sides has a regular polygon whose exterior angles are all 24°?

11. How many sides has a regular polygon whose interior angles are all 150°?

12. How many sides has a regular polygon whose interior angles are all 160°?

13. *ABCDE* is a regular pentagon.
  O is the centre of the pentagon such that $AO = BO = CO = DO = EO$

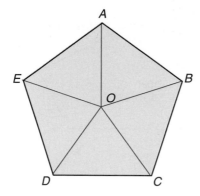

Find: (a) ∠*AOB*
    (b) ∠*OBC*
    (c) ∠*ABC*

14. *BCDEFG* is a regular hexagon.
  Find, giving reasons for your answer:

  (a) ∠*CDH*
  (b) ∠*CDE*
  (c) ∠*DCF*
  (d) What can you say about *CF* and *DE*?

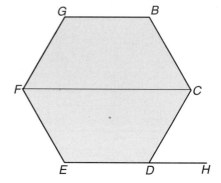

15. *ABCDEFGH* is a regular octagon with centre *O*.
  Find, giving reasons for your answer:

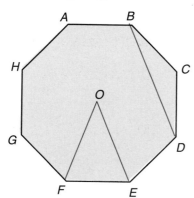

  (a) ∠*EOF*
  (b) ∠*FED*
  (c) ∠*OED*
  (d) ∠*BCD*
  (e) ∠*CDB*
  (f) ∠*BDE*
  (g) What can you say about
      BD and *OE*?

16. *ABCDE* is a regular pentagon and *EDFGHI* is a regular hexagon.
Find, giving reasons for your answer:

(a) ∠*CDE*
(b) ∠*EDF*
(c) ∠*CED*
(d) ∠*DEF*
(e) ∠*CDF*
(f) ∠*ECF*

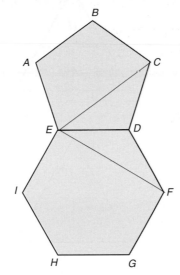

17. Here is the base of a regular polygon.
The interior angle is 11 times bigger than the exterior angle. How many sides has the polygon?

Int. angle

Ext. angle

Distance, speed and time formulae

The formula for the distance travelled, given the speed and time, is:

$d = st$ where d is the distance travelled, s is the average speed and t is the time taken.

From this formula we can derive the formula for the time taken: $t = \dfrac{d}{s}$

and the formula for the speed: $s = \dfrac{d}{t}$

You can think of these formulae in a triangle:

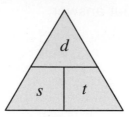

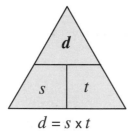

$$d = s \times t$$

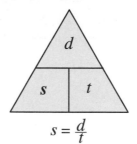

$$s = \frac{d}{t}$$

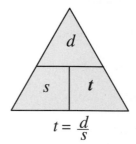

$$t = \frac{d}{s}$$

Here is an example to show how this speed triangle can be used:

Example:

I walk for 4 hours at 3 km per hour. How far do I walk?

Distance = speed × time

= 3 × 4

= 12 km

It is worth remembering that because the units of time do **not** follow the metric system – there are 60 seconds in a minute and 60 minutes in an hour – it is a good idea to convert time to a fraction or decimal fraction of the unit. Therefore, if speed is expressed as km per hour, then 2 hours and 30 minutes would be $2\frac{1}{2}$ hours or 2.5 hours. If you calculated time to be 3.3333 ... hours, then this is $3\frac{1}{3}$ hours or 3 hours and 20 minutes.

Example:

If I travelled 12 miles in 12 minutes what was my speed?

$$d = 12 \text{ miles} \qquad t = 12 \text{ minutes} = \frac{1}{5} \text{ hour} = 0.2 \text{ hours}$$

$$s = \frac{d}{t}$$

$$= \frac{12}{0.2}$$

$$= 60 \text{ mph}$$

Exercise 9.6

1. I travel at 60 mph for 45 minutes. How far do I go?

2. I drive 90 miles at a speed of 60 miles per hour. How long does the journey take?

3. I walk three quarters of a mile in twenty minutes. What is my speed in miles per hour?

4. A comet travels 5000 miles in 10 minutes. What is its speed in mph?

5. A space shuttle travels at 30 000 km per hour for 5 minutes. How far does it go?

6. My mother drives at 40 mph for 30 minutes and then drives at 30 mph for 40 minutes. How far does she go?

7. It took us three hours and twenty minutes to travel 300 kilometres. What was our speed?

8. We travelled 12 miles on the M25 at 10 mph, but then we travelled 80 miles on the M2 at 60 mph. What was our total journey time?

9. An aeroplane left Heathrow at 10:34 and arrived at Newark at 16:24. If the distance is 3605 miles, what was the speed of the aeroplane?

10. A ship travelled for 6 days and 4 hours on a journey from Southampton to Gibraltar, a distance of 3219 kilometres. What was the average daily distance covered, and what was the speed?

11. If a car travels twice as far as the distance between A and B, at the same speed it would have taken to travel from A to B, how much longer or shorter is the journey time?

12. If a car travels three times as far as the distance between A and B, in the same time it would have taken to travel from A to B, how much faster or slower is its speed?

13. If a car travels three times as far as the distance from A to B, in half the time it would have taken to travel from A to B, how much faster or slower is the its speed?

Average speed

Although the examples above talk about 'speed' it is hard in practice to drive 60 miles at a constant speed. That is why we talk about 'average speed':

$$\text{Average speed} = \frac{\text{total distance travelled}}{\text{total time taken}}$$

However, unlike most averages, you cannot find the average of two speeds by simply adding them together and dividing by two. Look at this next example:

Example: We travelled at 40 km per hour for 15 minutes and then travelled at 60 km per hour for 20 minutes. What was our average speed?

$\text{Speed}_1 = 40$ km/h $\qquad \text{Time}_1 = 15$ min $= 0.25$ h

$$d = st$$
$$d_1 = 40 \times 0.25$$
$$= 10 \text{ km}$$

$\text{Speed}_2 = 60$ km/h $\qquad \text{Time}_2 = 20$ min $= \frac{1}{3}$ h

$$d = st$$
$$d_2 = 60 \times \frac{1}{3}$$
$$= 20 \text{ km}$$

Total distance = 30 km $\qquad$ Total time = 35 minutes $= \frac{7}{12}$ hour

$$\text{average speed} = \frac{\text{total distance}}{\text{total time}}$$

$$= 30 \div \frac{7}{12}$$

$$= 51.428 \ldots$$

$$= 51.4 \text{ km/h (to 3 s.f.)}$$

Exercise 9.7

1. A car travels for 15 minutes at 45 km/h and then for 30 minutes at 60 km/h.
    (a) What distance did the car travel?
    (b) What was its average speed?

2. A man walked for 15 minutes at 4 km/h and then for 10 minutes at 5 km/h.
    (a) What distance did the man walk?
    (b) What was his average speed?

3. A train travelled at 60 km per hour for 20 minutes and at 120 km per hour for one hour and forty minutes.
    (a) What distance did the train travel?
    (b) What was his average speed?

4. An aeroplane travelled at 250 km/h for one and a half hours and then at 350 km/h for two and a half hours.
    (a) What distance did the aeroplane travel?
    (b) What was the average speed?

5. A car travelled at an average speed of 60 mph for 2 hours. In the first part of the journey, the car was driven in a town travelling at 25 mph for 20 minutes. What speed did the car travel in the second part of its journey?

6. A car travelled at an average speed of 80 km/h for 100 km. In the first part of the journey the car travelled at 40 km/h for 15 minutes. What speed did the car travel in the second part of the journey?

7. A London to Paris train travelled from London to Dover, a distance of 120 km, at 100 km/h. It then travelled 40 km under the channel at 80 km/h, before completing the remaining 240 km to Paris at 125 km/h.
    (a) What was the average speed of the train?
    (b) What was the total journey time?

Rearranging formulae

When we had to find the unknown lengths in the earlier exercise, we substituted numbers into the formula and then solved the resulting equation. However, there are times when we need to rearrange the formula, as we did in the previous exercise. In this instance we rearranged the formula:

$$d = st \quad \text{to give:}$$

$$t = \frac{d}{s} \quad \text{and} \quad s = \frac{d}{t}$$

When solving an equation we can do exactly the same sort of rearranging. Remember to **do the same thing to both sides** and always **write down** what you are doing on the right hand side:

Example:

Rearrange the formula $y = \frac{x}{4} + 7$ to give x in terms of y.

$$y = \frac{x}{4} + 7$$
$$(-7)$$
$$y - 7 = \frac{x}{4}$$
$$(\times 4)$$
$$4(y - 7) = x$$

$$x = 4(y - 7)$$

Note the use of brackets and the correct use of algebra. There are no $\times$ signs or $\div$ signs in the formula.

Exercise 9.8

Make x the subject of the following formulae:

1. $y = x + 3$
2. $y = x - 5$
3. $y = 4 + x$
4. $y = 8 - x$
5. $y = x + a$

6. $y = x - b$
7. $y = c + x$
8. $y = d - x$
9. $y = 2x$
10. $y = ax$

11. $y = \dfrac{x}{2}$

12. $y = \dfrac{x}{b}$

13. $y = 2x + 3$

14. $y = 3x - 4$

15. $y = 5 + 3x$

16. $y = 5 - 2x$

17. $y = 3x + 9$

18. $y = 2x - b$

19. $y = c + 3x$

20. $y = d - 3x$

21. $y = ax + b$

22. $y = cx - d$

23. $y = a - bx$

24. $y = a(x - b)$

25. $y = \dfrac{3x}{a}$

26. $y = \dfrac{ax}{b}$

27. $y = \dfrac{2a}{x}$

28. $y = \dfrac{3b}{2x}$

29. $y = \dfrac{ab}{x - 1}$

30. $y = \dfrac{x}{2} + 1$

Units of formulae

When writing formulae, or working with several formulae put together, it is important that we keep asking ourselves: "Does it look right? Does it seem sensible?"

It is as easy to do this with letters as it is with numbers. If we continually bear in mind the units of a formula it can help to check the validity of what we are doing.

Example:

If D = density in g/cm³, M = mass in g and V = volume in cm³, find the units of the following and hence the quantity (if any) being calculated:

(a) DV

$$DV = \frac{g}{cm^3} \times cm^3$$
$$= g$$
$$= \text{mass}$$

(b) $\dfrac{V}{M}$

$$\frac{V}{M} = \frac{cm^3}{g}$$
$$= ?$$
$$= \text{wrong formula}$$

Exercise 9.9

1. If d is a length in m, t is a time in seconds and s is a speed in m/s, what are the units of the following and what quantity do they represent?

   (a) st

   (b) $\frac{d}{s}$

2. If D = density in g/cm³, M = mass in g and V = volume in cm³ find the units of the following and hence the quantity being found:

   (a) $\frac{M}{V}$

   (b) $\frac{M}{D}$

3. If a, b, c and d are units of length in cm, for which quantity, length, area or volume are the following formulae?

   (a) $a(b+c)$

   (d) $\pi a^2(b+c)$

   (b) $\sqrt{a^2+b^2}$

   (e) $\sqrt[3]{abc}$

   (c) $\frac{\pi a^2}{b}$

   (f) $\frac{abc}{\pi}$

   (g) $\frac{\pi a^2(b+c)}{2a}$

4. If u and v are units of speed in m/s, t is a unit of time in sec, m of mass in g and a, b, c, and s units of length in metres, write down the units of the following formulae:

   (a) $A = \frac{m}{abc}$

   (b) $C = t\sqrt{u^2-v^2}$

   (c) $D = \frac{s}{u+v}$

Exercise 9.10: Extension questions – Rearranging formulae with factorising and roots

In Exercise 9.8 the only operations used when rearranging formulae were x, ÷, +, and –. However there are times when there is more than one x term and so you need to factorise:

Example: Make x the subject of the following formula:

$$y - x = \frac{a + x}{b}$$

(× b)

$$b(y - x) = a + x$$

(brackets)

$$by - bx = a + x$$

(+ bx)

$$by = a + x + bx$$

(– a)

$$by - a = x + bx$$

(factorise)

$$by - a = x(1 + b)$$

(÷ (1 + b))

$$\frac{by - a}{1 + b} = x$$

$$x = \frac{by - a}{1 + b}$$

Note that the rearrangement is made simpler if you keep the x term positive, just as you have done for equations and inequations. Do not miss out any stages of working, since this tends to lead to mistakes.

Make x the subject of the following formulae:

1. $y = \dfrac{a + x}{b + x}$

2. $y = \dfrac{a + x}{x - b}$

3. $b - x = \dfrac{a + x}{c}$

4. $ax = \dfrac{a + x}{b + c}$

5. $y = a(b + x) - c(a - x)$

6. $y(a - x) = b(a + x)$

7. $x - y = \dfrac{a + x}{b}$

8. $c(y + x) = a(x - b)$

9. $y = \dfrac{a(a - x)}{b + x}$

10. $y(a - x) = \dfrac{x(a - c)}{b}$

11. A motorbike courier spends part of his day in town and part of his time on a motorway. On the motorway he travels at an average speed of 60 mph and in town his speed is an average of 20 mph.

(a) On Monday he had a 40 mile journey, of which 30 miles were on the motorway:
  (i) What distance did he travel in town?
  (ii) What was the total time?
  (iii) What was his average speed?

(b) On Tuesday he had to make the same trip in the same time but he was held up in town and travelled at an average speed of 15 mph. Was he able to make the delivery without breaking the 70 mph speed limit on the motorway?

End of chapter 9 activity: Perigal's dissection

Take a sheet of A3 plain paper.

In the middle of it draw a right-angled triangle. It does not matter exactly what its dimensions are but make each side a different length. Draw your triangle askew like this:

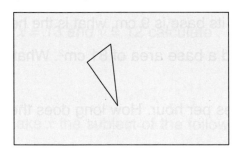

Now make each side of the triangle into a square like this:

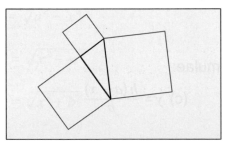

You should now have three squares, a big one, a little one and a middle-sized square. Dissect the middle-sized square by first drawing the two diagonals **very lightly** to find its centre:

The longest side of a right-angled triangle is the side opposite the right-angle and is called the **hypotenuse** (see page 203 chapter 10). Draw a line parallel to the hypotenuse through the centre of the middle-sized square. Using a set square and ruler to draw the parallel line:

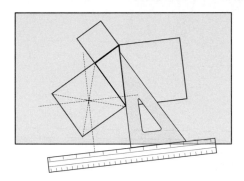

Slide your set square along a ruler to draw a parallel line.

Now draw a line at right-angles to the line you have just drawn also passing through the centre of the middle-sized square:

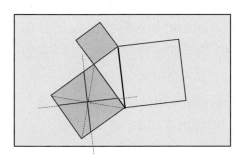

Slide your set square along a ruler to draw a parallel line.

Now trace over the little square and cut out the tracing. Then trace over the middle-sized square and cut out the four pieces. Can you fit all five pieces together in the big square? Does the area of the square on the hypotenuse equal the sum of the areas of the other two squares?

Chapter 10: Pythagoras' theorem

Pythagoras was a Greek Philosopher and mathematician. He was born on the island of Samos c.560 BC and travelled extensively as a young man. His contribution to mathematics was enormous. He was the first in the Western world (rather than the Eastern world of Ancient China and the Arabic world) to use letters on geometric shapes. This enabled him to deduce and prove many geometric and algebraic theorems.

Pythagoras equated the beauty of numerical properties with religion and his followers became a secret brotherhood following religious rites as well as mathematical and philosophical studies.

Pythagoras demonstrated the construction of the five regular solids and from his philosophical studies also claimed that this proved the world must be round – a concept that took centuries to be accepted!

While Pythagoras' exploration into number theory has been the starting point for much mathematical development, he is best known for proving the following:

> **For any right-angled triangle the square of the hypotenuse is equal to the sum of the squares of the other two sides.**
>
> (Note the capital H for hypotenuse – this avoids confusion with a lower case h, commonly used for height. Many calculations concerning right-angled triangles involve both the height and the hypotenuse.)

$$H^2 = x^2 + y^2$$

The special relationship between the sides of a right-angled triangle was known to many early civilisations, including the Babylonians 1000 years earlier, but Pythagoras seems to have been the first to have proved it.

Exercise 10.1

In a right-angled triangle the hypotenuse is the longest side – the side opposite the right-angle. Copy each of these triangles with a neat sketch and mark the hypotenuse with a capital H:

1.

3.

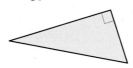

5.

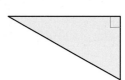

2.

4.

6.

Finding the hypotenuse

To find the hypotenuse of any right-angled triangle we can use Pythagoras' theorem. There are five steps in solving each problem:

> Step 1: Formula
> Step 2: Substitute
> Step 3: Calculate
> Step 4: Answer
> Step 5: Units

For each question you should draw a sketch of the triangle and label the hypotenuse with a capital H.

Example: Find the hypotenuse of this triangle:

7 cm

H

12 cm

$$H^2 = x^2 + y^2 \qquad \text{(Pythagoras' theorem)}$$

$$= 7^2 + 12^2 \qquad \text{(Substitute)}$$

$$= 49 + 144 \qquad \text{(Calculate)}$$

$$= 193$$

$$H = \sqrt{193}$$

$$= 13.892 \ldots \qquad \text{(Answer)}$$

$$= 13.9 \text{ cm (to 3 s.f.)} \qquad \text{(Units)}$$

Note that when writing down your calculations $H^2 = 193$

and $H = \sqrt{193}$

Exercise 10.2

Find the hypotenuse of these right-angled triangles, giving any non-exact answers to 3 s.f.

1.

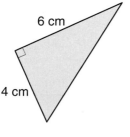

4 cm

3 cm

2.

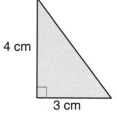

6 cm

4 cm

3.

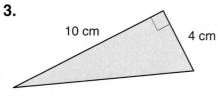

10 cm

4 cm

4.

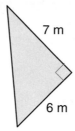

7 m

6 m

5.

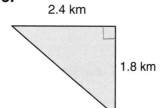

2.4 km

1.8 km

6.

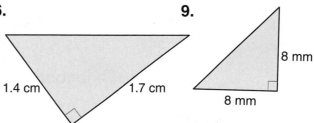

1.4 cm   1.7 cm

7.

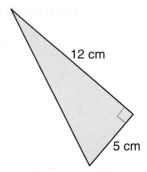

12 cm

5 cm

8.

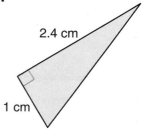

2.4 cm

1 cm

9.

8 mm

8 mm

Exercise 10.3

Now solve these problems, giving non-exact answers to 3 s.f.

Example: A man walked 400 m due North and then 500 m due West. How far was he from his starting point?

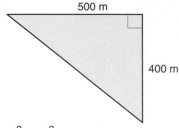

$$H^2 = x^2 + y^2 \qquad \text{(Pythagoras' theorem)}$$
$$= 400^2 + 500^2$$
$$= 160\ 000 + 250\ 000$$
$$= 410\ 000$$
$$H = \sqrt{410\ 000}$$
$$= 640.312\ 42\ldots$$
$$= 640 \text{ m (to 3 s.f.)}$$

---

1. A plane flew 6 miles due East and then 8 miles due South. How far was the plane from its starting point?

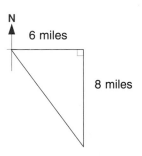

2. A ship sailed 240 km South East and then 320 km North East. How far was the ship from its starting point?

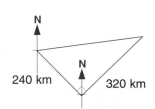

3. A hunter set out from home at *A* and walked 1.4 km on a bearing of 030º to a point *B* and then walked 2.7 km on a bearing of 120° to a point *C*. How far did he have to walk back home? (You must calculate angle *ABC* first!)

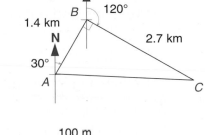

4. A school playground is in the shape of a rectangle 100 m by 50 m. John has to run around the whole perimeter of the rectangle and Janet has to run along the diagonal three times. Who runs further, Janet or John?

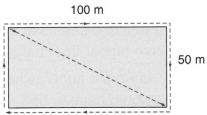

5. Find the length of a diagonal of a square with sides of 5 cm.

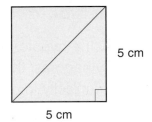

6. A doorway is 2 m tall and 1m wide. Can I get a piece of wood 2.3m square through the doorway? If not, how much must I shave off one side?

7. Freddie and Angus have a new ladder. Freddie reads the instructions and puts the foot of the ladder 2 m away from the foot of the wall. The top of the ladder reaches a point 4.6 m above the ground.

   (a) How long is the ladder?

   Angus complains that he cannot reach high enough up the wall. He wants to move the ladder 50 cm towards the wall and says that then he will be able to reach 50 cm higher than before.

   (b) Is Angus right? (Check the length the ladder would have to be.)

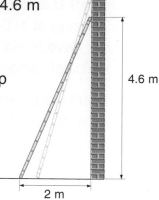

4.6 m

2 m

Finding a side other than the hypotenuse

If we know the hypotenuse and one other side of a right-angled triangle, we can use Pythagoras' theorem to find the third side. However, take care to substitute correctly into the equation.

Example: Find x in this triangle, giving your answer to 2 decimal places:

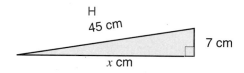

H
45 cm

7 cm

x cm

$$H^2 = x^2 + y^2 \qquad \text{(Pythagoras' theorem)}$$

$$45^2 = x^2 + 7^2$$

$$2025 = x^2 + 49$$

$$2025 - 49 = x^2 \qquad (-49)$$

$$x^2 = 1976$$

$$x = \sqrt{1976}$$

$$= 44.4522\ldots$$

$$= 44.45 \text{ cm (to 2 decimal places)}$$

Exercise 10.4

Find x in these triangles, giving any non-exact answers correct to 2 decimal places:

1.

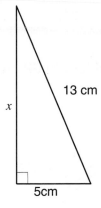

13 cm

x

5cm

4.

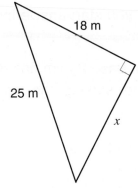

18 m

25 m

x

7.

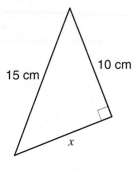

15 cm

10 cm

x

2.

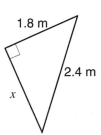

1.8 m

2.4 m

x

5.

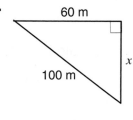

60 m

x

100 m

8.

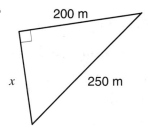

200 m

x

250 m

3.

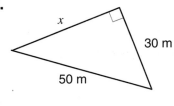

x

30 m

50 m

6.

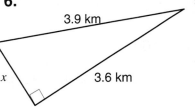

3.9 km

x

3.6 km

9.

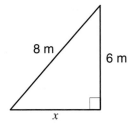

8 m

6 m

x

Exercise 10.5

Now solve the following problems, giving any non-exact answers correct to 2 decimal places. Remember, it is important to draw the right-angled triangle and mark the hypotenuse before you start answering each question.

Example: A rectangle of base 24 cm has diagonals of length 32 cm. What length are the other sides of the rectangle?

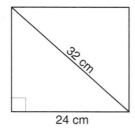 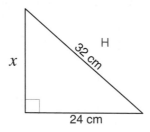

Let the other side of the rectangle be x cm long.

$$H^2 = x^2 + y^2 \qquad \text{(Pythagoras' theorem)}$$

$$32^2 = x^2 + 24^2$$

$$1024 = x^2 + 576$$

$$1024 - 576 = x^2 \qquad (-576)$$

$$x^2 = 448$$

$$x = \sqrt{448}$$

$$x = 21.166 \ldots$$

$$x = 21.17 \text{ cm (to 2 decimal places)}$$

1. A rectangle of base length 15 cm has diagonals of length 18 cm. What length are the other sides of the rectangle?

2. A ship sails 15 miles due North and she then sails due East until she is 30 miles from her starting point. How many miles did she sail due East?

3. A rambler walked 1.5 km North West, dropped his camera and then walked South West before he noticed. If he was now 2.4 km from his starting place, how far did he have to walk back to collect his camera?

4. A ladder 4 m long is leaning against a wall. If the foot of the ladder is 1 m from the base of the wall, how far up the wall does the ladder reach?

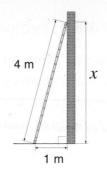

4 m

x

1 m

5. Another ladder is 3 m long and reaches 2 m up the wall. How far is the base of this ladder from the base of the wall?

6. The bracket for a hotel sign is in the shape of a right-angled triangle. How long is the top of the bracket?

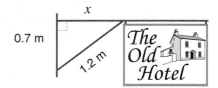

x

0.7 m

1.2 m

The Old Hotel

7. A square has diagonals of length 5 cm What is the length of a side of the square?

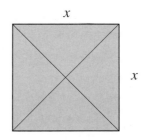

x

x

8. A rectangle has a diagonal of 12 cm and its long sides are twice the length of the short sides. What are the lengths of the sides of the rectangle?

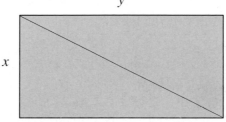

y

x

Isosceles triangles

Pythagoras' theorem can be used to find the height of an isosceles triangle, when you know the lengths of the sides. It is important to draw your sketches carefully first, so that you make sure that you have the correct dimensions in the right-angled triangle.

Example:

Find the height of an isosceles triangle ABC where $AB = AC = 12$ cm and $BC = 10$ cm.

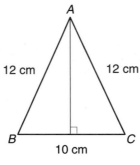

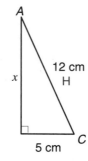

$$H^2 = x^2 + y^2 \qquad \text{(Pythagoras' theorem)}$$

$$12^2 = x^2 + 5^2$$

$$144 = x^2 + 25$$

$$144 - 25 = x^2 \qquad (-25)$$

$$x^2 = 119$$

$$x = \sqrt{119}$$

$$x = 10.908\ldots$$

$$x = 10.9 \text{ cm (to 3 s.f.)}$$

Exercise 10.6

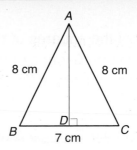

1. Find the height *AD* of an isosceles triangle where *AB* = *AC* = 8 cm and *BC* = 7 cm.

2. Find the height of an equilateral triangle of side 6 cm.

3. A tent has the dimensions shown: What is the height of the tent pole?

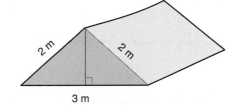

4. An isosceles triangle *XYZ* has height *AX* = 12 cm and sides *XY* = *XZ* = 13 cm. What is the length of *YZ*?

5. An equilateral triangle has a height of 8 cm. What is the length of a side?

Special triangles

In the last few exercises a small number of triangles had sides that were exact numbers. These were:

3 cm, 4 cm, 5 cm	1.8 km, 2.4 km, 3.0 km
5 cm, 12 cm, 13 cm	6 miles, 8 miles, 10 miles
30 m, 40 m, 50 m	60 m, 80 m, 100 m
3.9 km, 3.6 km, 1.5 km	150 m, 200 m, 250 m

Let's look at two of these triangles:

　　(i) 3 cm, 4cm, 5 cm　　and　　(ii) 5 cm, 12 cm, 13 cm

　　　Now let's consider:

$$3^2 + 4^2 = 9 + 16 \quad \text{and} \quad 5^2 + 12^2 = 25 + 144$$
$$= 25 \qquad\qquad\qquad\quad = 169$$

Both 25 and 169 are perfect squares:

25 = 5 x 5 and 169 = 13 x 13

The sum of the squares of the two smaller numbers equals the square of the largest number. Groups of three numbers that have this property are known as Pythagorean triplets. (We shall be looking at these in more detail in Exercise 10.10)

This makes the $3 : 4 : 5 \triangle$ (triangle) and the $5 : 12 : 13 \triangle$ very special. They frequently crop up in problems, either in this form or scaled up or down as in the examples below:

1.8 km, 2.4 km, 3.0 km	is a	$3 : 4 : 5 \triangle \times 0.6$
6 miles, 8 miles, 10 miles	is a	$3 : 4 : 5 \triangle \times 2$
30 m, 40m, 50m	is a	$3 : 4 : 5 \triangle \times 10$
60 m, 80 m, 100 m	is a	$3 : 4 : 5 \triangle \times 20$
150 m, 200m, 250 m	is a	$3 : 4 : 5 \triangle \times 50$
3.9 km, 3.6 km, 1.5 km	is a	$5 : 12 : 13 \triangle \times 0.3$

Spotting a $3 : 4 : 5 \triangle$ or a $5 : 12 : 13 \triangle$ can save a lot of time, so it is worth taking a little bit of time to look and check whether or not a triangle is 'special'.

Example: A flagpole is 2.4 m tall and is held up by wires 2.6 m long. How far from the base of the pole do the wires reach the ground?

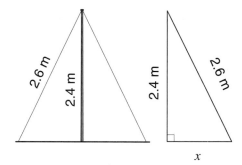

Let the distance on the ground be x m.

Write down your working like this:

Ratio of sides is $\quad x : 2.4 : 2.6$

which is $\quad 5 : 12 : 13 \times 0.2$

therefore $\quad x = 5 \times 0.2$

$x = 1$ m

The hypotenuse 2.6, is a multiple of 13, so check to see if it is a $5 : 12 : 13$ triangle. $(13 \times 0.2 = 2.6)$, so $5 : 12 : 13 \times 0.2$ is equivalent to $1.0 : 2.4 : 2.6$

We have two sides that are 2.4 and 2.6, and we can now say that this is a $5 : 12 : 13$ triangle. The third side is therefore 1 m.

Exercise 10.7

State if these triangles are 3 : 4 : 5 Δ or 5 : 12 : 13 Δ. If they are, write down the scale factor and find x.

1.

2.

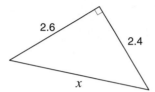

3.

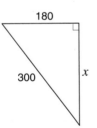

4.

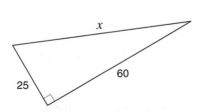

5.

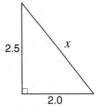

6.

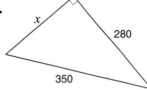

7.

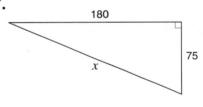

8.

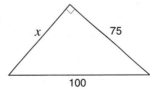

Exercise 10.8

Now solve these problems:

1. This is cross section through a porch. How long is the roof section *AD*?

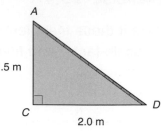

2. This is a radio aerial. It is held up by three wires attached to its top. The wires are 15 m long. How far from the base of the aerial are the wires attached to the ground?

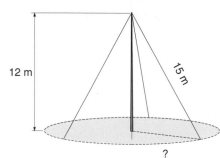

3. (a) A flagpole 18 m high is held up by wires that come $\frac{2}{3}$ of the way up the pole. How high up from the ground is this?

(b) The wires meet the ground 5 m from the base of the pole. How long are the wires?

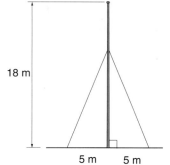

4. A hunter set out from home. He followed tracks 1200 m to the North and then 500 m West. The tracks then disappeared! How far did he have to walk home?

5. The hunter's wife, starting at home, tracked a bear 600 m to the North East and then 800 m South East, where she then lost its tracks. How far did she have to walk home?

6. Their son was out collecting firewood. He walked North West for a while and then walked 600 m North East before walking 650 m home. How far to the North West did he walk?

7. Find the height *AX* of an isosceles triangle where *AB* = *AC* = 15 m and *BC* = 18 m.

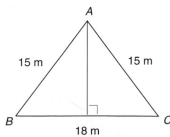

Mixed problems

There are times when you need to use an earlier result to answer the second part of a question. Remember not to calculate with a rounded answer but to use your full calculator display. It can sometimes be useful to leave answers in square root form.

Example:

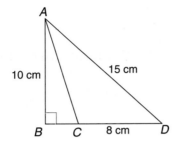

$AB = 10$ cm, $AD = 15$ cm, $CD = 8$ cm
Find (i) BC and   (ii) AC

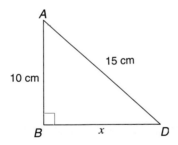

(i) We start this calculation by letting BD be x.

$$H^2 = x^2 + y^2 \qquad \text{(Pythagoras' theorem)}$$
$$15^2 = x^2 + 10^2$$
$$225 = x^2 + 100$$
$$225 - 100 = x^2 \qquad (-\,100)$$
$$x^2 = 125$$
$$x = \sqrt{125}$$
$$x = 11.1803\ldots$$

Now we know BD, we can calculate BC in the following way:
$BC = 11.1803\ldots - 8 = 3.18$ (to 3 s.f.)

(ii) Now we know *BC* we can calculate *AC*

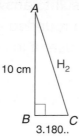

Let *AC* be H_2

$$H_2^2 = x^2 + y^2 \qquad \text{(Pythagoras' theorem)}$$
$$= 10^2 + 3.18^2 \ldots$$
$$= 100 + 10.114 \ldots$$
$$= 110.114 \ldots$$
$$H_2 = \sqrt{110.114 \ldots}$$
$$= 10.49 \ldots$$
$$= 10.5 \text{ cm (to 3 s.f.)}$$

Therefore *AC* = 10.5 cm

Exercise 10.9

Give all non-exact answers to 3 s.f.

1. *PR* = 8 cm, *PS* = 12 cm and
   QR = 6 cm
   Find *PQ* and *RS*.

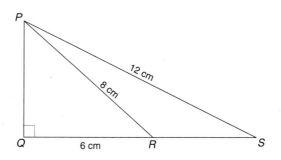

2. The diagonals of a kite are 40 cm and 60 cm.
   The shorter diagonal cuts the larger one a
   third of the way along its length.

   Calculate the lengths of the sides of the kite.

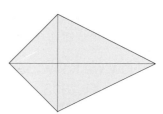

3. $ABC = 90°$ and $ADB = 90°$
$AB = 24$ cm, $AD = 19$ cm and
$BC = 12$ cm
Find CD and BD.

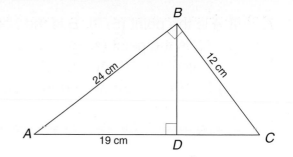

4. (a) A prince has a ladder 5 m long and
instructions that the base of the ladder must
be 2 m away from the base of the wall. Is the
ladder able to reach the princess' cell window
which is 4.7 m above the ground?
(b) How far forward must he move the base of
the ladder if he is to reach the window?

5. $ABCD$ is a square with diagonal AC 10 cm long.
EF bisects CD and AE bisects BC.
G is the point where EF cuts AC.
Calculate: (a) CD (b) CF (c) EF (d) CG

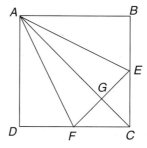

6. Look at this cuboid. It is an open-topped box with a base measuring 10
cm by 7 cm and a height of 5 cm:

A spider sitting at A spies a bug
tucked inside the corner of the
box at B. The spider wants to
take the most direct route to the
bug.

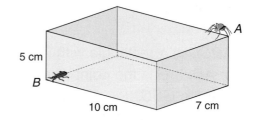

To find out the spider's route you
have to draw a net of the box.
Mark the positions A and B and then draw the spider's route. How far
does the spider have to go?

7. If *A* is the point (5, 5), *B* is the point (2, 4) and *C* is the point (4, −1):

    (a) Calculate *AB*, *AC* and *BC*.

    (b) Is *ABC* a right-angled triangle?

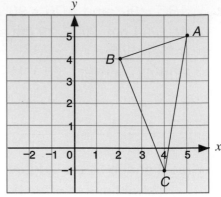

8. The mist came down on the moor in the middle of our Duke of Edinburgh expedition. My group had walked 5 km from our starting point on a bearing of 310° and then we walked another 3.75 km on a bearing of 220°

    It was lucky that we had Ella with us. She managed to work out the distance we were from our starting point without using a calculator. How did she do it and what was her answer?

9. The square *ABCD* has sides of 12 cm. Calculate:

    (a) *AC*

    (b) *FC*

    (c) The areas of triangles *AFB*, *BCF* and *AFC*.

    (d) The areas of triangles *GBC* and *AGF*.

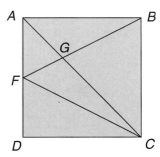

10. *ABCD* is a rectangle with *AB* = 12 cm and *AD* = 8 cm and *F* the mid point of *AD*. If *G* is the point where *BF* crosses *AC,* work out the area of triangle *GBC*.

Exercise 10.10: Extension questions – Pythagorean triplets

The 3 : 4 : 5 $\triangle$ and the 5 : 12 : 13 $\triangle$ are special because the sum of the squares of the smaller two numbers equals the square of the largest number.

Remember that groups of three numbers that have this property are known as Pythagorean triplets.

How many more can you find (excluding multiples of 3 : 4: 5 and 5 : 12 : 13)?

You might like to use the spreadsheet application on a computer to investigate this problem. If so, you will need to find the correct formulae for finding squares and square roots. If you are using Microsoft Excel, squares are given by typing =POWER(number,power) e.g. =POWER(4,2) for calculating 4^2 and square roots by typing =SQRT(number or cell ref.). If you are using a different application, you may need to refer to a manual.

Step 1. Start by making a table of numbers and their squares. You will need to go up to 40 or even 50:

Number	Square	Subtract	Answer
1	1		
2	4	4 − 1	3
3	9	9 − 4	5
4	16	16 − 9	7
5	25	25 − 16	$9 = 3^2$
6			
7			
8			
9			
10			

Step 2. Then look at the differences between the consecutive squares:
For example $17^2 − 16^2 = 33$
See if any of these differences are perfect squares.

Step 3. Next try looking at the differences between non-consecutive squares and see if any of those are perfect squares.

Step 4. Look for a pattern in your answers, can you find and repeat a pattern, or is this a random property of certain sets of numbers?

We have used our calculators or computers to do this search, but spare a thought for the ancient Greeks who found their triplets without such aids to calculation!

Exercise 10.11: Summary exercise

1. Write out Pythagoras' theorem in words.

2. A hunter starts from home and travels 4 km East and then 2.5 km North. She then shoots a pheasant which falls at her feet. How far does she have to carry the pheasant home?

3. An isosceles triangle ABC has base $BC = 32$ cm and two equal sides $AB = AC = 63$ cm. Calculate its height and then its area.

4. This diagram shows the cross section of our roof.

   The total height of the roof is 2.6 m, and the heights BE and CF are both 1.3 m.

   The sloping lengths AG and GD are both 4 m.

   Calculate:
   (a) The length AD.
   (b) The total cross-sectional area of the roof.
   (c) The length AE and thus the length AB (compare the total height to height BE).
   (d) The rectangular area of usable of roof space $BCFE$.

5. A similar roof with height CF of 2.6 m and base AB of 7m has a dormer window inserted. The height of the window DE is 1.5 m and the length CD is 2 m. Calculate the length BE.

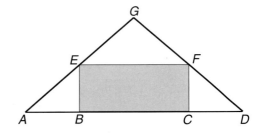

6. A company logo is in the form of two triangles as shown. The total width of the logo is 5 cm and the height is 3 cm. The ratio of $BC : CE$ and thus the lengths $AB : DE$ is 3 : 2

Calculate:

(a) The length AD.

(b) The areas of the two triangles ABC and CDE.

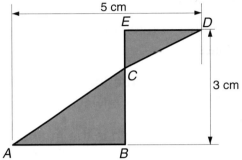

End of chapter 10 activity: Truthful twins?

There is famous pair of twins where one of them always tells the truth and the other always lies. This is very difficult for anyone talking to the twins because, as, like all twins, it is impossible to tell them apart and people never know which twin they are talking to.

1. Which twin, the liar or the truthful one, (or both or neither) could make these statements?

   (a) 'I always tell the truth'

   (b) 'I always tell lies'

   (c) 'I never tell lies'

   (d) 'My brother always tells the truth'

   (e) 'My brother always tells lies'

   (f) 'I always tell lies but my brother always tells the truth'

2. What question could you ask one twin to decide which one is the truth teller and which is the liar?

Chapter 11: Area and volume

In chapter 9 we saw some formulae for area and volume, and in **Maths Prep Book 2** we learnt some special formulae for circles.

Circles

Remind yourself of the names of the parts of a circle.

The **circumference** is the distance round the outside.
The **radius** is the distance from the centre to the outside.
The **diameter** is the distance across the centre.
Diameter = 2 × radius

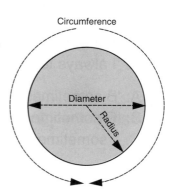

Do you remember the formulae for finding the circumference and area of a circle?

$$C = \pi d \quad \text{or} \quad C = 2\pi r \quad \text{and} \quad \text{Area} = \pi r^2$$

Exercise 11.1

Use the π button on your calculator for this exercise and give non-exact answers to 3 s.f.

Example : Find the circumference of a circle of diameter 14 cm:

d =14 cm
$C = \pi d$
$\quad = \pi \times 14$
$\quad = 43.982...$
$\quad = 44.0$ cm (to 3 s.f.)

---

1. Find (i) the circumference and (ii) the area of each of these circles:

(a) diameter of 8 cm
(b) radius of 31 cm
(c) diameter of 1.2 m

(d) radius of 4.5 m
(e) diameter of 50 cm
(f) radius of 12 m

2. My bicycle has wheels of diameter 95 cm. How far will my bicycle go in one turn of the wheel?

3. This table mat has a diameter of 14 cm. Find its area and circumference.

4. I have a glass with a base diameter of 8 cm. Find the area of the base of my glass.

5. My frisbee has a radius of 9 cm. What is the circumference?

6. I bought a large sheet of MDF (medium density fibreboard) measuring 1.25 m by 2.5 m. I cut from the board the largest circle that I could. What area of MDF is left?

Parts of circles: Perimeter

Often there are shapes that are not whole circles but parts of circles:

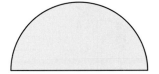

A half circle is a semi-circle   A quarter circle is a quadrant

To find the perimeter of a **semi-circle** we have to first find **half** the circumference and then **add** on the length of the straight side.

Example: Find (i) the area and (ii) the perimeter of this semi-circle:

$d = 14$ cm
$r = 7$ cm

(i) Remember that because this is half a circle, you must halve the area formula:

$$\text{Area} = \frac{1}{2}\pi r^2$$

$$= \frac{1}{2}\pi \times 7^2$$

$$= \frac{1}{2} \times \pi \times 49$$

$$= 76.969 \ldots$$

$$= 77.0 \text{ cm}^2 \quad \text{(to 3 s.f.)}$$

(ii) Curved length $\qquad = \pi d$

$\qquad\qquad\qquad\qquad = \pi \times 14$

$\qquad\qquad\qquad\qquad = 21.991\ldots$

Straight side is the diameter measuring 14 cm

$\qquad$ Perimeter $= 21.991\ldots + 14$

$\qquad\qquad\qquad = 35.991\ldots$

$\qquad\qquad\qquad = 36.0$ cm (to 3 s.f.)

Exercise 11.2

1. Find the perimeter of this semi-circular carpet:

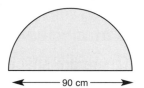

— 90 cm —

2. Find the area and perimeter of this quadrant:

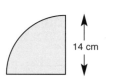

14 cm

3. Find the area of this three-quarter circle:

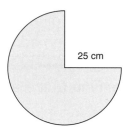

25 cm

4. (a) Calculate the distance round the outside of this running track:

(b) What is the area enclosed by the running track?

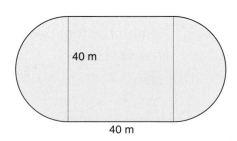

40 m

40 m

5. Find the area of this lily pad:

For the next few questions use $\pi = \dfrac{22}{7}$

6. Here is the cross-section through the building that won this year's architectural prize. Calculate the area of the cross-section:

7. This is the pattern for my new petticoat. What length of ribbon do I need to trim the whole outside edge of the petticoat?

8. This is the cross-section through a spinning toy. The top semi-circle has a diameter of 49 mm and the bottom semi-circle a diameter of 98 mm. What is the area of the cross-section?

Finding the radius

Example:

Find the radius of a circle of area 100 cm²:

$$\text{Area of circle} = \pi r^2$$
$$100 = \pi r^2$$
$$100 \div \pi = r^2$$
$$r^2 = 31.8309 \ldots$$
$$r = \sqrt{31.8309\ldots}$$
$$= 5.6418\ldots$$
$$= 5.64 \text{ cm (to 3.s.f.)}$$

Exercise 11.3

1. Find the diameter of a circle of circumference 14 cm.

2. Find the radius of a circle of area 100 cm².

3. Find the radius of a circle of circumference 12 m.

4. Find the diameter of a circle of area 250 cm².

5. Find the radius in cm of a circle of area 4 m².

6. I have a length of wooden trim measuring 2 m. What is the radius of the largest circle that I could trim with it?

7. I have a circular tablecloth of area 5 m². What is the radius of the largest table that it could cover?

8. The perimeter of a semi-circle is 20 cm. What is the diameter?

More circle problems

Some questions need a little more thought. For some of the following problems you may need to use Pythagoras' theorem. Make sure your working is clearly set out.

Exercise 11.4

Use the π button on your calculator for this exercise and give non-exact answers to 3 s.f.

1. (a) Find the diameter of the circle inscribed in a square of side 10 cm:
   (b) Now find the length of the diagonal of the square.

10 cm

2. Find the diameter and thus the area of the circle drawn around a square of side 10 cm:

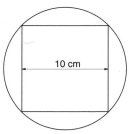

10 cm

3. Find the area of the shaded part of this circle:

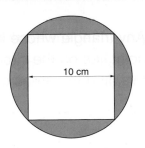

10 cm

4. (a) Here is a square inscribed inside a circle of diameter 22 cm. Find the length of a side of the square:

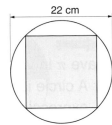

22 cm

(b) Now find the shaded area in the second diagram.

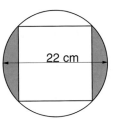

22 cm

5. A square is inscribed in a circle of radius 7 cm. What is the area of the square?

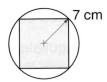

7 cm

6. A circle of radius 12 cm is inscribed in a square. What is the area of the square?

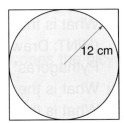

12 cm

7. A circle of diameter 25 cm is inscribed inside a square. What is the length of a diagonal of the square?

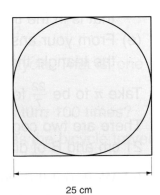

25 cm

More about volume

In **Maths Prep** Book 2 we looked at prisms.

A prism is a shape that has a **constant cross-section**. This means that the shape can be sliced into slices of the same area. The formula for the volume of a prism is:

Volume of a prism = area of cross-section × length (or height or depth)

Here are some examples:

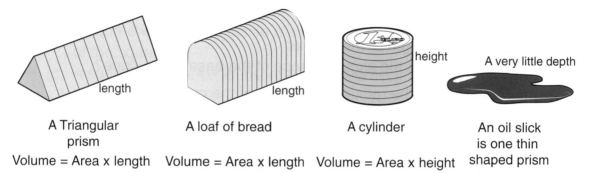

A Triangular prism	A loaf of bread	A cylinder	An oil slick is one thin shaped prism
Volume = Area x length	Volume = Area x length	Volume = Area x height	Volume = Area x depth

---

Example:

Find the volume of a prism of length 15 cm and a triangular cross section of base 8 cm and height 6 cm.

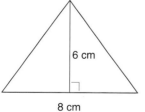

Always draw the cross-sectional area first

$$\text{Area of triangle} = \frac{1}{2} bh$$

Next calculate the cross-sectional area

$$= \frac{1}{2_1} \times \cancel{8}^{4} \times 6$$

$$= 24 \text{ cm}^2$$

Finally use the formula to work out the volume

$$\text{Volume of prism} = \text{area} \times \text{length}$$
$$= 24 \times 15$$
$$= 360 \text{ cm}^3$$

Do not forget the cubic units.

Exercise 11.5

1. Find the volume of a triangular prism of length 18 cm. The triangle has height 2.5 cm and base 3 cm.

2. A prism has a cross-sectional area of 15 m² and depth 14 cm. What is its volume in m³?

3. A wooden bar has a cross-sectional area of 5 cm² and length 2 m. What is its volume in cm³?

4. A hexagonal paving stone is a prism with a cross-section in the shape of a hexagon. The hexagon is made up from two trapezia, each base 12 cm, top 6 cm and height 5.5 cm. If the paving stone is 3 cm thick, what is its volume?

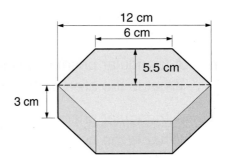

5. A prism has a cross-sectional area in the shape of a parallelogram of height 95 cm and base 1.2 m. The depth of the prism is 1.4 m. What is the volume, in m³, of the prism?

6. This builder's skip is 3 m wide. What volume of rubbish can we put in it?

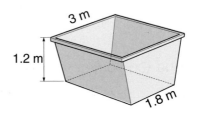

7. I have three hollow blocks, all 15 cm tall. The cross-section of one is a rectangle of width 8 cm and length 12 cm, one is a square of side 10 cm and the last is a triangle with base 14 cm and height 12 cm.

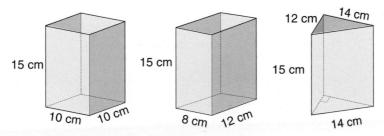

   (a) Which has the greatest volume?
   (b) If I were to pour 1.5 litres of water into each prism which ones would overflow?

8. A bird nesting box is made up of the following pieces:

Calculate the volume of the box.

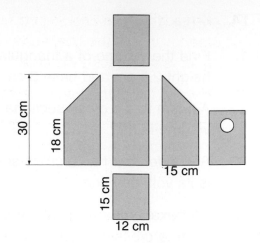

9. A triangular prism has volume 120 cubic centimetres and length 15 cm. What is the area of the cross-section?

10. A triangular prism has a volume of 200 ml and a base of area 10 cm². What is the height of the prism?

11. Find the volume of this prism:

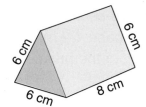

12. Find the volume of this prism:

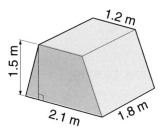

13. Find the volume of this prism:

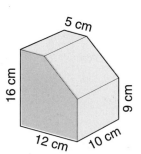

14. For each of the prisms in q.11, q.12 and q.13 above sketch the net and then work out the total surface area (the cross-section of the prism in q.12 is an isosceles trapezium).

15. Here is the plan of an ornamental pond:

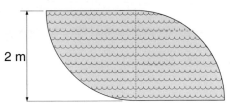

(a) Calculate the surface area of the pond.

2 m

(b) The pond is half a metre deep. A goldfish requires 10 litres of water. What is the maximum number of goldfish that I could keep in the pond?

Volume of a cylinder

As we saw above the volume of a prism is given by the formula

---

Volume of a prism = area of cross-section × height (or length or breadth)

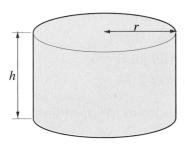

The cross-section of a cylinder is in fact a circle, so the formula for the volume of a cylinder can be written:

Volume of cylinder = $\pi r^2 h$

Example:

Find the volume of a cylinder of radius 5 cm and height 10cm.
Give your answer in litres.

$r = 5$ cm $\qquad h = 10$ cm $\qquad 1000$ cm^3 = 1 litre

$$Volume = \pi r^2 h$$
$$= \pi \times 5^2 \times 10$$
$$= 785.398 \ldots$$
$$= 785 \text{ cm}^3$$
$$= 0.785 \text{ litres}$$

Exercise 11.6

Use the π button on your calculator for this exercise. Give non-exact answers to 3 s.f.

1. Find, in litres, the volumes of these cylinders:
    (a) radius 3 cm and height 5 cm.
    (b) radius 4 m and height 5 m.
    (c) diameter 60 cm and height 50 cm.
    (d) height 20 cm and radius 9 cm.
    (e) diameter 15 cm and height 8 cm.
    (f) height 1.2 m and radius 0.75 m.

2. Find the volume of a cylinder in m^3 of radius 80 cm and height 2.4 m.

3. Find the volume of a cylinder in litres of diameter 110 cm and height 1.2 m.

4. I have a glass of base diameter 6 cm and height 8 cm. How many glasses can I fill from a jug containing 2 litres of water?

5. This tin of 'WOOF' dog food has a radius of 5 cm and a height of 12 cm.
    What volume of 'WOOF' is in the can?

Surface area of a cylinder

In the q.5 above we had a can of dog food. If we took the label off and unwrapped it what shape would it be?

The label is a rectangle

The total surface area of a cylinder has to be calculated in two parts. If you think about unwrapping the label from a tin can you will see that it is a rectangle whose length is equal to the circumference of the cylinder:

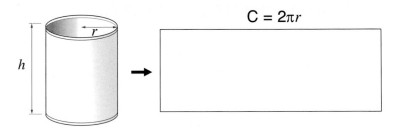

Therefore the curved surface area of a cylinder is given by the formula:

Surface area $(SA) = 2\pi rh$

But a solid cylinder has two ends (i.e. two circles) and so the formula for the surface area of a solid cylinder is:

$$SA = 2\pi rh + 2\pi r^2$$

or $\qquad SA = 2\pi r(h + r)$

Until you are used to working out surface area it is best to work the two parts out separately then add them together, especially as some cylinders are hollow and therefore don't have ends.

Example:

Find the surface area of a cylinder of radius 5 cm and height 10 cm.

$r = 5$ cm $h = 10$ cm

Curved $SA = 2\pi rh$
$= 2 \times \pi \times 5 \times 10$
$= 314.159...$

Round $SA = 2\pi r^2$
$= 2 \times \pi \times 5^2$
$= 157.079 ...$

Total $SA = 314.159 ... + 157.079 ...$
$= 471.23 ...$
$= 471$ cm^2 (to 3 s.f.)

In the example above, note that when we added together the two areas we used the unrounded answers.

Warning! If you calculate with rounded values you will get wrong answers!

Exercise 11.7

Use the π button on your calculator for this exercise. Give non-exact answers to 3 s.f.

1. What are the dimensions of the rectangular label from the WOOF can on page 239? What is its area?

2. (a) I have a cylindrical can of radius 5 cm and height 10 cm. What is the area of the label that wraps around the can?
    (b) What is the volume of the can?

3. Here is the top of a hat box. The radius of the circle is 25 cm and the height is 5 cm. What is the external surface area of the top of a hat box?

4. If you have an empty loo roll it can be unwrapped into a parallelogram:

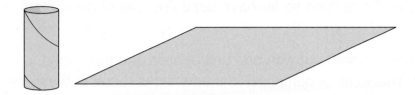

(a) If the parallelogram has base 15 cm and height 10 cm what is the surface area of the cylinder?

(b) What do you think the advantages are of a parallelogram rather than a rectangle?

5. This is a cylindrical drum. It has diameter 15 cm and height 7 cm. What is its surface area?

6. Which has the greater surface area, and by how much, a cube of side 10 cm or a cylinder of diameter and height 10 cm?

7. Which has the larger volume, a cylinder with radius 5 cm and height 6 cm or a cylinder with a radius of 6 cm and a height 5 cm? Can you answer the question without actually calculating the volumes of the two cylinders?

8. A can of tomato juice has a radius of 5 cm and a height of 12 cm. What volume of tomato juice is contained in a tray of 24 tins? Give your answer in litres.

9. My little sister has a cylindrical paddling pool of radius 1.2 m, filled to a depth of 14 cm. I had to fill up the pool using a cylindrical bucket of radius 12 cm and height 30 cm. How many bucket loads did I have to carry?

10. A prism has a cross-section in the shape of a circle of circumference 15 cm. The volume of the prism is 268 cm³. What is the length of the prism? (Clue: find r from the circumference first.)

Units of area and volume

All the calculations we have done so far have used one unit of area, mm², cm², m² or km².

There are times when we start out with one unit of area and then need to change to another. This is more complicated than it looks. Look at these two squares. We know that 1 m = 100 cm

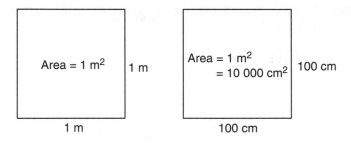

Therefore **1 m² = 10 000 cm²**

There are also occasions when we need to change units of volume.

Look at these two cubes:

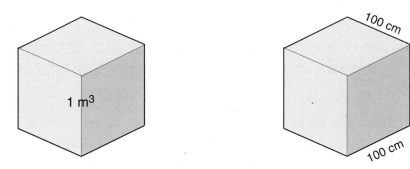

The volume of the second cube is $100 \times 100 \times 100 = 1\ 000\ 000$ cm³

Therefore **1 m³ = 1 000 000 cm³**

Exercise 11.8

1. Draw squares like the two on the previous page to find how many:
   (a) square millimetres are in a square centimetre.
   (b) square millimetres are n a square metre.
   (c) square metres are in a square kilometre.
   (d) square metres are in a square centimetre.
   (e) square metres are in a square millimetre.
   (f) square kilometres are in a square metre.

2. Draw cubes like the two above to find how many:
   (a) cubic millimetres are in a cubic centimetre.
   (b) cubic millimetres are in a cubic metre.
   (c) cubic metres are in a cubic kilometre.
   (d) cubic metres are in a cubic centimetre.
   (e) cubic metres are in a cubic millimetre.
   (f) cubic kilometres are in a cubic metre.

3. (a) How many litres are there in a cubic metre?
   (b) How many cubic mm are there in a litre?

More volume problems

When calculating with π, leave π in your answer until the last possible moment – it frequently cancels out. It is perfectly acceptable to leave a length or volume in the form 100π, for example, and only multiply out the final answer.

Example:

A cylindrical glass of radius 4 cm and height 8 cm is filled with water. All the water is poured into an empty cylindrical jug of radius 8 cm. What depth of water is now in the jug?

$$\text{Volume of glass} = \pi r^2 h$$
$$= \pi \times 4^2 \times 8$$
$$= 128\pi \text{ cm}^3$$

$$\text{Volume in jug} = \pi r^2 h$$
$$= \pi \times 8^2 \times h \text{ cm}^3$$
$$= 64\pi h \text{ cm}^3$$

Therefore $128\pi = 64\pi h$ \quad (depth of water now in the jug)
$$h = 2 \text{ cm}$$

Exercise 11.9: Extension questions 1

1. A cylindrical jug of radius 9 cm is filled with squash to a depth of 20 cm. All the squash is to be equally divided between 10 small cylindrical glasses of internal diameter 6 cm. What depth of squash should be poured into each glass?

2. A cube, 1 m by 1 m by 1 m, is filled with water. A cylinder with diameter 1 m contains the same amount of water. How high is the cylinder?

3. A cylinder of radius 5 cm and height 10 cm is filled with water. The water is then poured into a hollow cube, which it fills exactly. What is the length of an edge of the cube?

4. A cylindrical glass of radius 4 cm and height 8 cm is filled with water. All the water is poured into an empty cylindrical jug of radius 8 cm. What depth of water is now in the jug?

5. A fish tank has a rectangular base 20 cm by 35 cm and is filled with water from two cylindrical buckets of diameter 24 cm and depth 15 cm. What depth is the water in the fish tank?

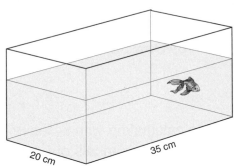

20 cm   35 cm

6. A rectangular block of clay, 5 cm by 6 cm by 10 cm, is fashioned into a cylinder of diameter 6 cm. How long is this cylinder?

7. A cylinder has a volume of 1 litre. Another cylinder has the same height as the first but twice the radius. What is its volume?

8. A cylindrical bucket is being used to fill up a rectangular water tank. The bucket has diameter 30 cm and height 50 cm. The rectangular tank has a base of 1 m by 1.5 m. How many buckets are needed to fill the rectangular tank up so that it contains 1050 litres?

Exercise 11.10: Extension questions 2 – Longer problems using area and volume formulae

In these problems you should not need to draw a 3-D diagram but you may need to use Pythagoras' theorem, so it is useful to draw sketches of a triangle when necessary.

Example: Find the volume of a prism of length 10 cm with the cross-section of an equilateral triangle of side 5 cm.

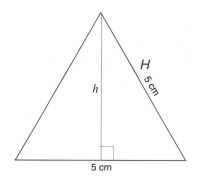
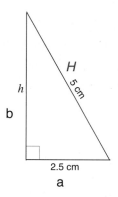

$$H^2 = a^2 + b^2 \qquad \text{(Pythagoras' theorem)}$$
$$5^2 = 2.5^2 + h^2$$
$$h^2 = 25 - 6.25$$
$$= 18.75$$
$$h = 4.330127...$$
$$= 4.33 \text{ cm (to 3 s.f.)}$$

$$\text{Volume} = \text{area of cross-section} \times \text{length}$$
$$= \frac{bh}{2} \times 10$$
$$= \frac{5 \times 4.330127}{2} \times 10$$
$$= 108.2531 ...$$
$$= \underline{108 \text{ cm}^3} \text{ (to 3 s.f.)}$$

Solve these problems, remembering that you may need to use Pythagoras' theorem to find some of the lengths. If the answer is not exact give it correct to 3 s.f.

1. I have to pack a cylindrical tube of circumference 21.5 cm and length 1.2 m into a rectangular box.

   (a) What is the volume of the smallest box that I could use?

   (b) Sketch the net of the box and work out the surface area.

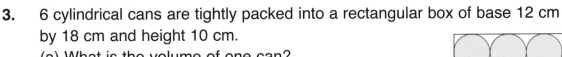

2. A fly walks around the inside of a cylindrical glass of height 12 cm and diameter 8 cm, The fly finishes at the top of the glass immediately above its starting point, but it has travelled twice around the glass.
   How far has the fly walked?

3. 6 cylindrical cans are tightly packed into a rectangular box of base 12 cm by 18 cm and height 10 cm.

   (a) What is the volume of one can?

   (b) What is the volume of the box?

   (c) What percentage of the volume of the box is not filled?

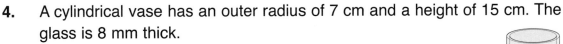

4. A cylindrical vase has an outer radius of 7 cm and a height of 15 cm. The glass is 8 mm thick.

   (a) Calculate the radius and height of the inside of the vase, and hence its volume.

   (b) Calculate the volume of glass used to make the vase.

5. This cylindrical glass of radius 5 cm has a volume of one litre. What is the length of the glass rod that just fits right across the inside of the glass as shown?

6. This parallelogram of cardboard rolls into a cylindrical tube and is then filled with pastry dough. The filled tube is sold in a supermarket (you may have bought one – the pastry makes jolly good croissants!).

The cylindrical tube has a radius of 4 cm and contains 800 cm³ of dough.

(a) What is the height and base length of the parallelogram?

(b) You will notice that the top corner of the parallelogram is immediately above the bottom corner. How long is the sloping side?

7. A chocolate bar is manufactured in the shape of a triangular prism. Each prism has length 15 cm and an equilateral triangular cross-section of sides 4 cm. Six of these bars are then packaged together to form a prism whose cross-section is a hexagon. Sketch the net of the hexagonal package that the six bars fit into and then calculate its surface area and its volume.

15 cm

4 cm

8. (a) Circle B has three times the area of circle A. What is the ratio of the radius of circle A to the radius of circle B?

(b) Cylinder C has twice the radius and twice the height of cylinder D. How much greater is the volume of cylinder C?

9. (a) A cylinder has a volume of 5 litres and the diameter of the cylinder is equal to its height. What is the radius of the cylinder?

(b) The contents of that cylinder are poured into a tank whose base is a square of side equal to the diameter of the cylinder. What is the depth of water in the tank?

10. Here is my birthday cake, before and after it was iced:

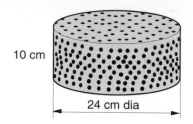 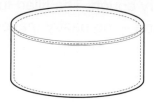

10 cm

24 cm dia

(a) The cake without the icing is in the shape of a cylinder 10 cm high and of diameter 24 cm. What is its volume?

(b) The icing is 0.5 cm thick and is made in two parts, a circle for the top, and a long rectangle to go round the sides. What is the diameter of the circle of icing?

(c) What are the height and length of the rectangle of icing?

(d) What is the total volume of the icing?

(e) If I mix icing sugar and water in the ratio 10:1 what volume of icing sugar was used?

11. A rope of length 100 m is wrapped around a cylindrical barrel of diameter 2 m.

(a) What length of rope is taken up by one turn around the barrel?

(b) How many turns are needed to take the whole 100 m?

(c) The rope is 10 cm in diameter, and the turns must lie flat on the barrel (i.e. a single thickness). What is the volume of the barrel?

12. Here is a tin of 'BowWow' dog food.
The radius of the tin is 6 cm and the height is 12 cm.

(a) The labels round the can overlap by one cm. Sketch a label and calculate its dimensions.

(b) In the dog food factory several labels are printed on each sheet of A0 paper and then cut up by machine before the individual labels are stuck on the cans of 'BowWow'. If a sheet of A0 paper is 84 cm by 118.8 cm, how many labels are there on every sheet?

13. (a) (i) I have two containers. One a cube, S, and
the other a cylinder, C. Both are the same
height h and both contain exactly a litre of
water. What is the ratio of the base area of
S to the base area of C?

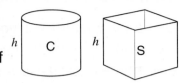

(ii) One tenth of a litre is now drawn off each
container. Which now contains the greater
depth of water, and by how much?

(b) I have another two containers, one a
cube, T, and one a cylinder, D. The
diameter of the cylinder is equal to the
height of the cube. Both containers are full
and contain one litre of water.

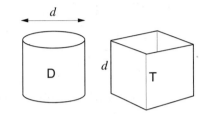

(i) What is the ratio of the area of the
base of T to the base of D?

(ii) One tenth of a litre is drained from each container. Which contains
the greater depth of water and by how much?

14. Here is the new logo for a record company.
The outside square is 25 cm long. Calculate:

(a) the area of one whole circle.

(b) the red area of one circle.

(c) the total red area of the shape.

(d) the percentage of red area in the square logo.

15. (a) 4 litres of chocolate are melted in a pan whose radius is 9 cm.
How deep is the melted chocolate in the pan?

(b) The chocolate is poured into a mould in the shape of an equilateral
triangular prism of side 18 cm. How deep is the chocolate in this
mould?

Exercise 11.11: Summary exercise

Use a calculator to solve these problems but make sure you show all formulae and working. Use the value of π given by the π button of your calculator and give non-exact answers to 2 decimal places.

1. Find the area and circumference of a circle of diameter 1.3 m.

2. Find the area and perimeter of this fan shaped garden pond:

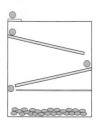

3. I put a two-pound coin in a charity box. The coin rolls down two slopes each of 15 cm before it falls into a hole. How many times does the coin rotate on its journey? The diameter of a two-pound coin is 28 mm.

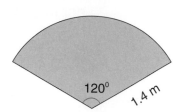

4. Find the volume in cm³ of a prism with cross-sectional area of 15 cm² and length 1.2 m.

5. Find the diameter of a circle with an area of 15 cm².

6. (a) A prism has a volume of 500 cm³ and a cross-sectional area of 81 cm². What is its height?
   (b) If the cross-section is in the shape of a triangle of base 18 cm what is the height of the triangle?

7. I pour 5 litres of water into a pan of radius 12 cm. How far does the water come up the pan?

8. Gasometers are large cylindrical containers holding domestic gas to feed the domestic supply. Gasometers are constructed so that as the gas is drawn out of the gasometer the height of the whole cylinder drops.
   (a) A gasometer is a cylinder with a diameter of 18 m and when it is full it stands 12 m high. What volume of gas is contained in it when it is full? Give your answer to the nearest 1000 litres.

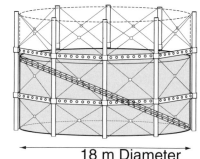

(b) 2 million litres of gas are drawn off the gasometer during the week and so its height decreases accordingly. How tall is it now?

(c) The rest of the gas drained out of the gasometer but something has gone wrong! The gasometer is stuck at the height in part (b). The repair man has to put a ladder across the inside of the gasometer. How long is his ladder?

End of chapter 11 activity: Packaging the litre

The litre is the most common unit of volume that we now use. Petrol is sold in litres. In the supermarket you will see that orange juice, milk, wine, shampoos and other fluids are also measured in litres or millilitres.

How many different packages with a volume of exactly one litre can you find?

Although the cube is an obvious shape for a container it is not usually used. Can you think why?

Can you design some prisms with a volume of exactly one litre? Their cross-sections could be circular, rectangular, triangular, trapezoid or any regular or irregular shape that you like.

Step 1: First decide what it is that you are going to package:

A bright green fizzy drink, a herbal shampoo, a latest chocolate bar, orange juice, talcum powder or just a pretty container to keep on your bedside table.

Step 2: Next think roughly about the shape you want your package to be: long and thin, small and squat.

Step 3: Now think about putting hundreds of these packages together. To do this efficiently and economically, they must fit closely together. In fact this could be part of your design - put several together and make a new shape (like those triangular prism chocolate bars we looked at earlier).

The net of your package is important too. How are you going to cut hundreds of these from one long strip of cardboard?

Step 4: Now calculate the dimensions of your package – you could use the spreadsheet programme of your computer to help you – making sure that you include the print out with your finished design.

Chapter 12: Simultaneous equations

What is an equation?

Equations can come in various forms, for example:

$$y = x^2 \qquad\qquad a + 3 = 5 \qquad\qquad 4 - 2x = 3x - 1$$

$$3(t + 1) = 1 - 2(2t + 4) \qquad\qquad 2u + 3v = 2$$

These equations all have one thing in common. They all contain an equals sign.

This means that the equation is **balanced**.

The expression on the left hand side **is equal in value** to the expression on the right hand side.

So far we have been familiar with looking at one equation on its own. This equation would contain one variable, often x but it could equally be y, h, p, s or a. The equation can be solved by simplifying, then adding, subtracting, multiplying and dividing values on both sides of the equation.

Most equations that we have come across so far have had only one variable, or unknown quantity.

Writing equations in two variables

As with any equation it is important to define your unknown quantities first.

Example:

I am thinking of two numbers whose sum is 12
Write this as an equation.

Let the numbers be x and y

$$x + y = 12$$

Exercise 12.1

1. I am thinking of two numbers whose sum is 24
   Write this as an equation.

2. I am thinking of two numbers whose difference is 8
   Write this as an equation.

3. I am thinking of two numbers. I double one and add this to the other and the answer is 20
   Write this as an equation.

4. My mother sends me to buy 15 cans of drink. I can buy either Cola or Orangeade. Show this as an equation.

5. I have £3 to buy some pencils and rulers. Pencils cost 25 pence each and rulers cost 30 pence each. Show this as an equation.

Using graphs to solve problems with two variables

Example:

I want to buy some avocados and some mangoes. Avocados cost 60 pence each and mangoes cost 80 pence each.

(a) Let the number of avocados I buy be a and the number of mangoes I buy be m. I spend exactly £12 altogether. Show how this can be given by the equation $3a + 4m = 60$

The cost of a avocados at 60 pence each $= 60a$
The cost of m mangoes at 80 pence each $= 80m$
The total cost is £12 or 1200 pence.
Therefore
$$60a + 80m = 1200$$
$$(\div 20)$$
$$3a + 4m = 60$$

(b) Plot a graph of $3a + 4m = 60$ and use it to show how many of each fruit I can buy.

To plot the graph it can help to choose $x = 0$ for your first point and $y = 0$ for your second and substitute it into the equation:

When $a = 0$, $m = 15$ and when $m = 0$, $a = 20$

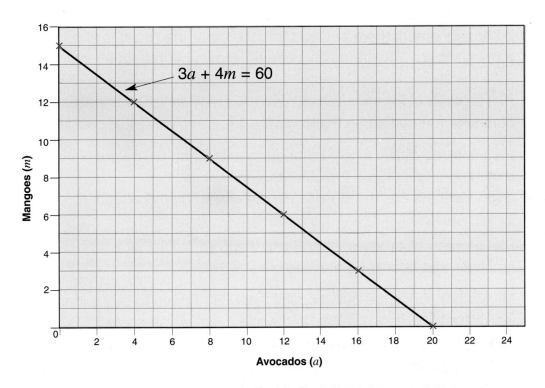

$3a + 4m = 60$

Mangoes (m)

Avocados (a)

From the graph I could buy 20 avocados and 0 mangoes
or 16 avocados and 3 mangoes
or 12 avocados and 6 mangoes
or   8 avocados and 9 mangoes
or   4 avocados and 12 mangoes
or   0 avocados and 15 mangoes

Exercise 12.2

1. (a) Plot a graph of $3x + 5y = 15$
   (b) Draw a table to show the whole number values of x and y that lie on the line.

2. (a) Plot a graph of $2x + 7y = 28$.
   (b) Draw a table of the whole number values of x and y that lie on the line.

3. I am thinking of two whole numbers greater than 0
   If I double one of them and add it to the other the result is 20
   If my numbers are x and y this can be shown by the equation
   $2x + y = 20$
   Plot a graph of $2x + y = 20$ and use the graph to list all the possible numbers that I could be thinking of.

4. I am thinking of two whole numbers greater than 0   If I double one of them and add it to half the other the answer is 12
   If my numbers are x and y this can be shown by the equation:
   $2x + \frac{1}{2}y = 12$
   Plot a graph of $4x + y = 24$ and use the graph to list all the possible numbers that I could be thinking of.

5. My Mother sends me out shopping with £8   I have to buy some milk, which costs 80 pence a litre, and some juice, which costs £1.60 a litre. Unfortunately I have forgotten how many litres of milk and juice I was supposed to buy.
   (a) If I let the amount of milk that I buy be m and the amount of juice I buy be j show that the total amount that I spend can be given by the equation: $m + 2j = 10$
   (b) Plot a graph of $m + 2j = 10$ and use your graph to show the numbers of litres each of milk and juice that I could buy for exactly £8
   (c) I suddenly remember that I should buy exactly 6 litres altogether. How many litres each of milk and juice is this?

6. I have to buy some batteries. Extra-long life batteries cost £4.50 per pack of 5, while normal batteries cost £1.50 per pack of 3   I have £13.50 to spend.
   (a) Let the number of packs of extra-long life batteries I buy be x and the number of packs of normal batteries I buy be y. Show that the total amount that I spend can be shown by the equation: $3x + y = 9$

(b) Plot a graph of $3x + y = 9$

(c) Use your graph to show how many packs of each type of battery I could buy for exactly £15

(d) I decide to buy as near as possible the same number of batteries of each type. How many of each pack do I buy?

7. I have £3 and I am going to buy some oranges and some lemons. Oranges cost 25 pence each and lemons cost 15 pence each.

(a) If I let the number of lemons I buy be x and the number of oranges I buy be y show that the total cost of my shopping can be shown by the equation: $3x + 5y = 60$

(b) Draw a graph of $3x + 5y = 60$ with a scale of 1 cm to 1 unit on both the horizontal and the vertical axes.

(c) From your graph draw up a table of the maximum numbers of oranges and lemons that I could buy.

(d) In fact my recipe calls for twice as many oranges as lemons. How many of each did I buy. If the total cost was not exactly £3 how much change did I receive?

What are simultaneous equations?

When we get a problem that involves two unknown quantities.

For example: The sum of two numbers is 13

We can let the two numbers be x and y, and write an equation: $x + y = 13$

We cannot solve this equation with a unique solution since we do not have enough information. As we have seen in earlier examples, there are several pairs of values of x and y which can satisfy this equation.

However, if we are also told that the difference between the two numbers is 3, then we can write another equation: $x - y = 3$

To solve the problem we now consider the graphs of both these equations:

$x + y = 13$

x	0	13	6
y	13	0	7

$x - y = 3$

x	0	3	6
y	-3	0	3

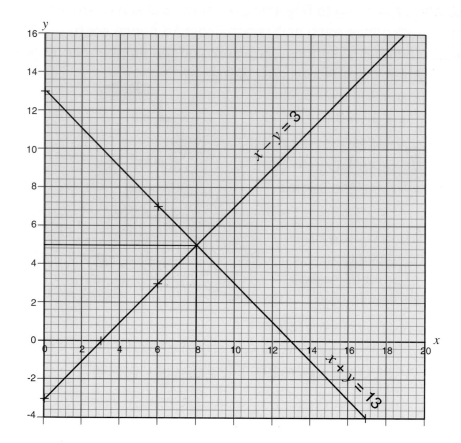

The solution to our equations is found where the two lines cross.
The solution is therefore $x = 8$ and $y = 5$

From the graph we can see that there is one, and only one, point that lies on both lines (8, 5).

Our two equations were solved by considering them together. These are called **simultaneous equations**. The solution to the problem above shows that the solution to a pair of simultaneous equations is a point which lies on the graphs of both equations.

There are various ways of solving simultaneous equations. The best method depends on the wording of the question and the format of the equation. It is often easier to understand things that can be seen and, although the graphical method of solving equations can take quite a long time, it is a good place to start.

The graphical method

Exercise 12.3

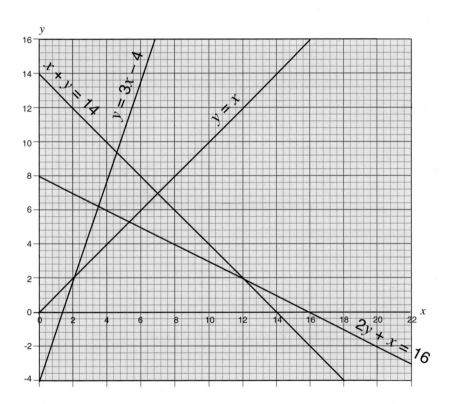

1. Use the graph above to find the solutions to the following pairs of simultaneous equations:

   (a) $x + y = 14$
       $y = x$

   (b) $x + y = 14$
       $y = 0$

   (c) $y = 3x - 4$
       $y = x$

   (d) $2y + x = 16$
       $x + y = 14$

   (e) $2y + x = 16$
       $x = 0$

   (f) $y = 3x - 4$
       $x + y = 14$

   (g) $2y + x = 16$
       $y = 3x - 4$

   (h) $2y + x = 16$
       $y = x$

Remember, when drawing a straight line graph you need at least two points. However it is better to have three so that you can check that your points are correct. It **does not matter** which three points you choose, they are only used for drawing the line. Any pair of points that fits that equation will lie on the line that you have drawn.

If your equation is in a simple form it can help to choose $x = 0$ for your first point and $y = 0$ for your second, then choose a third point that is not too close to the first two. Alternatively you could choose three points an equal distance apart such that $x = -3, 0, 3$. Either method is perfectly acceptable.

You must draw the line that represents your equation as long as possible since it does not stop at the limit of the points that you have chosen.

2. Solve these pairs of simultaneous equations graphically. (Use the worksheet for this question.)

(a) $x + y = 2$
$\quad\;\; x - y = 4$

(c) $\;x + y = 10$
$\quad\;\; 2x - y = 8$

(b) $x + 2y = 10$
$\quad\;\; x - y = 7$

(d) $3x + y = 15$
$\quad\;\; 2x - y = 0$

3. Draw a pair of axes with values of both x and y from -5 to 5 to solve each of these pairs of equations:

(a) $x + y = 3$
$\quad\;\; x - y = -5$

(c) $x - 2y = 2$
$\quad\;\; 2x - y = 4$

(b) $2x + 3y = 0$
$\quad\;\; x - y = -5$

(d) $3x + y = 8$
$\quad\;\; 2x - y = 7$

4. The answers to these equations may not always be a whole number. Using a scale of 1 cm to 1 unit draw pairs of axes with values of x from -8 to 8, and values of y from -5 to 12

Read off your graph carefully and give your answers in decimal form:

(a) $\;x + 2y = 6$
$\quad\;\; 3x - 4y = 4$

(b) $7x + 2y = 5$
$\quad\;\; x - 4y = 11$

5. Choose your own scale and axes for these pairs of equations:

(a) $2x + y = 1$
$\quad\;\; x - y = -7$

(b) $x - 3y = 9$
$\quad\;\; x + y = -5$

6.   Draw graphs for each of these pairs of equations. What is different about them?

(a) $x + y = -1$

$x + y = 3$

(b) $y = 2x + 1$

$2x - y = 3$

The elimination method

Drawing graphs accurately can be quite a time consuming process and thankfully most of the answers to the above equations were either whole numbers or quite simple decimals. There is, however, another, quicker, way to solve simultaneous equations.

Let's look at our original pair of equations:

$$x + y = 13$$
$$x - y = 3$$

You may notice that there are the same number of xs in each equation and the same number of ys. If we add y to $-y$ we get zero. Therefore if these two equations are added together the y terms will disappear altogether and we have:

$$2x = 16$$

and so

$$x = 8$$

As always in mathematics, it is very important to explain clearly to anyone reading your work exactly what you are doing. There is a conventional way of writing out the solution to a pair of simultaneous equations. It is important that you follow these conventions so that your work will be understood.

In Example (i) on the next page the equations are added together to eliminate the y terms. In Example (ii) one equation is subtracted to eliminate, in this case, the x terms. The next step is to substitute the first solution back into one of the equations to find the other variable. Finally you can check your answers in the second equation.

Examples:

(i) $2x + y = 5$ .... (1)

        $3x - y = 10$ .... (2)

(1) + (2) $5x = 15$

               $(\div 5)$

        $\underline{x = 3}$

Sub in(1) $6 + y = 5$

               $(- 6)$

       $\underline{y = -1}$

Check in (2) $9 - (-1) = 10$

      $\underline{x = 3}$ $\underline{y = -1}$

(ii) $2x + 3y = 10$ .... (1)

         $2x - y = 2$ .... (2)

(1) - (2) $4y = 8$

               $(\div 4)$

        $\underline{y = 2}$

Sub in (1) $2x + 6 = 10$

         $2x = 4$ $(- 6)$

               $(\div 2)$

         $\underline{x = 2}$

Check in (2) $4 - 2 = 2$

      $\underline{x = 2}$ $\underline{y = 2}$

Exercise 12.4

Solve these pairs of simultaneous equations using the elimination method:

1. $3x + y = 7$

      $x - y = 1$

2. $2x + y = 10$

      $3x - y = 5$

3. $2x + y = 12$

       $2x - 3y = 4$

4. $x + 2y = 7$

      $x + y = 4$

5. $3x + 2y = 15$

      $x + 2y = 9$

6. $3x - y = 8$

      $3x + y = 10$

7. $x + 2y = 7$

      $x - y = 1$

8. $x + 2y = 10$

       $3x - 2y = 6$

9. $3x + y = 7$

       $3x - 2y = -5$

However, often we find pairs of simultaneous equations that are not as easy to solve because they do not have the same number of xs or ys in each equation. In this instance another stage of working is necessary. In this extra stage we multiply either one or both of the equations by scale factors in order to have an equal number of x or y terms in both equations.

The scale factor method

In Example (i) below only one of the equations has to be multiplied by a scale factor. In the second both equations do. Note the convention of showing your working method by numbering each equation.

Examples:

(i) $\quad 2x + y = 5$ ....(1)
$\quad\quad 3x - 2y = 4$ ....(2)

$(1) \times 2 \quad 4x + 2y = 10$.........(3)
$(2) \quad\quad 3x - 2y = 4$

$(3) + (2) \quad 7x = 14$
$\quad\quad\quad\quad\quad (\div 7)$
$\quad\quad\quad\quad x = 2$

Sub in (1) $\quad 4 + y = 5$
$\quad\quad\quad\quad\quad\quad (-4)$
$\quad\quad\quad\quad\quad y = 1$

Check in (2) $6 - 2 = 4$

$\underline{x = 2} \quad\quad \underline{y = 1}$

(ii) $\quad 2x + 7y = 10$ ....(1)
$\quad\quad 3x - 2y = -10$.........(2)

$(1) \times 3 \quad 6x + 21y = 30$ ....(3)
$(2) \times 2 \quad 6x - 4y = -20$.........(4)

$(3) - (4) \quad 25y = 50$
$\quad\quad\quad\quad\quad\quad (\div 25)$
$\quad\quad\quad\quad\quad y = 2$

Sub in (1) $\quad 2x + 14 = 10$
$\quad\quad\quad\quad\quad\quad\quad (-14)$
$\quad\quad\quad\quad 2x = -4$
$\quad\quad\quad\quad\quad\quad (\div 2)$
$\quad\quad\quad\quad\quad x = -2$

Check in (2) $\quad -6 - 4 = -10$

$\underline{x = -2} \quad\quad \underline{y = 2}$

It is important that you check your answers by substituting back into the **original equations** and not back into the one that you have multiplied. This will give you easier numbers to work with and, if you have made a mistake, an error will be shown up by checking the original problem.

Exercise 12.5

Solve these pairs of simultaneous equations:

1. $3x + y = 5$
    $x + 3y = 7$

2. $3x + 2y = 8$
    $2x + y = 5$

3. $5x - 2y = 11$
    $x + 4y = 11$

4. $2x - y = 5$
    $x + 3y = 13$

5. $5x - 3y = -5$
    $2x + y = 9$

6. $5x + 2y = 22$
    $3x + y = 13$

7. $3x + 2y = 7$
    $2x - 3y = 3$

8. $2x + 3y = 11$
    $3x + 4y = 14$

9. $5x - 2y = 1$
    $3x + 5y = -18$

The re-arrangement and substitution methods

There are times when the equations are not in the same form. In these situations there are two options:

- either the equations can be re-arranged so that they are in the same form;

- or one equation can be substituted into another.

The two examples below show the same pair of equations. In the first, one equation is re-arranged, in the second, one equation is substituted into the other.

Examples:

(i) $3x + 2y = 6$.............(1)
                 $y = 5 - 2x$......(2)

(2) + 2x $2x + y = 5$.............(3)

(3) × 2 $4x + 2y = 10$..........(4)
                 $3x + 2y = 6$ ....(1)

(4) − (1) $\underline{x = 4}$

Sub in (1) $12 + 2y = 6$
                                 $(- 12)$
                 $2y = -6$
                                 $(÷ 2)$
                 $\underline{y = -3}$

Check in (2) $-3 = 5 - 8$
                 $\underline{x = 4}$ $\underline{y = -3}$

(ii) $3x + 2y = 6$......... (1)
                 $y = 5 - 2x$...(2)

Sub (2) in (1) $3x + 2(5 - 2x) = 6$
                         $3x + 10 - 4x = 6$
                                 $10 - x = 6$
                                                 $(+ x)$
                                 $10 = 6 + x$
                                                 $(- 6)$
                                 $\underline{4 = x}$

Sub in (2) $y = 5 - 8$
                 $\underline{y = -3}$

Check in (1) $12 - 6 = 6$
                 $\underline{x = 4}$ $\underline{y = -3}$

Exercise 12.6

Solve these pairs of simultaneous equations:

1. $3x + y = 6$
   $y = x + 2$

2. $2x + 3y = 25$
   $x = y - 5$

3. $3x = y - 9$
   $2y = 4 - x$

4. $y - 4x = 1$
   $3x = y$

5. $12 = 2x - 3y$
   $4x = 3 - y$

6. $2x + y = 1$
   $x = 2 + 7y$

7. $y - 6x = 4$
   $2y = 18 + 4x$

8. $\dfrac{x}{2} = -4 - 3y$
   $x + 2y = 2$

9. $4y - 2x = 15$
   $y = \dfrac{x}{4} + 3$

10. $x - y = 4$
    $3x = -4y$

11. $5x - y = 3$
    $3y = 10x + 9$

12. $2x + y = 3$
    $3y = 2 - 4x$

Solving problems with simultaneous equations

Many story problems are made easier by using simultaneous equations. It is very important to explain every step of your working as you solve these problems, otherwise it will be very difficult for anyone else to follow what you are doing. Start by defining your variables, e.g. x and y.

Example:

I buy 15 pencils. Coloured pencils cost 35p each and ordinary graphite pencils cost 22p each. If I receive 92p change from a £5 note, then how many of each type of pencil did I buy?

First identify and define the two equations:

Let the number of coloured pencils be x and the number of graphite pencils be y.

$$\text{The total cost} = £5 - £0.92$$
$$= £4.08 = 408\text{p}$$

So the two equations are:

$$x + y = 15 \quad \text{..........................(1)}$$
$$35x + 22y = 408 \text{.......................(2)}$$

(1) × 22 $\qquad\qquad$ $22x + 22y = 330\text{.........(3)}$

(2) − (3) $\qquad\qquad$ $13x = 78$
$\qquad\qquad\qquad\qquad\qquad$ (÷ 13)
$\qquad\qquad\qquad\qquad$ $\underline{x = 6}$

Sub in (1) $\qquad\qquad$ $6 + y = 15$
$\qquad\qquad\qquad\qquad\qquad$ (− 6)
$\qquad\qquad\qquad\qquad$ $\underline{y = 9}$

Check in (2) $\ 35 \times 6 + 22 \times 9 = 408$

$$\underline{x = 6} \qquad \underline{y = 9}$$

I bought 6 coloured pencils and 9 graphite pencils.

When you have finished your solution do check the original problem to make sure that you have answered the question.

Exercise 12.7

Solve these problems by forming simultaneous equations and solving them:

1. The sum of two numbers is 25, and the difference between the two numbers is 5
   What are the numbers?

2. I have two brothers. One of them is 4 years older than the other. The sum of their ages is 28
   How old are they?

3. I have saved up £25 more than my sister. We decided to pool our money to buy a CD player and found that we had £145 between us. How much had each one of us saved?

4. On a walking holiday I walked 4 miles further on the first day than I did on the second. If I walked a total of 17 miles in two days, how far did I walk on each day?

5. (a) Solve this pair of simultaneous equations:
$$c + g = 20 \quad \text{and} \quad 12c + 15g = 282$$

(b) I have to buy 20 apples. I buy some Coxs at 12p each and some Granny Smiths at 15p each. If I spend £2.82 in total, use your answer to part (a) to find out how many of each type of apple I bought.

6. (a) Solve this pair of simultaneous equations:
$$4p + s = 84 \quad \text{and} \quad 2p + 2s = 84$$

(b) My little sister collects stickers. For 84p she can either buy 4 sheets of plain stickers and one sheet of shiny ones, or she can buy 2 sheets of plain stickers and 2 sheets of shiny ones. Use your answer to part (a) to find out what it would cost her to buy 3 sheets of plain stickers and 2 sheets of shiny ones.

7. (a) Solve this pair of simultaneous equations:
$$3c + m = 127 \quad \text{and} \quad 2c + 3m = 136$$

(b) If I buy 3 cans of Cola and one Munchy bar, that will cost me £1.27
If I buy 2 cans of Cola and 3 Munchy bars, that will cost me £1.36

Use your answers to part (a) to find the cost of one can of Cola and one Munchy bar.

8. (a) Solve this pair of simultaneous equations:
$$y = x + 4 \quad \text{and} \quad 2y + 2x = 56$$

(b) The length of a rectangle is 4 cm longer than its width. The perimeter is 56 cm.
What is the area of the rectangle?

9. In my new computer game I have to zap aliens called Troggles and Gruggles. Zapping a Troggle scores 15 points and zapping a Gruggle scores 20 points. In the last round I zapped a total of 20 aliens and scored 365 points. Form a pair of simultaneous equations and then solve them to find how many Troggles and Gruggles I zapped.

10. This is a new game. I have to avoid hitting the Minkies but try to hit the Tankies. On my first go I hit 5 Minkies and 9 Tankies, and scored 83 points. On my second round I hit 2 Minkies and 12 Tankies and scored 134 points. Form a pair of simultaneous equations and solve them to find out how many more points I score for hitting a Tankie than a Minkie.

11. A straight line, given by an equation in the form $y = mx + c$, passes through a point $A(2, 4)$ and a point $B(1, 1)$. Form a pair of simultaneous equations and solve them to find m and c. Write down the equation of the line.

12. I have to buy a total of 15 Christmas cards. I buy some at 33p each for my relations and the rest at 25p each for my friends. If I spent a total of £4.15 how many of each type did I buy?

13. My Mother lets me spend only 2 hours a day playing computer games. Last Sunday I spent three times as long playing 'Prince of Persia' as I did playing 'Lemmings'. How long did I spend on each?

14. I have to buy 20 cans of drinks for my party. If I buy 12 cans of Cola and 8 cans of lemonade the total cost is £3.84 and if I buy 5 cans of Cola and 15 cans of lemonade the total cost is £3.70
What would be the cost of 10 cans of Cola and 10 of lemonade?

15. In my new computer game I have to shoot down asteroids and alien star ships. I shot 12 asteroids and 5 alien ships and scored 465 points on level one and then shot 15 asteroids and 4 alien ships and scored 480 points on level two. How many points did I score on level three when I shot down 20 asteroids and 6 alien ships?

Exercise 12.8: Extension questions

In the examples in this chapter you have had to solve two simultaneous equations to find two unknown quantities. There is no reason why you cannot have three unknown quantities and have three equations. Each equation need not necessarily have all three variables in it.

Example:

Consider this problem:

The sum of two numbers is 15

One of these numbers added to a third number makes 17 and the other number added to the same third number makes 14

Let us call our numbers a, b and c.

The three facts above give us three equations:

$$a + b \quad = 15 ....(1)$$
$$a + \quad c = 17 ....(2)$$
$$b + c = 14 ....(3)$$

Note that the equations are written out so that the letters stay in the same columns

It does not matter which pair of equations we take first. In this case we are going to take (3) from (2) to eliminate c.

(2) − (3)	$a - b = 3$	(4)
(1)	$a + b = 15$	(1)
(4) + (1)	$2a \quad = 18$	(÷ 2)
	$\underline{a = 9}$	
Sub in (1)	$9 + b \quad = 15$	(− 9)
	$\underline{b = 6}$	
Sub in (2)	$9 + c = 17$	(− 9)
	$\underline{c = 8}$	
Check in (3)	$6 + 8 = 14$	

$$\underline{a = 9} \qquad \underline{b = 6} \qquad \underline{c = 8}$$

1. Solve these three simultaneous equations:
$$x + y = 4$$
$$x + z = 8$$
$$y + z = 2$$

2. Solve these three simultaneous equations:
$$a + b + c = 7$$
$$a + b - c = 6$$
$$a - b - c = 2$$

3. Solve these three simultaneous equations:
$$2a + b - c = 1$$
$$4a + b - 3c = 5$$
$$a - c = 2$$

4. I have two brothers. The sum of our three ages is 41
The difference between the eldest and the youngest of us is 14
I am closer to my younger brother's age than my elder brother's age by two years. How old am I?

5. My mother sent me out to buy ten pieces of fruit, of 3 different varieties.
If I buy 3 apples, 6 bananas and 1 coconut it will cost me £1.59
However if I buy 2 coconuts, 7 bananas and 1 apple it will cost me £2.18
If I buy 1 coconut, 2 apples and 7 bananas it will cost me £1.55

   (a) Write 3 simultaneous equations and solve them to find the cost of the 3 types of fruit.
   (b) How can I buy my ten pieces of fruit at the minimum cost?

6. I am thinking of three numbers. The sum of two of them is 24
If I multiply the smallest number by the remaining number I have 49
If all my numbers are prime numbers, what are the numbers?

7. (a) (i) Show that it is impossible to solve the simultaneous equations:
   $$x + 2 = y \qquad y - 1 = z \qquad z - 1 = x$$

   (ii) Is there a limit to the possible solutions of these three equations?

   (b) (i) Show that it is impossible to solve the simultaneous equations:
   $$x - 3 = y \qquad y + 6 = z \qquad z - 4 = x$$

   (ii) Is there a limit to the possible solutions of these three equations?

8. Solve these three simultaneous equations:
$$x = (2y)^z \qquad y = 2^x \qquad x = 3^z$$

Exercise 12.9: Summary exercise

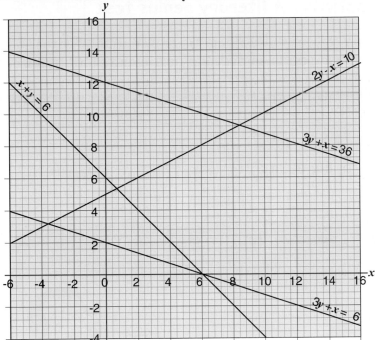

1. Use the above graph to solve the following pairs of simultaneous equations:

   (a) $x + y = 6$
       $2y - x = 10$

   (b) $3y + x = 36$
       $2y - x = 10$

   (c) $x + y = 6$
       $3y + x = 6$

   (d) Explain why you cannot find a solution to this pair of simultaneous equations:

   $3y + x = 6$
   $3y + x = 36$

2. Solve these pairs of simultaneous equations:

   (a) $x + 2y = 5$
       $x - y = 2$

   (b) $x - y = 6$
       $x + y = 4$

   (c) $x + 4y = 10$
       $4x - 5y = -23$

   (d) $2x - 3y = 7$
       $5x + 2y = 8$

   (e) $y = 1 - 2x$
       $x + 2y = -1$

   (f) $x = y + 4$
       $2x - 3y = 7$

3. I was supposed to buy my mother 3 clear light bulbs and 4 pearl light bulbs, which would have cost £3.10
   By mistake I bought 4 clear bulbs and 3 pearl bulbs and that cost me £3.20. What is the cost per bulb of each type of light bulb?

4. We bought 10 packets of sparklers for Guy Fawkes Day. Plain sparklers cost £1.20 per packet and coloured sparklers cost £1.50 per packet. If I spent £12.90 in all, how many packets of coloured sparklers did I buy?

End of chapter 12 activity: A literary genius test

These numbers occur as the titles of books, plays or are famous lines of a poem. How many of them can you fill in over the next twenty-four hours? (You are allowed to have help!)

Example: **3** M _ _   I _   A   B _ _ _

Answer: 3 Men in a Boat (Jerome K. Jerome)
(There are Bonus marks for the author!)

$\frac{1}{2}$ A L _ _ _ _ _, $\frac{1}{2}$ A L _ _ _ _ _, $\frac{1}{2}$ A L _ _ _ _ _   O _ _ _ _ _ _

1 F _ _ _ , **2** F _ _ _ , R _ _ F _ _ _ , B _ _ _   F _ _ _

1 F _ _ _   O _ _ _   T _ _   C _ _ _ _ _ ' _ N _ _ _

A T _ _ _   O _   **2** C _ _ _ _ _

3 S _ _ _ _ _ _

T _ _   **3** M _ _ _ _ _ _ _ _ _

4 Q _ _ _ _ _ _ _

4.50 F _ _ _   P _ _ _ _ _ _ _ _ _

5 C _ _ _ _ _ _ _ _   A _ _   I _

N _ _   W _   A _ _   **6**

T _ _   B _ _   **6**

G _ _ _   O _ _   S _ _ _ _ _   **7**

I' _   H _ _ _ _   T _ _   **8**th   I A _

T _ _   **9** T _ _ _ _ _ _

12 D _ _ _ _ _ _   P _ _ _ _ _ _ _ _

S _ _ _ _ _   D _ _ _ _   O _   A _ _ _ _ _   M _ _ _   A _ _ _   **13** A _ _ _   **3**

   Q _ _ _ _ _ _ _

19 E _ _ _ _ _ _   F _ _ _

20 T _ _ _ _ _ _ _ _   L _ _ _ _ _ _   U _ _ _ _   T _ _   S _ _

40 Y _ _ _ _   O _

101 D _ _ _ _ _ _ _ _

1066 A _ _   A _ _   T _ _ _

Chapter 13: Graphs

A graph is a pictorial representation of a relationship. It can be a bar graph, a column graph, a line graph or a curve. We are going to start this chapter by looking further at straight line graphs.

If a graph is a straight line then it represents a linear relationship between the two **variables** on the **axes**. If the graph goes through the origin (0, 0), this means that the two variables are directly proportional to one another. Examples of this type of relationship are the conversion graphs, such as foreign exchange, centigrade to Fahrenheit temperatures, miles to kilometres, that we looked at in *So you really want to learn Maths* Book 1

In Chapter 9 we looked at formulae for speed, distance and time. Showing journey as a graph on a grid is a useful way of seeing what is happening.

Travel graphs

A travel graph shows the relationship between distance travelled and time taken.

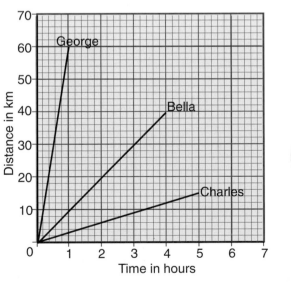

These graphs shows that Charles travelled 15 km in 5 hours, Bella travelled 40 km in 4 hours and George travelled 60 km in one hour.

From this we can see that Charles travelled 15 km in 5 hours. His speed was 3 km per hour which means he was probably walking. Similarly Bella travelled at 10 km per hour, possibly on a bicycle and George travelled at 60 km per hour, probably by car.

Exercise 13.1

1. Look at the three graphs on this grid:

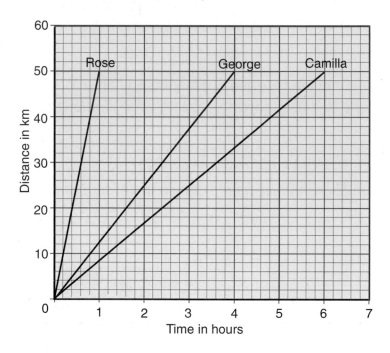

Rose, George and Camilla have all travelled 50 km but in different times.

From the graphs read off:

    (a) Rose's speed.
    (b) George's speed.
    (c) Camilla's speed.

How do you think each was travelling?

2. Here is the graph of another journey:

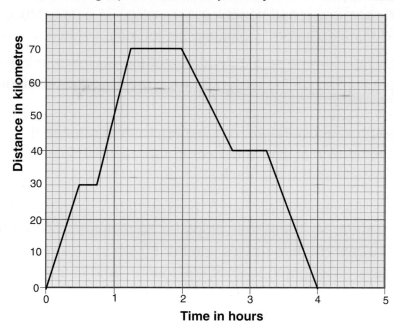

Describe this journey, including the time and different speed for each part of the journey.

3. These graphs shows two trains leaving Adamstown and Beesville at the same time.

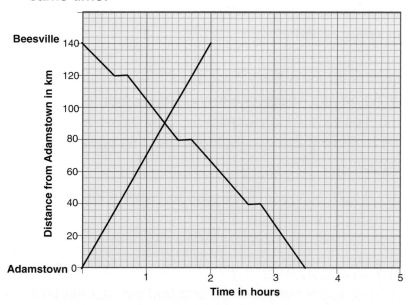

(a) What is the difference between the journeys of the two trains.

(b) How long after the start of the journeys do the two trains pass?

(c) How far from Beesville is this?

(d) At what speed does the Adamstown to Beesville Express travel?

(e) What is the fastest speed that the Beesville to Adamstown train travels?

4. The headmaster is going to a conference. He travels at 100 km/h along the motorway for one and a half hours. He then stops at a Jolly Muncher restaurant for 45 minutes before continuing his journey.

   The traffic is now heavier and so the headmaster travels for 30 minutes at 40 km/h before coming off the motorway and travelling for 15 minutes at 60 km/h.

   Draw a travel graph to show the journey, taking 1 cm to represent 30 minutes on the horizontal axis and 1 cm to represent 40 km on the vertical axis. How far was the journey?

5. (a) Mr Mattix's car leaves Ammersmith School at 10 a.m. and travels 100 km at 80 km/h. Mr Mattix then stops for 30 minutes while he has a McJimmy burger. He then travels another 80 km at 60 km/h to Bighton. Draw a travel graph to show the journey and use the graph to find out at what time Mr Mattix arrives at Bighton.
   (b) Miss Peinter leaves Bighton at 10.45 a.m. and travels at a steady 70 km/h to Ammersmith School. Add a graph of this car's journey. Use the graph to find out when Miss Peinter reaches Ammersmith School and at what time the two cars passed.

6. Fred leaves home at 9 a.m. He walks for 30 minutes at 4 km/h and then he takes a bus, which travels at 40 km/h for 45 minutes into town. He spends 1 and a quarter hours in town doing his Christmas shopping. He then starts to walk home at a speed of 5 km/h. His mother leaves home at 11.15 a.m. and drives to town to pick him up. She drives at 60 km/h. Draw travel graphs to show these two journeys and find out at what time Fred meets his mother.

7. Alfie and Bella set off from school at 4.00 p.m. to visit the local museum. Alfie walks at 4 km/h for 15 minutes and then catches a bus, which travels at 30 km/h for 20 minutes, directly to the museum.

   Bella cycles at 15 km/h for 44 minutes until she gets to the museum.

   Draw a travel graphs of these two journeys and find out at what time the bus overtakes the bicycle.

Everyday graphs

Journeys happen every day but there are other events that happen that can be shown on a graph. A graph gives a pictorial representation of the relationship between two variables.

Consider these two graphs of the monthly sales totals for two companies:

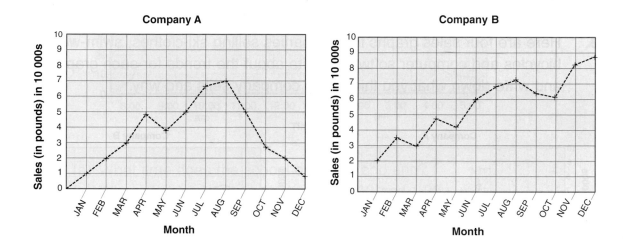

These graphs show trends – that is the general pattern of rise and fall of the total sales. At first glance it would seem that the prospects for Company B look a lot more healthy than those for Company A. But what else do the graphs tell us?

These graphs have a point for each monthly total and these points are joined by dotted lines. The line is dotted because there is no absolute value for the sales in between the points. Although Company A's sales have declined rapidly in the winter months they climbed from a low position at the start of the year to peak around June, July and August. This could suggest that the business is seasonal and possibly depends on good weather in the summer.

Company B had a steady rise in sales. Although there was a slight fall during August and September, it did not affect the overall growth in sales; indeed it probably reflects fewer purchases during and immediately after the holiday months.

Now look at some more equations:

3. On graph paper draw a pair of axes.
    Copy and complete these tables of values for the following functions:

(a) $y = 2x + 4$

x	−4	0	3
y			

(d) $y = 5x + 2$

x	−1	0	2
y			

(b) $y = 3x - 2$

x	−1	0	3
y			

(e) $y = \dfrac{x}{4} - 3$

x	−4	0	8
y			

(c) $y = \dfrac{x}{2} + 3$

x	−4	0	10
y			

Now draw the graphs. You should notice that the lines cut the y-axis at the value of the added or subtracted number in the equation. If you think about it, this makes sense because it is that number which moves the graph up and down.

Graphs of curves

All the graphs we have drawn so far have been straight lines but there is no reason why a graph should not be a curve. Indeed many graphs are curved. To draw a straight line you do not need to plot many points. You can in fact draw it with as few as two points but we usually plot three or four points to be sure. However to draw an accurate curve you will need to plot more than just two points.

The lines in the above exercise were all straight lines because there was only one possible value of x for each value of y.

Let us think about the function $y = x^2$ for the range of whole number values of x such that $-3 \leq x \leq 3$

Draw a table of values:

x	−3	−2	−1	0	1	2	3
y	9	4	1	0	1	4	9

Note that: y is equal to 9 when x is equal to both −3 and 3
y is equal to 4 when x is equal to both −2 and 2
y is equal to 1 when x is equal to both −1 and 1

With a function that contains an x^2 term there can be two values of x that give the same value of y. (For example if $x = -2$ or if $x = 2$ then y will be equal to 4 in both instances.) This is why the graph will be curved.

Draw the graph of $y = x^2$

(Note the neat + signs used to plot the points on the grid below. We need to be very accurate when plotting points and a + or x is the best way to do this. You should never use a splodge ● it is just not accurate enough!)

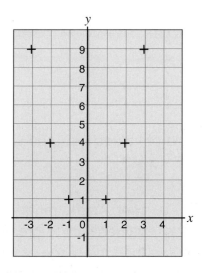
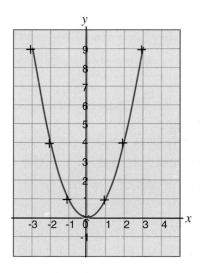

The shape of this particular curve is very distinctive. It is always symmetrical and is called a **parabola**. If the equation was of the form $y = -x^2$ then the parabola would be the other way up.

Exercise 13.4

Copy and complete these tables of values x and y. From each table draw the corresponding graph. (The worksheet may be used for this exercise. You will need one copy of the worksheet for each question.)

1. For the function $y = x^2 - 1$ complete this table of values for x and y, for whole number values of x in the range $-3 \leq x \leq 3$
    Draw the graph of $y = x^2 - 1$

x	−3	−2	−1	0	1	2	3
x^2	9	4		0			
y	8	3		−1			

2. For the function $y = x^2 + 2$ complete this table of values for x and y, for whole number values of x in the range $-3 \leq x \leq 3$
    Draw the graph of $y = x^2 + 2$

x	−3	−2	−1	0	1	2	3
x^2	9						
y	11	6		2			

3. For the function $y = 2x^2$ complete this table of values for x and y, for whole number values of x in the range $-3 \leq x \leq 3$
    Draw the graph of $y = 2x^2$

x	−3	−2	−1	0	1	2	3
x^2		4					
y	18	8		0			

    Hint: As the range of values for y is greater than the range of values for x you should change the scale on the y-axis.

4. For the function $y = \dfrac{x^2}{2}$ complete this table of values for x and y, for whole number values of x in the range $^-3 \leq x \leq 3$

Draw the graph of $y = \dfrac{x^2}{2}$

x	-3	-2	-1	0	1	2	3
x^2	9	4		0			
y	4.5	2		0			

5. For the function $y = 2x^2 - 3$ complete this table of values for x and y for whole number values of x in the range $^-3 \leq x \leq 3$

Draw the graph of $y = 2x^2 - 3$

x	-3	-2	-1	0	1	2	3
x^2		4					
y							

Points of intersection

The point where two lines cross is called a point of intersection. In the last two exercises there has only been one graph on each grid but we can have two graphs on the same grid.

Consider the graphs of the functions $y = x^2 - 2$ and $y = 2x + 1$

First of all we need a table of values for each function:

$y = x^2 - 2$

x	-3	-2	-1	0	1	2	3
x^2	9	4	1	0	1	4	9
y	7	2	-1	-2	-1	2	7

$y = 2x + 1$

x	-2	0	2
$2x$	-4	0	4
y	-3	1	5

Now draw the two functions on the same pair of axes:

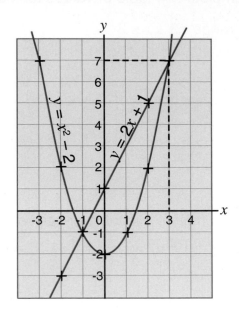

The two lines interesct at the two points:

$(-1, -1)$ and $(3, 7)$

Exercise 13.5

(The worksheet may be used for this exercise. You will need one copy for each question.)

Draw graphs of the following pairs of functions and find the points of intersection. You will need to complete tables of values for x and y for each function first.

1. $y = x^2$ $y = x + 2$

2. $y = x^2 + 2$ $y = x + 4$

3. $y = x^2 - 1$ $y = x - 1$

4. $y = \frac{1}{2}x^2 + 2$ $y = x + 1\frac{1}{2}$

5. $y = x^2 - 4$ $y = 2 - x$

6. $y = x^2 + 1$ $y = 1 - 2x$

Exercise 13.6: Extension questions 1 – The reciprocal curve

1. Copy and complete this table of values for $y = \frac{1}{x}$

x	−5	−3	−1	−0.5	−0.25	0	0.25	0.5	1	3	5
y											

The value of y for $x = 0$ has been blocked out. Try this on your calculator and see what you get.

Try calculating values of y for smaller and smaller values of x. What do you notice?

You should notice that as x gets smaller the value of y gets closer to 0 but never actually reaches it.

Using a scale of 1 cm to 1 unit on the x-axis for values of x in the range $-5 \le x \le 5$, and 1 cm to 1 unit on the y-axis for values of y in the range $-5 \le y \le 5$, draw a graph of $y = \frac{1}{x}$. Your graph should approach the axes, but not touch them. The axes in this case are known as **asymptotes**, that is lines that the curve approaches but does not touch. The shape of the reciprocal curve is called a **hyperbola**.

2. Draw graphs of the following equations:

(a) $y = \frac{4}{x}$

(b) $y = \frac{1}{x-4}$

(c) $y = \frac{1}{x^2}$

(d) $y = \frac{1}{2x}$

(e) $y = \frac{1}{2-x}$

(f) $y = -\frac{1}{x^2}$

Exercise 13.7: Extension questions 2 – Other curves

1. Complete this table of values and draw the graph of the function $y = x^3$

x	−5	−4	−3	−2	−1	0	1	2	3	4	5
y											

2. Complete this table of values and draw the graph of the function
$y = x^2 - x$

x	−5	−4	−3	−2	−1	0	1	2	3	4	5
x^2											
y											

3. Complete this table of values and draw the graph of the function
$y = x^2 + 2x$

x	−5	−4	−3	−2	−1	0	1	2	3	4	5
x^2											
y											

4. Complete the table of values and draw the graph of the function
$y = \sqrt{x}$ or $x = y^2$ (N.B. you cannot have the square root of a negative
number!):

x	−5	−4	−3	−2	−1	0	1	2	3	4	5
y	*	*	*	*	*						

5. A rectangle has a perimeter of 20 cm and a length of x cm:

$P = 20$

x

(a) Show that the area A of the rectangle can be given by the formula
$A = 10x - x^2$

(b) Take values of x from 0 to 10 and calculate the corresponding values
of A.

(c) Draw a graph with x along the horizontal axis and y on the vertical
axis. Choose a suitable scale for each axis.

(d) From your graph find the maximum possible area of the rectangle
and its corresponding length and width.

6. A cuboid has a square base and a total surface area of 100 cm².

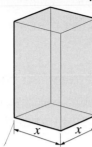

(a) If the base has a side of x cm show the height of the cuboid can be given by expression

$$\frac{50 - x^2}{2x}$$

(b) Show that the volume V of the cuboid is given by the formula

$$V = \frac{50x - x^3}{2}$$

(c) By calculating V for suitable values of x draw a graph of x against V and find the maximum possible value for the volume of the cuboid.

Exercise 13.8: Summary exercise

1. Here is the graph of a car journey:

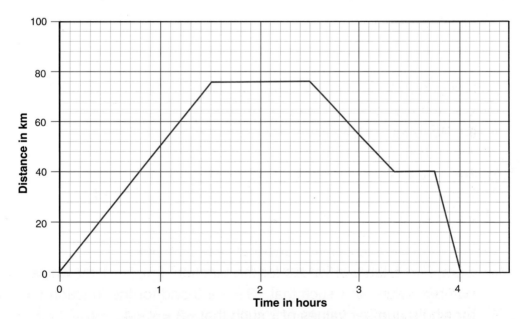

(a) At what speed was the car travelling for the first hour and a half?
(b) What did the car do after the first hour and a half?
(c) At what speed did the car travel after that?
(d) At what speed did the car travel for the last quarter of an hour of the journey?

(e) Describe what you think the purpose of this car journey was.

2. Which of these graphs of a car journey best fits each of these statements:

(a) The car accelerated, decelerated, stopped, and travelled back again.
(b) The car stayed in the garage.
(c) The car decelerated and then travelled at a constant speed.
(d) The car decelerated slowly and then stopped.

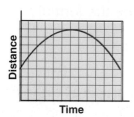
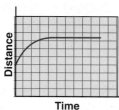
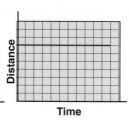
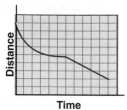

3. Complete this table of values for the function $y = 2x - 4$

x	−2	−1	0	1	2
$2x$					
y					

Draw a graph of this function on a grid with an x-axis numbered from −2 to 2 and a y-axis numbered from −8 to 1
Where does this graph cross:
(a) the x-axis
(b) the y-axis
(c) the line $x = -1$
(d) the line $y = -6$

4. You could use a copy of worksheet for this question.
(a) Complete a table of values for the function $y = x^2 - 1$ for whole number values of x such that $-3 \le x \le 3$ and for the function $y = x + 1$ for whole number values of x such that $-2 \le x \le 1$.
(b) Draw a pair of axes with x co-ordinates from −3 to 3 and a scale of 2 cm to 1 unit and y co-ordinates from −2 to 10 with a scale of 1 cm to 1 unit.
(c) Draw the graphs of both functions from part (a).
(d) Give the co-ordinates of the points where the two graphs intersect.

End of chapter 13 activity: Experiments and graphs

Are there any experimental results that will produce a straight line when you plot the results?

You know that, if you draw a graph of time against distance travelled for a car travelling at a constant speed, that graph will be a straight line. Are there any other situations which can be investigated over a period of time to give a straight line?

Here are some examples that you could investigate:

1. The distance travelled by the tip of the minute hand of a clock.

2. The length of your shadow on a sunny day.

3. The number of pupils in the school from an hour before school starts to the start of school.

4. The height of a bean plant over three weeks.

5. The temperature of a cup of tea in the first 30 minutes from when it was brewed.

6. The height of an ice cube when it is left out of the fridge.

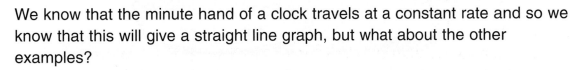

We know that the minute hand of a clock travels at a constant rate and so we know that this will give a straight line graph, but what about the other examples?

Look at each experiment and state what other variables, apart from the ones you are recording, might effect the result of your experiment. Write down the steps you would take to ensure that your experiment is a fair test.

Here is an example for Experiment 6: Measuring the height of an ice cube.

Step 1: Make a big block of ice so that it is easier to measure. Take a clean empty yoghurt pot, fill it with tap water and place it in the freezer for 48 hours before you carry out the experiment.

Step 2: Take the pot out of the freezer and turn it upside down on a flat plate. Put the plate in a position so that any melted water can drain away.

Step 3: Keep testing the pot every five minutes until you can lift the pot off the ice. Measure the height of the ice block.

Step 4: Measure the height of the ice block every ten minutes until it is too small to be measured. Record your results.

Step 5: Draw a graph of height against time.

Chapter 14: Equations and brackets

We have been using brackets in our calculations for quite a while but, until now, we have been using only one pair of brackets. In this chapter we are going to revise the use of brackets and then look at how we deal with two pairs of brackets.

In a calculation, the numbers within brackets indicate that this part of the calculation must be done first:

$$3 \times (4 + 5) = 3 \times 9$$
$$= 27$$

In algebra it is not always possible to do the calculation inside the bracket. However the number outside the bracket indicates the number that **everything** inside the bracket must be multiplied by:

Example:

$$3(2x + 4) = 3 \times 2x + 3 \times 4$$
$$= 6x + 12$$

Exercise 14.1

Multiply out these brackets:

1. $3(3x + 1)$
2. $4(2x - 5)$
3. $2(5 - 3x)$
4. $7(3 + x)$
5. $6(2x + 5)$

6. $x(3x + 1)$
7. $2x(4x - 3)$
8. $a(5a - 2b)$
9. $a(5b + c)$
10. $3x(4 - 3x)$

Factorising algebraic expressions

A number can be written as a product of its prime factors, for example:

$$36 = 4 \times 9$$
$$= 2^2 \times 3^2$$

An algebraic expression can also be written as a product of factors:

$$3x = 3 \times x$$
$$x^2 = x \times x$$

Some expressions have common factors:

Example:

$$x^2 + 3x = x \times x + 3 \times x$$
$$= x(x + 3)$$

We call this 'factorising'.

Exercise 14.2

Factorise the following expressions:

1. $3x + 9$

2. $8x - 12$

3. $15 - 3x$

4. $7x + x^2$

5. $x^2 + 2x$

6. $4x^2 + 2x$

7. $4x^2 + 2x + 6$

8. $6x^2 - 9x$

9. $10x^2 - 2x + 4$

10. $6x^2 - 6$

Exercise 14.3: More brackets

Multiply out these brackets and simplify the answer if possible. Remember you have to take care when there is a minus sign before the brackets:

Example:

$$3(2x + 4) - 4(2 - x) = 3 \times 2x + 3 \times 4 - 4 \times 2 - 4 \times (-x)$$
$$= 6x + 12 - 8 + 4x$$
$$= 10x + 4$$

1. $2(x + 3) + 3(2x - 2)$ **6.** $2x(x + 5) + 3(3x - 1)$

2. $2(x + 2) - 3(x - 2)$ **7.** $x(4x + 2) - 3(x + 5)$

3. $2(4x - 3) + 4(2x + 1)$ **8.** $7(5 - 2x) - 3x(2x + 3)$

4. $4(3 - x) - 3(x - 3)$ **9.** $3(x + 3) + x(2 - 5x)$

5. $5(2x - 1) - (2 - 5x)$ **10.** $5x(3 - 2x) - 3(x + 5)$

Multiply out these brackets and simplify the answer if possible:

11. $2(x + 3) + 3x(x + 3)$ **14.** $a(a - b) + b(a - b)$

12. $3(2x - 5) - x(2x - 5)$ **15.** $3x(1 - 2x) + 3(1 - 2x)$

13. $3a(a - b) + 4(a - b)$ **16.** $x(2x - y) - 2y(2x - y)$

Two sets of brackets

Look carefully at q.11–16 from the last exercise. In each question the expression within both sets of brackets is the same:

$$2(x + 3) + 3x(x + 3)$$

This in fact could also be written: $(2 + 3x)(x + 3)$

Examples:

(i) $\quad (2 + x)(x + 1) = 2(x + 1) + x(x + 1)$
$$= 2x + 2 + x^2 + x$$
$$= x^2 + 3x + 2$$

(ii) $\quad (2x - 2)(x - 1) = 2x(x - 1) - 2(x - 1)$
$$= 2x^2 - 2x - 2x + 2$$
$$= 2x^2 - 4x + 2$$

It can help if you think of this multiplication like the multiplication you would do to find the area of a rectangle:

Example (i) $(2 + x)(x + 1)$

	2	x
x	$2x$	x^2
1	2	x

You then add the terms together: $x^2 + 3x + 2$

Exercise 14.4

Multiply out these brackets and simplify:

1. $(x + 1)(x + 4)$

6. $(x + 3)(x + 4)$

2. $(x + 3)(x + 2)$

7. $(x + 2)(x + 4)$

3. $(x + 4)(x + 6)$

8. $(x + 3)(x + 3)$

4. $(x + 7)(x + 7)$

9. $(x + 8)(x + 3)$

5. $(x + 1)(x + 1)$

10. $(x + 2)(x + 7)$

Once you have mastered this you can start to omit the first line of the working above by remembering the following rule:

First pair   **O**uter pair   **I**nner pair   **L**ast pair

$$(2 + x)(x + 1)$$

11. $(x + 1)(x - 2)$

16. $(x - 2)(x + 6)$

12. $(x + 3)(x - 2)$

17. $(x + 5)(x - 3)$

13. $(x + 1)(x - 5)$

18. $(x - 3)(x + 3)$

14. $(x + 4)(x - 4)$

19. $(x + 5)(x - 4)$

15. $(x - 1)(x + 3)$

20. $(x + 1)(x - 1)$

21. $(x - 1)(x - 2)$

22. $(x - 4)(x - 2)$

23. $(x - 3)(x - 5)$

24. $(x - 7)(x - 1)$

25. $(x - 2)(x - 2)$

26. $(x - 5)(x - 8)$

27. $(x - 2)(x - 6)$

28. $(x - 4)(x - 7)$

29. $(x - 5)(x - 4)$

30. $(x - 1)(x - 1)$

31. $(x + 4)(x - 2)$

32. $(x - 3)(2 - x)$

33. $(x + 3)(x + 2)$

34. $(2 + x)(2 + x)$

35. $(x - 1)(x - 9)$

36. $(x - 5)(x + 5)$

37. $(x + 2)(3 - x)$

38. $(x - 4)(2 + x)$

39. $(x - 5)(3 + x)$

40. $(3 - x)(3 - x)$

Squares and the difference between them

In the examples above there were some where the two brackets had the same expression inside them. These could have been written as squares:

$$(x + 7)(x + 7) = (x + 7)^2$$
$$(x - 2)(x - 2) = (x - 2)^2$$
$$(3 - x)(3 - x) = (3 - x)^2$$

These brackets can be multiplied out just as before:

Example:

Expand these brackets: (i) $(x + 7)^2$ and (ii) $(x - 2)^2$

(i) $(x + 7)^2 = (x + 7)(x + 7)$
$= x(x + 7) + 7(x + 7)$
$= x^2 + 7x + 7x + 49$
$= x^2 + 14x + 49$

(ii) $(x - 2)^2 = (x - 2)(x - 2)$
$= x(x - 2) - 2(x - 2)$
$= x^2 - 2x - 2x + 4$
$= x^2 - 4x + 4$

Exercise 14.5

Multiply out these brackets:

1. $(x + 2)^2$

2. $(x + 5)^2$

3. $(x - 6)^2$

4. $(3 + x)^2$

5. $(4 - x)^2$

6. $(1 + x)^2$

Look at your answers above. You will see that in each case the term x^2 is a square, the number term is a square and the coefficient of x is even. Note also that the x^2 term and the number term are always positive.

Therefore in general terms:

$(x + a)^2 = x^2 + 2ax + a^2$

$(a + x)^2 = a^2 + 2ax + x^2$

$(x - a)^2 = x^2 - 2ax + a^2$

$(a - x)^2 = a^2 - 2ax + x^2$

Use this pattern to multiply out the squares below:

7. $(x + 4)^2$

8. $(x - 2)^2$

9. $(x + 10)^2$

10. $(x - 8)^2$

11. $(7 - x)^2$

12. $(4 + x)^2$

13. $(6 - x)^2$

14. $(2 + x)^2$

You can use the pattern in reverse to factorise:

$x^2 + 2ax + a^2 = (x + a)^2$

$a^2 + 2ax + x^2 = (a + x)^2$

$x^2 - 2ax + a^2 = (x - a)^2$

$a^2 - 2ax + x^2 = (a - x)^2$

Example:

$x^2 + 4x + 4 = (x + 2)(x + 2)$ 2 is the square root of 4 and the sign must be +

$x^2 - 6x + 9 = (x - 3)(x - 3)$ 3 is the square root of 9 and the sign must be −

Exercise 14.6

Factorise these:

1. $x^2 - 4x + 4$
2. $x^2 + 6x + 9$
3. $x^2 + 8x + 16$
4. $x^2 - 2x + 1$
5. $x^2 + 14x + 49$

6. $25 - 10x + x^2$
7. $100 + 20x + x^2$
8. $b^2 - 2bx + x^2$
9. $b^2 - 2bc + c^2$
10. $x^2 + 2xy + y^2$

Now try these. It might be sensible to check by multiplying out the brackets:

11. $4x^2 - 4x + 1$
12. $16x^2 + 8x + 1$
13. $9x^2 + 6x + 1$
14. $4x^2 - 8x + 4$
15. $49x^2 + 28x + 49$

16. $100 - 20x + x^2$
17. $100 + 40x + 4x^2$
18. $4b^2 - 4bx + x^2$
19. $9b^2 - 6bc + c^2$
20. $4x^2 + 8xy + 4y^2$

Those were squares. Now we are going to look at close relations.

The difference between two squares

Exercise 14.7

Multiply out these brackets:

1. $(x - 3)(x + 3)$
2. $(x - 4)(x + 4)$
3. $(x + 1)(x - 1)$
4. $(x + 5)(x - 5)$
5. $(x - 7)(x + 7)$

6. $(2 - x)(2 + x)$
7. $(6 + x)(6 - x)$
8. $(8 - x)(8 + x)$
9. $(a - x)(a + x)$
10. $(y + x)(y - x)$

From these examples you can see that the middle term has cancelled itself out and you are left with one perfect square less another perfect square.

An expression in this form is known as 'the difference between two squares'.

Now try a few more:

11. $(x - 10)(x + 10)$

12. $(x - 9)(x + 9)$

13. $(11 - x)(11 + x)$

14. $(2x + 5)(2x - 5)$

15. $(3x - 3)(3x + 3)$

16. $(2a - x)(2a + x)$

17. $(6 + ax)(6 - ax)$

18. $(8 - \frac{x}{2})(8 + \frac{x}{2})$

19. $(a - \frac{x}{2})(a + \frac{x}{2})$

20. $(y - \frac{x}{4})(y + \frac{x}{4})$

You can factorise an expression, where there are two squares separated by a minus sign, by taking the square roots of the terms:

$$x^2 - a^2 = (x - a)(x + a)$$
$$x^2 - 16 = (x - 4)(x + 4)$$
$$25x^2 - 16 = (5x - 4)(5x + 4)$$

Exercise 14.8

Factorise these expressions, **if possible**:

1. $x^2 - 9$

2. $x^2 - b^2$

3. $x^2 - 81$

4. $x^2 - 16$

5. $x^2 - 100$

6. $x^2 - y^2$

7. $4x^2 - 1$

8. $9x^2 - 1$

9. $16x^2 - 1$

10. $x^2 - 4a^2$

11. $x^2 + 1$

12. $4x^2 - b^2$

13. $9x^2 - 25$

14. $144 - x^2$

15. $81 + x^2$

16. $25x^2 - y^2$

17. $x^2 - 9y^2$

18. $2x^2 - 9y^2$

19. $x^2 - 6y^2$

20. $36x^2 - 121a^2$

Solving equations by factorising

When an expression is factorised, the result is a multiple – one number or expression multiplied by another.

However consider these: $7 \times 0 = 0$

$$0 \times x = 0$$
$$4x^2 \times 0 = 0$$

any number multiplied by 0 is 0

If we have $xy = 0$ then either $x = 0$ or $y = 0$
and if $(x + 3)(x - 4) = 0$ then either $(x + 3) = 0$ or $(x - 4) = 0$

Therefore to solve an equation such as $9x^2 + 3x = 0$ all the non-zero terms have to be grouped on one side and then factorised.

Examples: Solve these equations:

(i)
$$9x^2 + 3x = 0$$
$$3x(3x + 1) = 0$$
Either $3x = 0$ or $3x + 1 = 0$
$$x = 0 \qquad 3x = -1$$
$$x = -\frac{1}{3}$$

(ii)
$$x^2 - 9 = 0$$
$$(x - 3)(x + 3) = 0$$
Either $x - 3 = 0$ or $x + 3 = 0$
$$x = 3 \qquad x = -3$$

Note that when an equation is a quadratic equation (i.e. it contains an x^2 term) it has two solutions. When the quadratic expression is a perfect square these two solutions are the same.

Exercise 14.9

Solve these equations:

1. $2x^2 - 8x = 0$

2. $x^2 - 4x = 0$

3. $12x^2 - 15x = 0$

4. $x^2 - 16 = 0$

5. $x^2 - 4x + 4 = 0$

6. $x^2 - 10x + 25 = 0$

7. $4x^2 - 16x = 0$

8. $x^2 - 25 = 0$

9. $15x^2 - 25x = 0$

10. $x^2 - 100 = 0$

11. $x^2 + 8x + 16 = 0$

12. $5x^2 - 15x = 0$

13. $12x^2 + 27x = 0$

14. $36 - x^2 = 0$

15. $36x - 60x^2 = 0$

16. $x^2 + 14x + 49 = 0$

17. $10x - 16x^2 = 0$

18. $9x^2 - 36 = 0$

19. $81 - 18x + x^2 = 0$

20. $35x + 49x^2 = 0$

To solve these equations, you may need to rearrange them before you can factorise:

21. $x^2 + 16 = 8x$

22. $9x^2 = 15x$

23. $x^2 = 121$

24. $6x = 9 + x^2$

25. $36x = 4x^2$

26. $1 = 4x^2$

27. $16x + x^2 = -64$

28. $10x + x^2 = 25x$

29. $4(2x - 4) = x^2$

30. $x(x + 6) = -9$

Solving problems with factorising and brackets

Certain problems can be solved by letting an unknown quantity be x. When the resulting equation is quadratic then the equation may be solved by factorising. This may give two answers in which case both need to be considered and one may be discarded because it doesn't make sense:

Example:

A rectangle has one side 3 times as long as the other and an area of 27 cm². How long are the sides?

Let the short side be x cm:

$$3x \times x = 27$$
$$3x^2 = 27$$
$$3x^2 - 27 = 0$$
$$x^2 - 9 = 0$$
$$(x - 3)(x + 3) = 0$$

Either $x - 3 = 0$ or $x + 3 = 0$
$$x = 3 \qquad\qquad x = -3$$

A length cannot be negative, therefore $x = 3$ and so the sides are 3 cm and 9 cm.

Exercise 14.10

1. One side of a rectangle is twice as long as the other and the area of the rectangle is 72 cm². Find the lengths of the sides.

2. One side of a rectangle is four times as long as the other and the area of the rectangle is 100 cm². Find the lengths of the sides.

3. Two numbers have a difference of 6
   Their squares have a difference of 120
   What are the two numbers?

5. Two numbers have a sum of 20
   Their squares have a difference of 40
   What are the two numbers?

6. The sides of a rectangle are $(7 - x)$ cm and $(x + 3)$ cm respectively, and the area of the rectangle is 25 cm². Find the lengths of the sides.

7. A square of side x cm and a square of side $(x + 3)$ cm have a difference in area of $9x$ cm². Find the lengths of the sides of the squares.

8. These two rectangles have the same area. Find the value of x:

9. This square and this rectangle have the same area. Find the lengths of the sides of the rectangle.

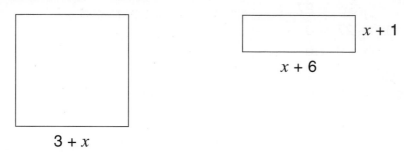

10. Two squares, one of which has sides 3 cm longer than another have a difference in area of 57 cm². What are the lengths of the sides of the two squares?

Exercise 14.11: Extension questions

1. Two consecutive numbers can be written as n and $n + 1$
    (a) (i) Find the sum of these two consecutive numbers.
        (ii) Explain if the sum is always odd, always even or if it is not possible to tell.
    (b) (i) Find the difference between these two consecutive numbers.
        (ii) Explain if the difference is always odd, always even or if it is not possible to tell.
    (c) (i) Find the product of these two consecutive numbers.
        (ii) Explain if the product is always odd, always even or if it is not possible to tell.

2. Three consecutive numbers can be written as $n - 1$, n and $n + 1$
    (a) (i) Find the sum of these three consecutive numbers.
        (ii) What are the factors, if any, of the sum of any three consecutive numbers?
    (b) (i) Find the product of these three consecutive numbers.
        (ii) Explain if the product is always odd, always even or if it is not possible to tell.

3. (a) Multiply out $(p + q)(p - q)$

(b) You know that $5^2 - 4^2 = 3^2$
For $(p + q)(p - q) = 9$ what are the values of p and q?

(c) What values of p and q give a difference of two
squares of: (i) 16   (ii) 25?

(d) Write your answers above in the form of a Pythogorean triplet:
$x^2 + y^2 = z^2$
and use the same method to find one more.

4. (a) A right-angled triangle has one of the shorter sides of length
15 cm and a perimeter of 40 cm. Draw a sketch of the triangle and
show that the other two sides are of lengths x and $25 - x$ cm.

(b) Multiply out $(25 - x)^2$

(c) Use Pythagoras' theorem to form an equation in x. Solve it to find the
lengths of the three sides of the triangle.

5. (a) Show that any odd number can be written as $(2x + 1)$

(b) Multiply out $(2x + 1)^2$

(c) Use your answer to explain why dividing the square of an odd
number by four always gives a remainder of 1

(d) What will be the remainder when the square of an even number is
divided by 4?

(e) Divide these numbers by 4 and say which of them cannot be perfect
squares, and why:
(i) 144   (ii) 517   (iii) 523   (iv) 625   (v) 1067

6. (a) Show that $(a - b)^2 = a^2 - 2ab + b^2$

(b) Use you answer to (a) to expand and simplify:

(i) $(5 - \frac{1}{5})^2$ (ii) $(x - \frac{1}{5})^2$ (iii) $(x - \frac{1}{x})^2$

(c) Explain why $(x - \frac{1}{x})^2$ is never negative, whatever the value of x

(d) Find the least possible value of $x^2 + \frac{1}{x^2}$

(e) What is x when $x^2 + \frac{1}{x^2}$ equals 2?

7. (a) Simplify $(a + b)^2 - (a - b)^2$

   (b) Using your result find values of $(a + b)$ and $(a - b)$ such that:
   $(a + b)^2 - (a - b)^2 = 16$

   (c) Find as many pairs of values of a and b as you can.

8. (a) Simplify $(x + y)^2 - (x - y)^2$

   (b) Using your result and choosing suitable values of x find two positive whole numbers, m and n, such that $m^2 - n^2 = 120$

   (c) Find as many pairs of values of m and n as you can.

9. (a) Multiply out $(p + q)(p - q)$

   The odd number 7 can be written as the difference of two squares:
   $$4^2 - 3^2 = 16 - 9$$
   $$= 7$$

   (b) Express the numbers (i) 11 and (ii) 19 as differences between two squares.

Comparing our answers to q.9 (a) and (b) we could say that:

The difference between two squares p^2 and q^2 is equal to $(p + q)(p - q)$.

If the difference is 7, 7 has two factors, 7 and 1;
therefore: $p + q = 7$ and $p - q = 1$

Solving these as simultaneous equations gives us:
$$p = 4 \text{ and } q = 3$$

   (c) Use the method above to find two numbers whose squares have a difference of 31

   (d) Now use the method above to find as many pairs of numbers as possible whose squares have a difference of 36

10. (a) Without using your calculator and leaving $\sqrt{2}$ in your answer find the values of:

   (i) $(2 + \sqrt{2})^2$ (ii) $(2 - \sqrt{2})^2$

   (b) Find a general result in terms of m for (i) $(m + \sqrt{m})^2$ and (ii) $(m - \sqrt{m})^2$

Exercise 14.12: Summary exercise

1. Multiply out these brackets and simplify if possible:

   (a) $2x(3 - 3x)$

   (b) $3(b + 2) + 2(2b - 1)$

   (c) $2(a - 5) - 3(a - 2)$

   (d) $2x(x + 6) - 3(4x - 3)$

2. Factorise these expressions:

   (a) $9x + x^2$

   (b) $12a + 3a^2$

   (c) $10x^2 - 5x + 15$

   (d) $36x^2 - 6$

3. Multiply out these brackets:

   (a) $(x + 1)(x + 3)$

   (b) $(x - 4)(x + 7)$

   (c) $(2 + b)(5 - b)$

   (d) $(a - b)(5 - a)$

4. Multiply out these brackets :

   (a) $(x + 5)^2$

   (b) $(x - 6)^2$

   (c) $(5 - a)^2$

   (d) $(2a - b)^2$

5. Factorise these expressions:

   (a) $x^2 - 6x + 9$

   (b) $a^2 + 10x + 25$

6. Multiply out these brackets:

   (a) $(x + 5)(x - 5)$

   (b) $(x - 7)(x + 7)$

   (c) $(6 - a)(6 + a)$

   (d) $(2a - b)(2a + b)$

7. Factorise these expressions:
   (a) $x^2 - 36$

   (b) $a^2 - 144$

8. I take a number and square it. I add 2 to the original number and then square the result. The difference between my two numbers is 144

   What was my first number?

End of chapter 14 activity: The dragon curve or Jurassic Park fractal

Have you ever read *Jurassic Park*? You possibly saw the film, but did you read the book? Did you notice the drawings on the chapter heading pages? They look like partial squares. They're labelled *First Iteration, Second Iteration, etc.*, and they get more and more complex with each iteration. They are in fact a fractal sequence, like the ones we looked at in Chapter 8.

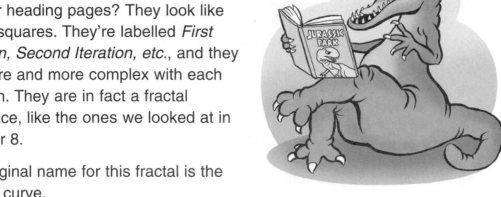

The original name for this fractal is the dragon curve.

How does the dragon curve fractal work?

The dragon curve fractal is an interesting one. You can imagine a long strip of paper that gets folded in half many times until you get a pretty small piece of folded paper or a small line. You then unfold it 90° to get something that looks like an L. As with all fractals the next iteration or generation has self-similarity to the first. So fold the paper again with an extra fold and then unfold. You get a shape that looks like two L's connected together.

With real paper there is a physical limit regarding how many times one can fold a paper in half. Even though in theory there is no real limit in a computer, the limit becomes the amount of memory and the processor. Even though this is one of the slowest growing fractals, you probably **won't be able to go past iterations 13 or 14**

Go ahead and give it a try.

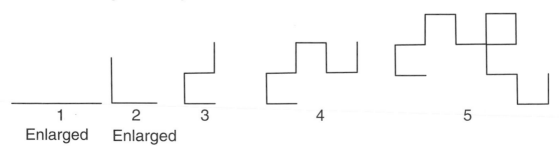

| 1 | 2 | 3 | 4 | 5 |
| Enlarged | Enlarged | | | |

How quickly do the numbers of points (ends and corners) grow?

We want to find out the general formula to predict the number of points at any iteration. As a hint, start by figuring out the number of lines at each iteration. You may also want to fill in this table:

Iteration	Number of Lines	Number of Points
0	1	2
1	2	3
2	4	
3		
4		
5		
6		

You might also want to consider right and left L bends. How do you define them?

Now use strips of paper or pipe cleaners to make the next iterations.

Iteration 7

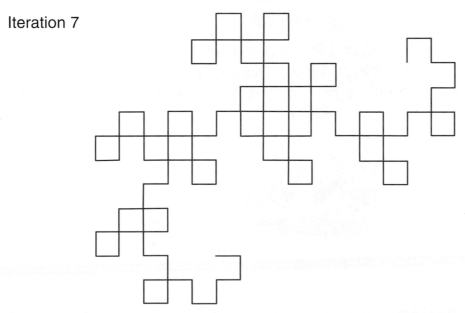

If you could fold the paper about 50 times, it would look like this:

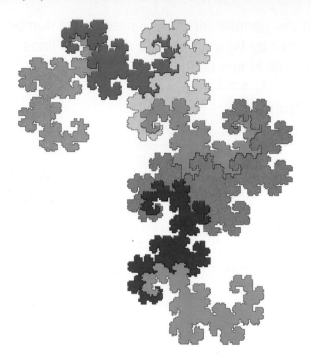

But of course, you **can't** fold the paper 50 times, so you have to let the mathematics take over the paper-folding process.

Chapter 15: Probability

Let us start by reminding ourselves of what we learned in *So you really want to learn Maths* Books 1 and 2.

Calculating probability

The probability of an event can be calculated by considering the possible outcomes of that event, if all outcomes of the event are equally likely.

For example, if a normal die is thrown the possible outcomes are 1, 2, 3, 4, 5 and 6; that is six equally likely outcomes. The probability of throwing a 6 is one out of the six possible outcomes. This is written:

$$\text{Probability of an outcome } P(6) = \frac{1}{6}$$

In general terms when all the possible outcomes are equally likely the probability of an outcome can be found by the following rule:

$$P(\text{outcome}) = \frac{\text{frequency of the outcome}}{\text{number of equally likely outcomes}}$$

Using this rule we can see that the probability of an outcome must lie between 0 and 1

Example:

When throwing a normal die what is the probability of throwing:
(i) an odd prime number (ii) 7 (iii) a number less than 7?

(i) Possible outcomes are 1, 2, 3, 4, 5, 6
     2 of these are odd primes

$$P(\text{odd prime}) = \frac{2}{6} = \frac{1}{3}$$

(ii) Not one of the numbers is 7
     $P(7) = 0$

(iii) All six of the numbers are less than 7

$$P(\text{less than 7}) = \frac{6}{6} = 1$$

We can say:

P(certainty) = 1
P(impossibility) = 0
and also that P(outcome not happening) = 1 – P(outcome happening)

Example: A bag contains 12 balls. 5 are blue, 4 are green, 2 are white and the rest are black. If one ball is taken out of the bag at random, what is the probability that it is: (i) blue (ii) white (iii) not green?

(i) $P(blue) = \dfrac{5}{12}$

(ii) $P(white) = \dfrac{2}{12} = \dfrac{1}{6}$

(iii) $P(green) = \dfrac{4}{12} = \dfrac{1}{3}$

$P(not\ green) = 1 - \dfrac{1}{3}$

$= \dfrac{2}{3}$

Exercise 15.1

1. A normal pack of 52 cards is cut and one card is taken at random, give the probability the card is:
   (a) black
   (b) a heart
   (c) not a royal card
   (d) a King
   (e) not a diamond
   (f) the Ace of hearts

2. If a normal die is rolled, give the probability that the score is:
   (a) three
   (b) a square number
   (c) an even number
   (d) less than 6

3. If a letter is picked at random from the alphabet, write down the probability that the letter is:
   (a) a vowel
   (b) not a vowel
   (c) one that appears in the word MATHEMATICS

4. A letter is chosen at random from the letters in the word PROBABILITY. Write down the probability that the letter is:
   (a) a vowel
   (b) the letter I
   (c) the letter L
   (d) the letter S

5. A bag contains 3 orange sweets, 5 red sweets, 6 green sweets and 4 purple sweets. If I select one sweet at random, write down the probability that it is: (a) red or green   (b) not orange or purple

6. Another bag of sweets contains only orange sweets and lemon sweets.
   (a) If the probability of picking a lemon sweet is $\frac{4}{7}$, what is the probability of picking an orange sweet?
   (b) If there are 12 lemon sweets in the bag how many orange ones are there?

7. (a) If I have 4 pairs of white socks, 3 pairs of black socks and 5 pairs of grey socks and I take one pair of socks at random what is the probability that I pick a pair of grey socks?
   (b) If my socks are not in pairs but are lying loose in my sock drawer and I take one sock at random what is the probability that it is a grey sock?

8. I am asked to pick a number between one and 20 (inclusive) at random. Give the probability that I pick:
   (a) a prime number
   (b) a multiple of 5
   (c) a square number
   (d) a negative number
   (e) a number with more than two factors (other than itself and 1)
   (f) a number that is not a multiple of 3

Using theoretical probability

In the examples above you had to find the probability. Sometimes, as in q.6, you have to use the theoretical probability to predict a number.

Example:

A bag contains red and white balls. My teacher tells me that if I pick one ball at random the probability of it being a white ball is $\frac{2}{3}$
If there are 12 red balls how many white balls are there?

If P(white) = $\frac{2}{3}$ then P(red) = $\frac{1}{3}$

There are twice as many white balls as red balls.

Number of white balls = 2 × 12
                       = 24

Exercise 15.2

1. A bag contains green balls and red balls. My teacher tells me that if I pick one ball at random the probability of it being a green ball is $\frac{3}{4}$ If there are 12 red balls how many green balls are there?

2. A bag contains peppermints and toffees. My friend tells me that if I pick one sweet at random the probability of it being a toffee is $\frac{4}{5}$ If there are 12 peppermints how many toffees are there?

3. I buy a packet of seeds containing 20 seeds in total. The instructions warn that only $\frac{2}{3}$ of the seeds can be expected to germinate. How many seedlings can I expect?

4. In the Tombola at the School Fair the winning numbers all end in a 0 or a 5 If I buy 30 tickets how many prizes could I expect to win?

5. (a) If I toss a coin 20 times how many times would I expect it to land on heads?
   (b) If I toss a hairbrush 20 times will I expect it to land bristles up 10 times? Explain your answer.

6. If a die is rolled 60 times, write down how many times you should expect to score:
   (a) a 6
   (b) a number greater than 3
   (c) a number less than 3

7. In the school raffle 1000 tickets were sold.
   (a) If I bought 20 tickets, what is the probability of my winning 1st prize?
   (b) If there were 20 prizes, how many tickets would I have to buy to be sure of winning a prize in theory?
   (c) How many tickets would I have to buy to be absolutely sure of winning a prize?

8. The company that makes 'Luckychocs' say that every hundredth sweet they make is a Lucky choc. If I buy a bag of 12 'Luckychocs' what is the probability that I will be lucky? If I buy 9 bags of 'Luckychocs', can I be sure that I will be lucky?

The moral of that last exercise is that probability is theoretical – you cannot depend on it to win games of chance!

Probability with two events

The probability of two events can either be **dependent** or **independent**.

For example, picking a King or a 10 from a pack of cards are **independent events**. To calculate the probability you add the probability of one event to the probability of another:

$$P(\text{King or 10}) = \frac{4}{52} + \frac{4}{52} \qquad \text{where } P(\text{King}) \frac{4}{52} = \text{and } P(10) = \frac{4}{52}$$

$$= \frac{8}{52}$$

$$= \frac{2}{13}$$

However, if asked for the probability of picking a black card or an Ace from a pack of cards, there is a slight complication because two of the black cards are Aces. Half the pack is black i.e. 26 cards (including the 2 black Aces) and there are 2 red Aces. So:

$$P(\text{black card or Ace}) = \frac{28}{52}$$

$$= \frac{7}{13}$$

The probabilities of picking a black card and of picking an Ace are **dependent** and cannot be added. There is no simple rule to apply here. Each situation must be judged on its own merits.

Exercise 15.3

1. If a card is drawn at random from a full pack of 52 cards, write down the probability that it is:
    (a) a two or a three
    (b) a red card or a Knave
    (c) an Ace or a King
    (d) a red Ace or a heart
    (e) a black Queen or a red Knave
    (f) a black card or a royal card

2.   I have to pick any number from 1 to 30 at random. Give the probability
     that I pick:
     (a) 5
     (b) a multiple of 5
     (c) a prime number
     (d) a multiple of 5 or a prime number
     (e) an odd number or a prime number

Now consider bags of sweets. If I offer a bag of peppermints and humbugs to
my friend, he will probably take one. Therefore, when I offer the bag to my
next friend, the probability will change. However, if the first friend took a sweet
and then put it back, the probability would stay the same.

3.   A bag contains 8 green sweets, 6 red sweets and 4 yellow sweets.
     (a) If the first sweet I take out at random is red, give the probability that
         the second sweet is   (i) red   (ii) yellow
     (b) If the first sweet I take out at random is green, give the probability
         that the second sweet is   (i) green   (ii) yellow
     (c) If the first sweet I take out at random is yellow, give the probability
         that the second sweet is   (i) yellow   (ii) red

4.   A mixed bag of snack bars contained 5 caramel bars, 4 chocolate bars
     and 3 orange flavoured bars. I was allowed to choose one bar at random
     every day for my break time snack.
     (a) On Monday, what is the probability that the bar I picked was caramel?
     (b) In fact the bar on Monday was an orange flavoured bar, what was the
         probability that I would chose a caramel bar on Tuesday?
     (c) In fact the bar on Tuesday was a chocolate bar, what is the
         probability that I will choose a caramel bar on Wednesday?
     (d) In fact the bar on Wednesday was an orange flavoured bar, how
         many bars would I have to take out of the bag now to be sure of
         getting a caramel bar?

5.   I am dealt five cards from a pack of cards. These are 3 Kings and 2
     Queens. If no other cards have been taken from the pack, give the
     probability that the next card:
     (a) will be be a royal card
     (b) will not be a royal card

6.   I am dealt five cards from a pack of cards. These are 3 hearts and 2 diamonds. If no other cards have been taken from the pack, give the probability that the next card will be:
       (a) a heart
       (b) a spade

7.   I have a packet of 'N and N's. 12 are red, 6 are green, 5 are yellow and 4 are orange.
       (a) I offered the packet to my little sister. What is the probability that she took a green 'N and N'? (Assume the green 'N and N' is then put back in the bag.)
       (b) My little sister then takes a red 'N and N'. What is the probability that when I offer the bag to my mother she takes a red 'N and N' too? (Assume the red 'N and Ns' are put back in the bag.)
       (c) When I checked I found that my little sister had actually taken all the orange ones! What is the probability now that my mother will take a red one?

8.   There are 240 children in the school and they are grouped so that there are equal numbers in each of our 4 houses: Austen, Churchill, Nightingale and Wellington.
       (a) The headmaster chooses one child at random to run an errand. What is the probability that the child is from Churchill?
       (b) What is the probability that the next child the headmaster chooses will also be from Churchill?
       (c) (i) If half the children in each house are boys and half are girls, what is the probability that the first child was a boy from Churchill?
           (ii) What is the probability that the second child was a girl from Churchill?

9.   Have you heard of the bosun's locker? This is where the bosun (a ship's officer in charge of equipment and the crew) keeps his secret store of food supplies. Unfortunately the locker is wet and so all the labels have fallen off.

The bosun knows that he has 15 tins of rice pudding, 5 tins of fruit salad and 12 tins of emergency rations for the ship's cat. If the bosun takes two tins at random give the probability that:

(a) the first is rice pudding.

(b) if the first was rice pudding the second is fruit salad.

(c) if the first was cat food the second is also cat food.

10. In Aladdin's cave there were 10 bags of gold, 12 bags of silver, 13 bags of emeralds and 2 bags of diamonds.

(a) Aladdin had to leave in a rush. What was the probability that he took a bag of gold?

(b) The genie followed him out. If Aladdin had taken a bag of gold, what was the probability that the genie also took a bag of gold?

(c) Actually no-one knows which bag Aladdin took, but the bag that the genie took had a probability of $\frac{1}{18}$ of being selected. Can you tell who took which bag?

(d) If the genie took a bag that had a probability of $\frac{1}{3}$ of being selected, work out who took which bag?

Possibility space for combined events

When two coins are tossed together, the result could either be two heads, two tails or one head and one tail. It looks as though there are three possibilities, but there are in fact four possible combinations:

(head, head) (head, tail) (tail, head) (tail, tail)

It can be easier to see all the possibilities if we put the possible oucomes in a table like this:

First coin

	H	T
H	(H,H)	(T,H)
T	(H,T)	(T,T)

Second coin

This table is called a **possibility space** because it clearly shows all the possibilities. It is now clear that there are four possibilities, not three, as one head and one tail can be achieved in two ways.

Exercise 15.4

1. Copy and complete this possibility space to show the possible outcomes when throwing 2 dice:

		First die				
	1	2	3	4	5	6
1	(1,1)	(2,1)	(3,1)			
2	(1,2)	(2,2)	(3,2)			
3	(1,3)	(2,3)	(3,3)			
4	(1,4)	(2,4)				
5	(1,5)	(2,5)				(6,5)
6	(1,6)	(2,6)				(6,6)

(Second die)

When throwing 2 dice write down the probability of throwing:
(a) a total of 4
(b) a total more than 6
(c) a double
(d) a total that is an even number

2. Use the possibility space in q.1 to find the probability that:
(a) the total score is prime number
(b) there is a prime number on at least one die

3. Draw a possibility space to show all the outcomes when you throw together a normal die and a die with its faces numbered 1, 1, 1, 2, 2, 3
Use this possibility space to find the probability that:
(a) the total score is 2
(b) the total score is more than 4
(c) a double is thrown
(d) there is a multiple of 3 on each die
(e) the total score is a prime number
(f) the total score is 6 or more

4. I throw a die with 8 faces, numbered from 1 to 8, at the same time as I throw a die with 6 faces. Draw a possibility space to find all the possibilities. Use this probability space to find the probability that:
    (a) the total score is 12
    (b) the total score is more than 12
    (c) a double is thrown
    (d) there is a multiple of 2 on each die
    (e) the total score is a prime number
    (f) What is the most likely total score?

5. Here are two spinners from the game of 'Tops'. For each move they are spun together. The score is the sum of the two numbers.

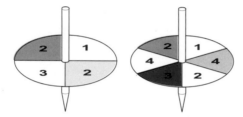

    (a) Draw a possibility space to find all the possible outcomes from the two spinners.
    (b) From the possibility space find:
        (i)   the highest and lowest possible scores
        (ii) the most likely score
        (iii) the probability of throwing a score that is even
        (iv) the probability of throwing a score that is odd
        (v)   the probability of a score of 4
        (vi) the probability of a score of 6

6. I have the four Aces from a pack of cards in one pile and the four Kings in another.
    (a) Draw a possibility space to show all the possible outcomes from selecting a card from each pile.
    (b) If I take one card from each pile give the probability of selecting:
        (i)   two red cards
        (ii) a red card and a black card
        (iii) two cards of the same suit
        (iv) two Kings

Exercise 15.5: Extension questions – Drawing diagrams to help solve problems

Sometimes we have to handle lots of information. It can be useful, in some cases, to put the numbers in a Carroll diagram first. Here is an example:

Example:

There are 24 students in my class. 16 are boys and 12 play the violin. 6 girls play the violin. What is the probability that a child chosen at random is a boy that plays the violin?

	Girls	Boys	Total
Violin	**6**	6	**12**
No Violin	2	10	12
Total	8	**16**	**24**

P(boy that plays violin) $= \dfrac{6}{24}$

$\qquad\qquad\qquad\qquad = \dfrac{1}{4}$

The Carroll diagram is the table showing how many pupils there are of each sex and how many play or do not play the violin. The numbers in bold are the figures we have been given. From these you can work out all the missing ones.

For each of the following questions first draw a Carroll diagram and then answer the questions.

1. In our class there are 10 boys and 12 girls. 16 of us have pets and the rest do not. 7 of the pet owners are girls. If one of the class is picked at random give the probability that it is:
   (a) a girl
   (b) a pet owner
   (c) a boy that owns a pet

2. In a school of 240 children there are 70 boys that board and 90 day girls. 130 children board altogether.
   (a) Draw a Carroll diagram to show this information.
   (b) If a child is picked at random, what is the probability that this is a day boy?
   (c) All the boarders went to Long Hall to do Prep. Matron then picked a day child at random. What was the probability that she picked a girl?

3. On a school trip to France we ate in a restaurant. We had to choose a main course and a pudding. 43 of us chose coq au vin and the rest chose an omelette. 49 chose crème caramel and the rest chose a glace. 8 of us had coq au vin and a glace. 29 of those who had the omelette did not have crème caramel.
   (a) How many of us had coq au vin and a crème caramel (comme moi!)?
   (b) One child was sick on the way home. What was the probability that he or she had omelette and glace?

Sometimes you can fill in your Carroll diagram with percentages.

4. We are allowed to make some choices about our school uniform. 30% of the girls choose to wear trousers and the rest choose skirts. 55% of the pupils in the school are girls. Funnily enough not one of the boys chooses to wear a skirt but 40% of them wear shorts and the rest wear trousers.
   (a) What is the probability that a girl picked at random will be wearing a skirt?
   (b) What is the probability that a boy picked at random is wearing shorts?
   (c) What is the probability that a child picked at random will be wearing trousers?

5. All sorts of people come to school by car, not only the children but the teachers, the cooks, and even some of the cleaners. One day we did a survey.
   16% of the cars coming into school contained exactly two people. Another 4% contained only one person (the driver!). The rest had more than two people. All of those with more than two people had at least one child. Altogether, 95% of the cars contained at least one child.
   (a) Show this information on a Carroll diagram. You will need three columns (one person, two people and more than two people) this time.

(b) What is the probability that a car picked at random will have one adult and one child?

(c) What is the probability that a car picked at random will contain no adults?

(d) What is the probability that a car picked at random will contain exactly two adults?

Sometimes you can fill in your Carroll diagram with fractions.

6. In the school exactly one half the pupils are boys and one half are girls. A recent survey shows that $\frac{1}{3}$ of the pupils walk to school, $\frac{1}{4}$ of the pupils come by car and the rest come by public transport. If a pupil is picked at random, what is the probability that it is a boy coming to school by public transport. What assumptions, if any, have you made?

Exercise 15.6: Summary exercise

1. If I cut a normal pack of cards and select one card at random write down the probability that this card will be:
   (a) an Ace
   (b) a diamond
   (c) the ten of hearts
   (d) either an Ace or a King
   (e) either a heart or a Queen

2. There are eight tins of soup in my cupboard, 3 tomato, 2 chicken, 2 beef and 1 farmhouse vegetable. If I pick one tin at random write down the probability that it is:
   (a) tomato
   (b) suitable for vegetarians
   (c) not beef

3. I roll an ordinary die and a die numbered 1,2,3,3,5,6
   (a) Draw a possibility space.
   (b) Use the possibility space to find the probability that I throw:
       (i) a double
       (ii) a six on either die
       (iii) a total greater than 5
       (iv) a total less than 4
   (c) If I rolled both the dice together 30 times, how many doubles would I expect?

4. A box contains 3 red balls and 7 white balls. Two balls were taken from the box.
    (a) What is the probability that the first ball was red?
    (b) If the first ball was red, what is the possibility that the second ball was also red?
    (c) If the first ball was white, what is the possibility that the second ball was red?
    (d) How many balls would I have to take out to be sure of removing one ball of each colour.

5. I offer a bag containing a mixture of sherbet lemons and mint humbugs to my sister. There is a $\frac{3}{5}$ chance that she will pick a mint humbug. If there are 6 sherbet lemons in the bag, how many mint humbugs are there?

6. (a) My maths master, Mr Chance, is very absent minded. There is a 20% chance that he will forget to set us any maths prep and a 30% chance that he will forget to ask for it to be given in. However if Mr Chance does remember to ask for it and we have not done it (regardless of whether it was set or not), then the class gets a detention. Write down the probability that:
        (i)   no prep was set and none was asked for.
        (ii) prep was set but we were not asked to give it in.
        (iii) the class got a detention.
    (b) Actually I am quite absent minded too! There is a 40% chance that I forget to do my homework if it is set. What is the probability that I am given a detention for not handing in prep when it was asked for?
    (c) If there are 20 nights in a term when I am supposed to have Maths prep, how many detentions could I expect to get?

End of chapter 15 activity: Probability experiments

Using the random number key

On your calculator you should find a button marked RAN (usually a second function). Press this button and you should be presented with a three figure number preceded by a decimal point.

Ignore the decimal point and record the number. Do this again and again until you have recorded twenty numbers, or 60 single digits.

If these numbers are produced in a truly random fashion, how many of each digit from 0 to 9 would you expect to find in your 60 digits?

How many of each digit have you actually recorded?

Is this a good way of generating random numbers? (If your results were not truly random, try repeating this experiment until you have 120 digits and see if this looks any better.)

Look also at the first digit of each of your three digit numbers. With twenty numbers, you should theoretically get about 2 examples of each digit. Do you?

It is quite likely that you do not. It is probable that you will have more of some digits than others. This is not a mistake. It is because random events in real life do tend to bunch together. (Accidents happen in threes, pairs of consecutive numbers appear in three lottery draws in a row.) This is an important fact to remember when planning something using random events.

A random event happens at random. Time does not divide itself into equal intervals such that each time interval is equal to:

$$\frac{\text{time under consideration}}{\text{number of probable occurences}}$$

Using statistics from past history, disasters such as floods and severe rain storms are classified under the probability of them occurring:

'a once in every fifty years storm,' or 'a once a century flood.'

However you could get two 'once every fifty years rainfall' in ten years and then no more for another eighty years.

Statisticians use random numbers to help them model real probability problems. Let us look at some simple modelling.

Picking a pupil at a random

There are five year groups in my school, with approximately the same number of pupils in each year. I can therefore allocate random numbers as follows:

0–1	1st Year	2–3	2nd Year	4–5	3rd Year
6–7	4th Year	8–9	5th Year		

The headmaster picks a child in the school at random each day to bring him the day's notices. Use your random number button on your calculator (select the first digit of each three digit number generated) to see which years the five pupils chosen this week come from. Repeat this several times. How many weeks pass before the year groups are fairly represented?

Random Cricket

Here's an interesting exercise. We can make a model of a cricket game by using the random number generator on your calculator.

In this case we will use the first digit for the bowler and the second digit for the batsman. For example:

0.312	3: the bowler	1: the batsman
0.784	7: the bowler	8: the batsman

and so on, but note:

0.4	4: the bowler	0: the batsman

And now to cricket: Firstly, let us consider the bowler. He could bowl a 'true' ball, or a 'no ball' or could bowl the batsman out. We will allocate the bowler's randomly generated numbers as follows:

0 – 5 to a 'true' ball
6 – 8 to a 'no ball'
9 is bowling the batsman out

Secondly, let us look at the batsman. He could make runs, be caught, be run out or be LBW. We will allocate his randomly generated numbers as follows:

0 – 1 to 1 run
2 – 6 to the equivalent number of runs
7 is caught out
8 is run out
9 is LBW

Now to play: Use this chart to record the results of our game of cricket:

1st Over							
Ball	Random no.	Result	Batsman no.	Random no.	Runs	Total runs	Out?
1							
2							
3							
4							
5							
6							

Let us assume we generate random numbers:

3, 9,   0, 6,   4, 1,   9, 4,   7, 2,   2, 8

Ball 1:   3 means the bowler bowled true
9 means that batsman 1 was out LBW

Ball 2:   0 means the bowler bowled true
6 means that batsman 2 made 6 runs

Ball 3:   4 means the bowler bowled true
1 means that batsman 2 made 1 run

Ball 4:   9 means the bowler bowled batsman 2 out
4 has no effect because the batsman was bowled out

Ball 5:   7 means the bowler bowled a no ball and the batting team get 1 "Extra" run
2 means that batsman 2 made 2 runs

Ball 6:   2 means the bowler bowled true
8 means that batsman 3 is run out

Our score card for the first over looks like this:

1st Over							
Ball	Random no.	Result	Batsman no.	Random no.	Runs	Total runs	Out?
1	3	True	1	9	LBW	0	Out
2	0	True	2	6	6	6	
3	4	True	2	1	1	7	
4	9	Out	2		0	7	Out
5	7	No ball	3	2	3	10	
6	2	True	3	8	Run out	10	Out

You can see that, in this over (6 balls), Batsman 1 was out LBW for a Golden duck (i.e. out on the first ball with no runs), Batsman 2 was bowled out with 7 runs and Batsman 3 was run out with 2 runs (the run given as a result of the no ball goes towards the batting teams score).

1. Try some more overs of your own and see how soon the batting side gets out.

2. It seems from the first over that the bowling team have the advantage. Do the statistics of your own team's results look like this? Do you think you should adjust the allocation of the random numbers? Try a variation and see if that changes the outcome of the game.

3. Look carefully at your own team's statistics and allocate the random numbers in a completely different way. Then see if you get similar results to your own.

4. Look carefully at a test match team's statistics and allocate the random numbers in an appropriate way. Then see if you get similar results to the test

5. Take another game: rounders, tennis, netball, or anything else you fancy (Quidditch?) and use a random number simulation to generate the results.

Chapter 16: Transformations

Most of the geometry that we study has its origins in Ancient Greece. A prominent Greek mathematician, Euclid (born in around 325 BC) wrote a book called *The Elements*. This famous work was a compilation of mathematical knowledge that became the centre of mathematical teaching for 2000 years and forms the basis of any work on geometric construction.

The Elements begins with five postulates. The first three postulates are postulates on construction:

1. It is possible to draw a straight line between any two points.

2. Any straight line can be extended indefinitely in a straight line.

3. It is possible to describe a circle with any centre and radius.

The fourth and fifth are of a different nature:

4. All right-angles are equal to one another.

5. If two lines are drawn which intersect a third in such a way that the sum of the inner angles on one side is less than two right-angles, then the two lines inevitably must intersect each other on that side if extended far enough.

(A postulate is a statement which is taken to be true without proof and it is interesting to note that Euclid's fifth postulate cannot be proven as a theorem, although this was attempted by many people. Euclid himself used only the first four postulates.)

For centuries the study of geometry was based on Euclidean rules. It was only as recently as the nineteenth century that this was questioned. The German mathematician Felix Klein wrote about a different approach to geometry in 1872 when he was only 23 years old. In his *Erlanger Programm* he wrote about a means by which shapes could be moved around by a group of transformations in space without altering their essential properties.

Klein was also notable for his encouragement of female mathematicians and it was through his influence that the University of Göttingen opened its doors to women in 1893. It sounds as if Klein was a great teacher – his favourite motto was 'Never be Dull'.

Transformation geometry

A point can be mapped onto another point by a transformation. Transformations that you will have come across in **Maths Prep** books 1 and 2 are reflections, rotations, translations and enlargements.

A point P is mapped onto its image and the image can be by called another letter, e.g. Q, or P'. If it is the first of a series of transformations the images can be known as P_1, P_2, P_3, etc …

Reflections

An object can be **reflected** to give a **mirror image** of itself. The object is reflected in a mirror line or a line of reflection. On a co-ordinate grid this could be a horizontal or a vertical line such as the x-axis or the y-axis, or a line such as $x = 2$, or $y = -3$, or a sloping line such as $y = x$ or $y = -x$ or $y = 3x - 2$

If a reflection is not on a co-ordinate grid then the image will need to be constructed:

In this reflection of $ABCD$ in the mirror line PQ the point A maps on to A',

B to B'
C to C'
D to D'

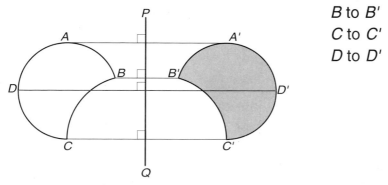

Note that the lines AA', BB', CC', DD' are at right-angles to PQ and are bisected by PQ. If you take any other line from a point on $ABCD$ to its reflection on $A'B'C'D'$, you will see that this is always true.

Also note that AA', BB', CC', DD' are parallel.

To construct a reflection of a line *PQ* in a line *AB*:

Draw a line from point *P* to meet *AB* at right-angles at a point *X*.

A line is then drawn to *P'* on the opposite side of the mirror line that is a continuation of *PX* and equal in length to *PX*. The end of the line is *P'*, the reflection of *P*.

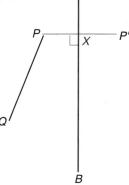

Q' can be constructed in the same way and the line *P'Q'* is drawn; the reflection of *PQ* in the line *AB*.

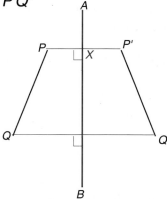

Exercise 16.1

You will need the worksheets for this exercise.

1. The diagram on the following page is also drawn on the worksheet. Some of these triangles may have a reflected image and some may not.
    (a) Draw any mirror line that maps one triangle onto its image on the worksheet.

(b) List any pairs of triangles and their reflected images.

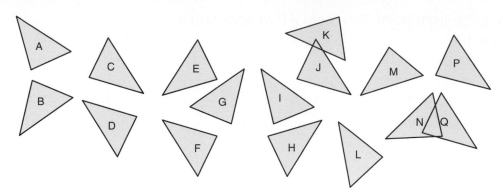

2. On the worksheet you will see this shape with various mirror lines. Construct the image of the shape after a reflection in each of the different mirror lines.

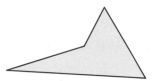

3. Construct a shape like this one using your compasses. Draw a mirror line and then construct the image of your shape.

When a shape has to be reflected in two mirror lines, then not only is the shape reflected twice but both images are reflected to give a congruent fourth image:

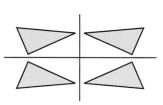

On the worksheet you will see these shapes and two mirror lines. Draw reflections of the following shapes in the mirror lines marked on the worksheet:

4.

5.

6.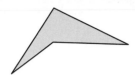
7.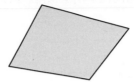

8. The new logo for a computer company is a design in the form of a shape and its three reflections. Design the logo.

Rotations

A rotation describes the transformation of an object that is rotated about a point. A rotation can be either clockwise or anticlockwise and needs to be described, not only by the centre of rotation, but also by the size of the angle of rotation and the direction:

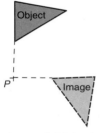

A rotation of 90° clockwise about a point *P*.

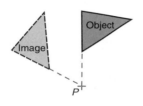

A rotation of 60° anticlockwise about a point *P*.

To construct the image of an object after a rotation you need a pair of compasses and a protractor.

For a rotation of 90° clockwise about a point *P*:

Draw lines from the centre of rotation *P* to each point on the object. Construct lines lines at 90° to each.

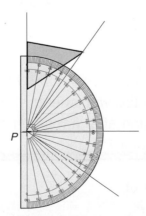

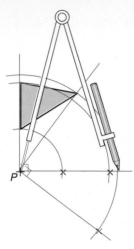

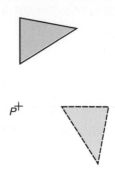

With compasses centre *P,* draw arcs from each point on the object to cross the construction lines.

Draw the image.

Exercise 16. 2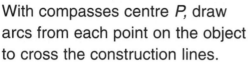

You will need the worksheet for this exercise:

1. You will see this shape on the worksheet:
   Draw the image of the shape after a rotation of:
   (a) 90° clockwise about point *P* marked on the worksheet.
   (b) 180° about *P.*
   (c) 270° clockwise about *P.*

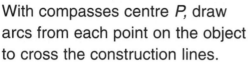

2. You will see this shape on the worksheet:
   Draw the image of the shape after a rotation of:
   (a) 60° clockwise about the point *P* marked on the worksheet.
   (b) 120° anticlockwise about *P.*
   (c) 60° anticlockwise about *P.*

3. You will see this shape on the worksheet:
   Draw the image of the shape after a rotation of:
   (a) 45° clockwise about point *P* marked on the worksheet.
   (b) 135° anticlockwise about *P.*
   (c) 135° clockwise about *P.*

4. Draw a shape on isometric paper or on the worksheet and then construct its image after a rotation of 120° anticlockwise.

Rotational symmetry

When some shapes are rotated about their own centre they may have images that are identical to them. These shapes have rotational symmetry:

| Rotational symmetry of order 2 | Rotational symmetry of order 4 | Rotational symmetry of order 6 | Rotational symmetry of order 3 | No rotational symmetry |

Exercise 16.3

You will need the worksheet for this exercise.

1. Write down the order of rotational symmetry of these shapes:

   (a)   (b)   (c)   (d)   (e)

Now write down the number of lines of symmetry of each shape.

2. Write down the order of rotational symmetry of these shapes:

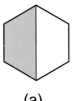  

   (a)   (b)   (c)   (d)   (e)

Now write down the number of lines of symmetry of each shape.

3. Write down the order of rotational symmetry of these shapes:

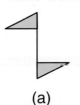 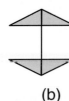 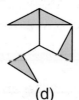 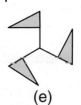

   (a)   (b)   (c)   (d)   (e)

Now write down the number of lines of symmetry of each shape.

4.-6. On the worksheet for this exercise you will find various incomplete shapes. Complete each shape so that it has the number of lines of symmetry and the order of rotational symmetry given. Note that not all of them may be possible!

Translations

A transformation which does not change the shape or orientation of an object but moves it is called a **translation**. A translation needs to be given in two parts – horizontal and vertical.

As with co-ordinates the horizontal movement (x-direction) is given first. A movement to the right is positive and a movement to the left is negative.

The vertical movement (y-direction) is given second. A movement up is positive and a movement down is negative.

We write a translation as a vector:

A movement of 5 units right and 2 units up is given by the vector $\begin{pmatrix} 5 \\ 2 \end{pmatrix}$

and is shown on a grid by an arrow used to show the direction of movement:

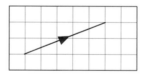

Exercise 16.4

You will need the worksheet for this exercise.

1. Write down the translations shown by these vectors:

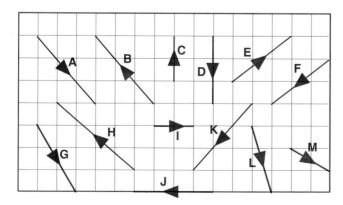

2. On the worksheet draw the vectors given by these translations:

(a) **A** = $\begin{pmatrix} 3 \\ 4 \end{pmatrix}$ (c) **C** = $\begin{pmatrix} -2 \\ -4 \end{pmatrix}$ (e) **E** = $\begin{pmatrix} 0 \\ 3 \end{pmatrix}$ (g) **G** = $\begin{pmatrix} 3 \\ -1 \end{pmatrix}$ (i) **I** = $\begin{pmatrix} -3 \\ 1 \end{pmatrix}$

(b) **B** = $\begin{pmatrix} 3 \\ -4 \end{pmatrix}$ (d) **D** = $\begin{pmatrix} 4 \\ -2 \end{pmatrix}$ (f) **F** = $\begin{pmatrix} -3 \\ 0 \end{pmatrix}$ (h) **H** = $\begin{pmatrix} 5 \\ -2 \end{pmatrix}$ (j) **J** = $\begin{pmatrix} 0 \\ -5 \end{pmatrix}$

When a shape is transformed by a translation the whole object moves. This movement can be seen as the result of a horizontal movement followed by a vertical movement, by distances given by the vector. In this diagram the triangle *PQR* is mapped onto the triangle *P'Q'R'* by a translation given by the vector $\begin{pmatrix} 8 \\ 2 \end{pmatrix}$:

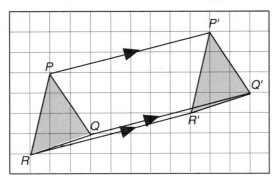

3. On the worksheet translate:

(a) triangle *ABC* by the vector $\begin{pmatrix} 3 \\ 5 \end{pmatrix}$

(b) quadrilateral *PQRS* by the vector $\begin{pmatrix} -4 \\ -2 \end{pmatrix}$

(c) *GHIJ* by the vector $\begin{pmatrix} 4 \\ 0 \end{pmatrix}$

(d) *DEF* by the vector $\begin{pmatrix} 0 \\ -2 \end{pmatrix}$

(e) *WXYZ* by the vector $\begin{pmatrix} -3 \\ -1 \end{pmatrix}$

(f) *KLMN* by the vector $\begin{pmatrix} -4 \\ 2 \end{pmatrix}$

Translations are often applied to shapes on a co-ordinate grid.

4. (a) On the worksheet plot the following points on the co-ordinate grid:

    $A(1, 0)$ $B(-2, 5)$ $C(0, -2)$ $D(3, 2)$ $E(-2, -4)$

    (b) Write down the co-ordinates of the image of these points after a translation by the given vectors:

    A to A' by the vector $\begin{pmatrix} -3 \\ 0 \end{pmatrix}$ B to B' by the vector $\begin{pmatrix} 4 \\ -4 \end{pmatrix}$

    C to C' by the vector $\begin{pmatrix} -1 \\ 3 \end{pmatrix}$ D to D' by the vector $\begin{pmatrix} -1 \\ -2 \end{pmatrix}$

    E to E' by the vector $\begin{pmatrix} 0 \\ 4 \end{pmatrix}$

5. Without drawing, write down the co-ordinates of the image of these points after a translation by the given vectors:

    (a) $A(-1, 3)$ to A' by the vector $\begin{pmatrix} 2 \\ 3 \end{pmatrix}$

    (b) $B(0, -3)$ to B' by the vector $\begin{pmatrix} -2 \\ 4 \end{pmatrix}$

    (c) $C(2, 4)$ to C' by the vector $\begin{pmatrix} -3 \\ -5 \end{pmatrix}$

    (d) $D(-1, -2)$ to D' by the vector $\begin{pmatrix} -2 \\ 5 \end{pmatrix}$

    (e) $E(-4, 0)$ to E' by the vector $\begin{pmatrix} 6 \\ -5 \end{pmatrix}$

6. On the worksheet draw the position of the points A, B and C after a translation by one vector followed by another. In each case write down the co-ordinates of the image:

    (a) $A(1, 0)$ after a translation by the vector $\begin{pmatrix} 3 \\ 2 \end{pmatrix}$ followed by $\begin{pmatrix} 1 \\ 3 \end{pmatrix}$

    (b) $B(-2, 5)$ after a translation by the vector $\begin{pmatrix} -1 \\ -3 \end{pmatrix}$ followed by $\begin{pmatrix} 1 \\ 3 \end{pmatrix}$

    (c) $C(0, -2)$ after a translation by the vector $\begin{pmatrix} 3 \\ -2 \end{pmatrix}$ followed by $\begin{pmatrix} -4 \\ -1 \end{pmatrix}$

Enlargements

A transformation that changes the size of the object and thus also the position of an object is called an **enlargement**.

The enlargements you have met before have all had a scale factor that is a positive whole number. However scale factors can be negative and they can be less than one.

Consider these figures:

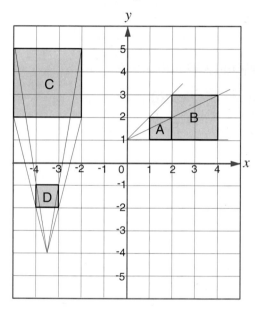

B is the enlargement of A by a scale factor 2 and centre of enlargement (0, 1) but A is half the size of B and so we can also say :

A is the enlargement of B by a scale factor $\frac{1}{2}$ and centre of enlargement (0, 1)

C is the enlargement of D by a scale factor 3 and centre of enlargement $(-3\frac{1}{2}, -4)$

but D is a third the size of C and so we can also say :

D is the enlargement of C by a scale factor $\frac{1}{3}$ and centre of enlargement $(-3\frac{1}{2}, -4)$

A fractional scale factor means that the lengths of the image are reduced.

Exercise 16.5

You will need the worksheet for this exercise

1.-4. On the worksheet you will see 4 pairs of quadrilaterals, an object *ABCD* and its image *A'B'C'D'*. For each pair join the corresponding vertices and hence find the centre of enlargement and the scale factor.

5.-8. Enlarge each of the shapes on the worksheet by the given scale factor and with the given centre of enlargement.

Transformations on a grid

A transformation is a general term for an application that transforms the original object onto its image.

A transformation can be a rotation, a reflection, a translation or an enlargement.

A transformation could be more than one of these:

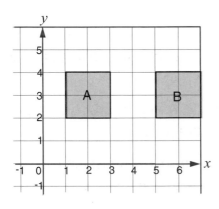

B is the image of A after either:

- a translation by the vector $\begin{pmatrix} 4 \\ 0 \end{pmatrix}$

- a reflection in the line $x = 4$

- a rotation of 180° about the point (4, 3)

- a rotation of 90° clockwise about the point (4, 1)

- a rotation of 90° anticlockwise about the point (4, 5)

To differentiate between these you may need to add letters:

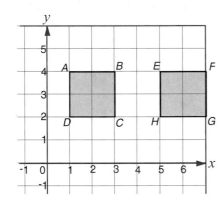

- *EFGH* is the image of *ABCD* after a translation by the vector $\begin{pmatrix} 4 \\ 0 \end{pmatrix}$

- *FEHG* is the image of *ABCD* after a reflection in the line $x = 4$

- *GHEF* is the image of *ABCD* after a rotation of 180° about the point (4, 3)

- *FGHE* is the image of *ABCD* after a rotation of 90° clockwise about the point (4, 1)

- *HEFG* is the image of *ABCD* after a rotation of 90° anticlockwise about the point (4, 5)

The order of the letters is important. If we compare the last three examples:

In the first rotation $A \rightarrow G$, $B \rightarrow H$, $C \rightarrow E$ and $D \rightarrow F$
In the second rotation $A \rightarrow F$, $B \rightarrow G$, $C \rightarrow H$ and $D \rightarrow E$
In the third rotation $A \rightarrow H$, $B \rightarrow E$, $C \rightarrow F$ and $D \rightarrow G$

Note the description of each transformation. It is important to describe these in full taking care not to miss out any piece of information.

A **reflection** *in* a *line*

A **translation** *by* a *vector*

An **enlargement** *by scale factor* and *centre of enlargement*

A **rotation** *through* an *angle*, *clockwise* or *anticlockwise*, *about* a *point.*

Exercise 16.6

1.

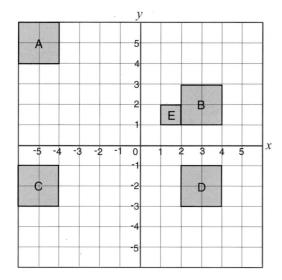

(a) Describe the reflection that maps A to C

(b) Describe the rotation that maps C to D

(c) Describe the translation that maps A to B

(d) Describe the enlargement that maps E to B

(e) Describe the enlargement that maps B to E

2. Describe as many single transformations as you can to map:

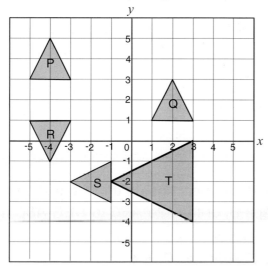

(a) P to R

(b) Q to P

(c) R to S

(d) S to T

(e) S to Q

3. Describe in full the single transformation that maps:

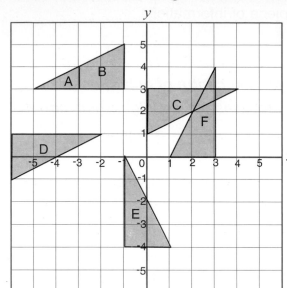

(a) C to D

(b) B to D

(c) A to B

(d) B to A

(e) C to F

(f) D to E

4. Describe in full the single transformation that maps:

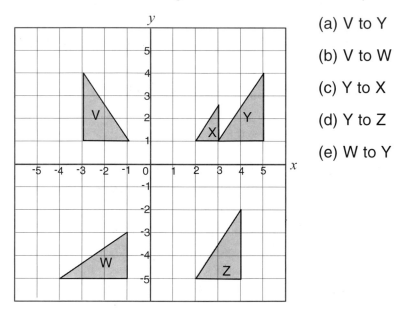

(a) V to Y

(b) V to W

(c) Y to X

(d) Y to Z

(e) W to Y

You will need the worksheet for the next six questions. In these questions instead of shape A mapping on to shape B, or triangle *ABC* to *DEF*, *ABC* maps on to $A_1B_1C_1$ and then to $A_2B_2C_2$.

5. (a) Draw a triangle *ABC* with vertices at *A*(−5, 1), *B*(−3, 5) and *C*(−1, 2)

   (b) Draw the image $A_1B_1C_1$, the rotation of *ABC* through 90° clockwise about (−5, 1)

   (c) Draw the image $A_2B_2C_2$, the rotation of $A_1B_1C_1$ through 180° about (0, 1)

   (d) Describe a single transformation that maps *ABC* onto $A_2B_2C_2$

6. (a) Draw a triangle *XYZ* with vertices at *X*(−3, −2), *Y*(−2, −4) and *Z*(−4, −4)

   (b) Draw the image $X_1Y_1Z_1$, the enlargement of *XYZ* by scale factor 2 and centre of enlargement (−6, −2)

   (c) Draw the image $X_2Y_2Z_2$, the enlargement of *XYZ* by scale factor 2 and centre of enlargement (−3, −5)

   (d) Describe a single transformation that maps $X_1Y_1Z_1$ onto $X_2Y_2Z_2$

7. (a) Draw a rhombus *PQRS* with vertices at *P*(4, 5), *Q*(6, 2), *R*(4, −1) and *S*(2, 2)

   (b) Draw the image $P_1Q_1R_1S_1$, the rotation of *PQRS* through 90° anticlockwise about (4, −3)

   (c) Draw the image $P_2Q_2R_2S_2$, the reflection of $P_1Q_1R_1S_1$ in the line $y = -x$

   (d) Describe a single transformation that maps *PQRS* onto $P_2S_2R_2Q_2$

8. (a) Draw a kite *ABCD* with vertices at *A*(−5, 2), *B*(−3, 4), *C*(1, 2) and *D*(−3, 0)

   (b) Draw the image $A_1B_1C_1D_1$, the reflection of *ABCD* in the line $y = x$

   (c) Draw the image $A_2B_2C_2D_2$, the rotation of *ABCD* through 90° clockwise about (−3, 0)

   (d) Describe a single transformation such that $A_1B_1C_1D_1$ maps onto $A_2D_2C_2B_2$

9. (a) Draw a square *KLMN* with vertices at *K*(3, 3), *L*(4, 2), *M*(3, 1) and *N*(2, 2)

   (b) Draw the image $K_1L_1M_1N_1$, the enlargement of *KLMN* by scale factor 2 and centre of enlargement (1, 2)

   (c) Draw the image $K_2L_2M_2N_2$, the translation of $K_1L_1M_1N_1$ by the vector $\begin{pmatrix} -4 \\ -2 \end{pmatrix}$

   (d) Describe a single transformation that maps $K_2L_2M_2N_2$ onto *KLMN*

10. (a) Draw a triangle *XYZ* with vertices at *X*(−2, 0), *Y*(−1, 2) and *Z*(1, 0)

   (b) Draw the image $X_1Y_1Z_1$, the enlargement of *XYZ* by scale factor 3 and centre of enlargement (−1, 1)

   (c) Draw the image $X_2Y_2Z_2$, the translation of *XYZ* by the vector $\begin{pmatrix} 0 \\ -4 \end{pmatrix}$

   (d) Describe a single transformation that maps $X_2Y_2Z_2$, onto $X_1Y_1Z_1$

Exercise 16.7: Extension questions
Finding a general rule for a transformation

When looking at vectors, it became apparent that there was a simple rule to find the image of a point *P* (*a*, *b*) after a translation by a vector $\begin{pmatrix} a \\ b \end{pmatrix}$

The image will be the point *P'*(*a* + *a*, *b* + *b*)

To find a rule for **other** transformations use the worksheet for this exercise.

There are two co-ordinate grids on the worksheet. The first has a triangle **A** with vertices at (4, 5), (5, 1) and (1, 2) and the second has a triangle **B** with vertices at (−5, 4), (−5, 1) and (−2, 2).

Draw the image of each triangle (A and B) after the following transformations:

1. A reflection in the *x*-axis   (Label the images A_1 and B_1)

2. A reflection in the *y*-axis   (Label the images A_2 and B_2)

3. A reflection in the line $y = x$ (Label the images A_3 and B_3)

4. A reflection in the line $y = -x$ (Label the images A_4 and B_4)

Now copy and complete the following table for your first transformation, a reflection in the *x*-axis, for both triangles A and B:

A	A_1	B	B_1
(4, 5)		(−5, 4)	
(5, 1)		(−5, 1)	
(1, 2)		(−2, 2)	
(*a*, *b*)		(*a*, *b*)	

By considering the co-ordinates of each image, you should be able to write down the co-ordinates of P' the image of any point $P(x, y)$ after a reflection in the x-axis.

Now make appropriate tables and find a rule for transformations 2, 3, and 4

Once you have done that you might like to take a fresh copy of the worksheet and try to find the rule for these:

5. A rotation through 90° clockwise about the origin.

6. A rotation through 180° about the origin.

7. A rotation through 270° clockwise about the origin.

8. A rotation through 90° anticlockwise about the origin.

9. An enlargement of scale factor 2 and centre of enlargement (0, 0)

10. Now investigate some further transformations and see if you can find any other rules. Here are some you might consider:
(a) A reflection in the line $x = 3$
(b) A reflection in the line $y = 2x + 1$
(c) A rotation through 90° clockwise about (1, 1)
(d) A rotation through 180° about (2, 1)
(e) An enlargement of scale factor 2 and centre of enlargement (1, −1)

Exercise 16.8: Summary exercise

Use the worksheet with this exercise.

1. On the worksheet you will see this shape with various mirror lines. Construct the image of the shape after a reflection in each mirror line.

2. On the worksheet you will see this shape:

Draw the image of the shape after:
(a) a rotation of 60° clockwise about point P on the worksheet.
(b) a rotation of 120° clockwise about P.
(c) a rotation of 60° anticlockwise about P.

3. (a) Write down the order of rotational symmetry of these shapes:

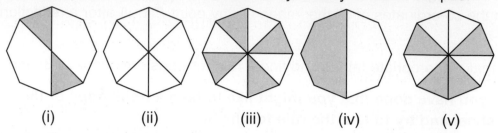

(i)   (ii)   (iii)   (iv)   (v)

    (b) Write down the number of lines of symmetry in each shape.

    (c) Draw a sixth octagon with rotational symmetry of order 2 but no lines of symmetry.

4. On the worksheet draw these vectors:

    (a) $\mathbf{A} = \begin{pmatrix} 4 \\ 1 \end{pmatrix}$ (b) $\mathbf{B} = \begin{pmatrix} 4 \\ -1 \end{pmatrix}$ (c) $\mathbf{C} = \begin{pmatrix} -4 \\ 0 \end{pmatrix}$ (d) $\mathbf{D} = \begin{pmatrix} 0 \\ -2 \end{pmatrix}$ (e) $\mathbf{E} = \begin{pmatrix} -1 \\ -5 \end{pmatrix}$

5. Describe in full the transformation that maps:

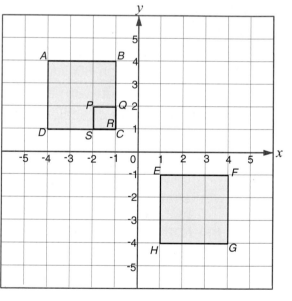

    (a) *ABCD* onto *EFGH*

    (b) *ABCD* onto *GHEF*

    (c) *ABCD* onto *GFEH*

    (d) *RSPQ* onto *CDAB*

6. Draw x and y-axes with values of x and y from −5 to 5. Draw the kite *ABCD*, which has vertices $A(1, 3)$, $B(3, 4)$, $C(4, 3)$ and $D(3, 2)$.

    (a) Draw the image $A_1 B_1 C_1 D_1$, the reflection of *ABCD* in the line $y = -x$

    (b) Draw the image $A_2 B_2 C_2 D_2$, the rotation of *ABCD* through 90° clockwise about the point (0, 2).

    (c) Describe the single transformation such that $A_1 B_1 C_1 D_1$ maps to $A_2 D_2 C_2 B_2$.

End of chapter 16 activity: Hexaflexagons

A hexaflexagon is a paper hexagon made from a strip of paper. When you flex the hexaflexagon the faces change, just like magic!

This is how you make the simplest hexaflexagon:

Step 1:   Construct an equilateral triangle with sides of four centimetres. Now add to it so you have a row of 10 triangles and colour them like the strip below:

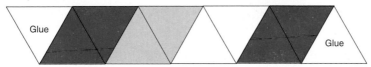

Step 2:   Fold the strip over and colour the other side like this:

Step 3:   Now fold the strip along the lines so that each pair of coloured triangles lies on top of each other. Glue together the two triangles marked Glue. You will now have a pink hexagon on one side and a white hexagon on the other.

Pinch together and down two adjacent triangular sections with a crack between them. Push the opposite corner under and down. Then, open the flexagon from the centre:

Your red hexagon will now appear!

Now you have made your first flexagon you can go on to make a hexahexaflexagon. This is made from a row of 19 triangles: Colour it like pattern A below, then fold it as in diagrams B, C, and D on the next page.

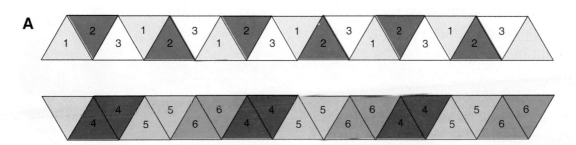

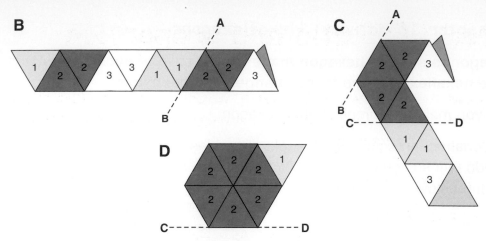

The flexagon flexes just as before. See if you can find all 6 coloured faces.

The tritetraflexagon

The tritetraflexagon is a variation on a hexaflexagon but made from squares. It is folded from a strip of seven squares of paper like this:

Fold this so that all the white squares are hidden and glue the two marked squares together. Now you have a square that is red on one side and pink on the other. To find the white square fold the red square in half on one centre line and then open it up again from the pink side.

Hexaflexagons are used by mathematicians to send each other secret pictures or notes, or even love letters! They were invented in 1939 when an English student at Princeton University called Arthur H. Stone trimmed an inch from his American notebook sheets to fit his English binder. After folding the trimmed-off strips for amusement, he came upon the first hexaflexagon. Martin Gardner wrote about hexaflexagons for the magazine 'Scientific American' and you can find out more about them in his book *Mathematical Puzzles and Diversions*.

Chapter 17: Ratio and proportion

When we looked at enlargement in Chapter 16 we considered the effect of the scale factor. Now we are going to look more closely at what happens to the area and volume of enlargements.

Comparing area and volume

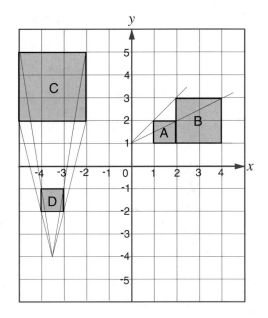

Let's look once again at the original enlargements we first saw on page 339 in chapter 16:

B is the enlargement of A by a scale factor 2 and centre of enlargement (0, 1)

A has an area of 1 square unit and B has an area of 4 square units.

C is the enlargement of D by a scale factor 3 and centre of enlargement $(-3\frac{1}{2}, -4)$

D has an area of 1 square unit and C has an area of 9 square units.

What we can see is that the **area of the image is increased by the square of the scale factor of the enlargement**.

This is true for any enlargement:

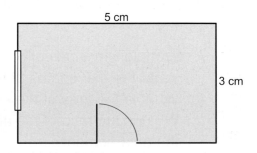

Here is a drawing of my bedroom drawn to a scale of 1:100

The drawing measures 5 cm by 3 cm and so has an area of 15 cm²

The bedroom measures 5 m by 3 m (500 cm by 300 cm) and has area 15 m² (150 000 cm²).

The ratio of the lengths is 1 : 100
The ratio of the areas is 1 : 10 000 (100²).

Exercise 17.1

1. A square of side 3 cm is enlarged by scale factor 2
    (a) What are the lengths of the sides of the enlargement?
    (b) What is the area of the enlargement?
    (c) What is the ratio of the area of the original square to the area of the enlargement?

2. A square of side 4 cm is enlarged by scale factor 3
    (a) What are the lengths of the sides of the enlargement?
    (b) What is the area of the enlargement?
    (c) What is the ratio of the area of the original square to the area of the enlargement?

3. A square of side 3 cm is enlarged by scale factor 4
    (a) What are the lengths of the sides of the enlargement?
    (b) What is the area of the enlargement?
    (c) What is the ratio of the area of the original square to the area of the enlargement?

4. A square of side 2 cm is enlarged by scale factor of $\frac{1}{2}$
    (a) What are the lengths of the sides of the enlargement?
    (b) What is the area of the enlargement?
    (c) What is the ratio of the area of the original square to the area of the enlargement?

5. A rectangle with sides of 3 cm and 4 cm is enlarged by scale factor 2
    (a) What are the lengths of the sides of the enlarged rectangle?
    (b) What is the area of the enlargement?
    (c) What is the ratio of the area of the original rectangle to the area of the enlargement?

6. A rectangle with sides of 5 cm and 6 cm is enlarged by scale factor 3
    (a) What are the lengths of the sides of the enlarged rectangle?
    (b) What is the area of the enlargement?
    (c) What is the ratio of the area of the original rectangle to the area of the enlargement?

7. A triangle of base 8 cm and height 5 cm is enlarged by scale factor 3
   (a) What is the base and the height of the enlarged triangle?
   (b) What is the area of the enlargement?
   (c) What is the ratio of the area of the original triangle to the area of the enlargement?

8. A right-angled triangle with perpendicular sides of lengths 6 cm and 8 cm is enlarged by scale factor 4
   (a) What is the length of the hypotenuse of the enlargement?
   (b) What is the area of the enlargement?
   (c) What is the ratio of the area of the original triangle to the area of the enlargement?

9. This kite is enlarged by scale factor 4
   What is the area of the enlargement?

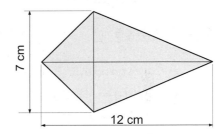

10. This trapezium is enlarged by scale factor 3
    What is the area of the enlargement?

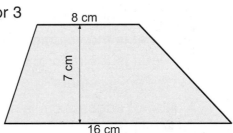

11. The ratio of the areas of two squares is 1 : 4
    If the smaller square has sides of 3 cm, what are the lengths of the sides of the larger square?

12. The ratio of the areas of two squares is 1 : 9
    If the smaller square has sides of 2 cm, what are the lengths of the sides of the larger square?

Volumes of enlargements

Consider this cube and the enlargement of the cube by a scale factor 3:

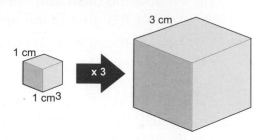

The **sides** of the enlarged cube will all be 3 cm.
The **area** of each face of the enlargement will be 9 cm².
The **volume** of the enlargement will be 27 cm³.

The ratio of the volume of the original to the volume of the enlargement is:
     1 : 27 (1 : 3³)

Exercise 17.2

1.   A cube of volume 1 cm³ is enlarged by scale factor 2
    (a) What is the volume of the enlarged cube?
    (b) What is the ratio of the volume of the original cube to the volume of the enlargement?

2.   A cube of volume 2 cm³ is enlarged by scale factor 2
    (a) What is the volume of the enlarged cube?
    (b) What is the ratio of the volume of the original cube to the volume of the enlargement?

3.   A cube of edges 2 cm is enlarged by scale factor 3
    (a) What is the volume of the original cube?
    (b) What is the volume of the enlarged cube?
    (c) What is the ratio of the volume of the original cube to the volume of the enlargement?

4.   A cuboid of volume 5 cm³ is enlarged by scale factor 3
    (a) What is the volume of the enlarged cuboid?
    (b) What is the ratio of the volume of the original cuboid to the volume of the enlargement?

5.   A cube has been enlarged by scale factor 4
    The enlarged cube has a volume of 192 cm³. What is the volume of the original cube?

6.   A cuboid has been enlarged by scale factor 2
    The enlarged cuboid has a volume of 192 cm³. What is the volume of the original cuboid?

More questions on area and volume

In general terms we can say that, if an object is enlarged by a scale factor k

> The lengths of the image are enlarged by scale factor k
> The area of the image is enlarged by scale factor k^2
> The volume of the image is enlarged by scale factor k^3

> Examples:
>
> 1. A square of side 4 cm is enlarged by scale factor 5
>   What is the area of the enlarged square?
>
> $$\text{Scale factor } k = 5$$
> $$\text{Area scale factor } k^2 = 25$$
> $$\text{Area of image} = 25 \times \text{area of object}$$
> $$= 25 \times 16$$
> $$= 400 \text{ cm}^2$$
>
> 2. A model shed is made to a scale of $\frac{1}{20}$th of the original.
>   (a) If the height of the model is 12 cm, what is the height of the original?
>
> $$\text{Scale factor } k = 20$$
> $$\text{Height of original} = 20 \times \text{height of model}$$
> $$= 20 \times 12$$
> $$= 240 \text{ cm} = 2.4 \text{ m}$$
>
> Height of original shed is 2.4 m
>
> (b) If the volume of the original is 45 m³, what is the volume of the model?
>
> $$\text{Volume scale factor} = k^3 = 8000$$
> $$\text{Volume of original} = 30 \text{ m}^3 = 30\,000\,000 \text{ cm}^3$$
> $$\text{Volume of original} = k^3 \times \text{volume of model}$$
> $$30\,000\,000 = 8\,000 \times \text{volume of model}$$
> $$\text{Volume of model} = \frac{30\,000\,000}{8000}$$
> $$= 3750 \text{ cm}^3$$
>
> Volume of model is 3750 cm³

Exercise 17.3

1. On the worksheet you will find a plan of a study bedroom drawn to a scale of 1 : 25
   (a) Fill in the scale details at the top of the sheet.
   (b) Write down the real life measurements of:
      (i) length and width of the desk.
      (ii) length and width of the bed.
      (iii) length of the radiator.
   (c) Calculate the real life floor area of:
      (i) the desk.
      (ii) the bed.
      (iii) the wardrobe.
   (d) Carpet costs £15 per square metre. Calculate the cost of carpeting the room, including the bathroom.
   (e) I have been given a rug 1.5 m by 2 m. Draw the rug on the floor plan of the bedroom.
   (f) The bookcase is 1 m high. Calculate the volume of the real bookcase.
   (g) The volume of the real room is 45 m³. Calculate the height of the real room.

2. I have a model of a water tower. My model is exactly one hundredth of the height of the original tower.
   (a) If my model is 5 cm tall how tall is the original tower?
   (b) If the original tower contains 250 cubic metres of water, what volume of water is contained in my model? Give your answer in cubic cm.
   (c) If the water tower is in the shape of a cylinder, estimate its radius.

3. Here is a family of jugs. Each is an exact enlargement of the smallest jug:

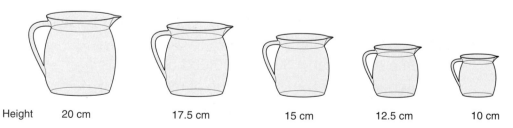

| Height | 20 cm | 17.5 cm | 15 cm | 12.5 cm | 10 cm |

   (a) If the smallest jug contains 0.25 litres, what volume will each of the other jugs contain?
   (b) What height of jug would have a volume of one litre?

4. I am making a model of a water tower. The actual water tower is in the shape of a cylinder and has a diameter of 10 m. It contains 200 m³ of water. My model is being made to a scale of 1 cm to 1 m.
    (a) How tall is the real water tower?
    (b) How tall is my model?
    (c) What will be the volume of my model?
    (d) What is the curved surface area of the real water tower?
    (e) What is the curved surface area of the model?

5. 'Superclean' fluid comes in two sizes, a small container for domestic use and a large drum for commercial use. The large drum is an enlargement of the small drum, by a scale factor of 10

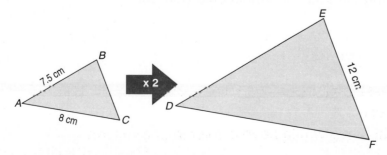

    (a) If the label on the large drum has an area of 45 000 cm², what is the area of the label on the small drum?
    (b) If the height of the small drum is 12 cm, what is the height of the large drum?
    (c) If the large drum contains 1.5 m³, how many litres does the small drum contain?

Exercise 17.4 – Finding missing lengths

1. Triangle *DEF* is an enlargement of triangle *ABC* by scale factor 2
    Copy the diagram and fill in all the missing dimensions:

2. Triangle *XYZ* is an enlargement of triangle *PQR* by scale factor 3
Copy the diagram and fill in all the missing lengths, including *PQ* and *XY*,
and find the area of triangle *PQR*:

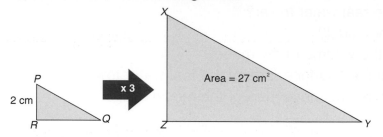

3. *XYZ* is an enlargement of *ABC*. Find the scale factor of the enlargement
and hence the lengths *AB* and *YZ*.

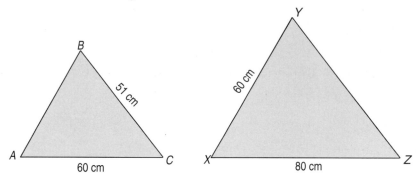

4. In this enlargement the area of the object is given. This should help you
to find the missing dimensions.

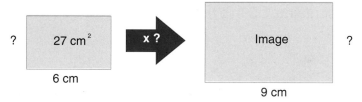

What is the ratio of the area of the object to the area of the image?

5. Find the missing dimensions in this enlargement:

More ratio questions: Proportion

Treating the ratio 2 : 5 as a fraction $\frac{2}{5}$ can be the simplest way of solving ratio questions.

If two quantities are in the ratio 2 : 5, then the smaller is always $\frac{2}{5}$ of the larger.

If the larger is 10 the smaller is $\frac{2}{5}$ of 10 = 4

If the larger is 15 the smaller is $\frac{2}{5}$ of 15 = 6

Some questions about quantities that are in the same proportion do not immediately present as ratio questions but can also be solved in this way.

Exercise 17.5

Give non-exact answers correct to 2 decimal places.

Example:
1 kg is equivalent to 2.2 lb.
How many kg are equivalent to 5 lb.?

Let x be the no. of kg equivalent to 5 lb.

$$\frac{1}{2.2} = \frac{x}{5}$$

$$\frac{5 \times 1}{2.2} = x$$

$$x = 2.2727 \ldots$$
$$= 2.27 \text{ (to 2 d.p.)}$$

---

1. I can buy 15 packets of crisps for £1.20
   How many packets can I buy for £1.68?

2. Four of my hand spans make 60 cm. How many hand spans will I need to make 2 m?

3. 13 feet are equal to 4 metres. How many feet are there in 7 metres?

4. I sell 4 dozen cakes for a total of £6.00
   How much should I sell a pack of 5 cakes for?

5. To cook rice, you add two cups of rice to seven cups of water. How many cups of water will I need for five cups of rice?

6. If 77 000 people form 88% of the local electorate, how many people make up the remaining 12%?

7. 3 crates of oranges weigh 720 kg. How much do 8 crates of oranges weigh?

8. My bicycle is geared in the ratio 1 : 3   One turn of the pedals turns the wheels round 3 times. The circumference of the wheel is 210 cm.
(a) How far does the bicycle go in one turn of the pedals?
(b) How many turns of the pedals do I need to go 1 km?

9. A metal alloy is made up of tin and copper in the ratio 2 : 7
If I have 14 g of tin, how many grams of the alloy will I make?

10. Three children are left some money in their grandfather's will. The money is in proportion to their ages:
Alf receives £495, Bertha £315 and little Charlie £270
Charlie is 12 years old. How old are Bertha and Alf?

Exercise 17.6: Extension questions – More area and volume

Many of the questions in this exercise are not difficult, but need some thought. Use what you have learnt about proportion and ratio to solve them and set out all your working clearly.

1. Write down which of these shapes will always be in proportion regardless of their dimensions:
(a) a pair of cones.
(b) a pair of cylinders.
(c) a pair of spheres.
(d) a pair of square based pyramids.
(e) a pair of regular tetrahedra.

2. A large metal sphere is melted down and used to make several smaller spheres of radius $\frac{1}{5}$ the length of the radius of the original sphere. How many little spheres can be made?

3. A sphere T has a volume of V cm³ , surface area A cm² and radius r cm.

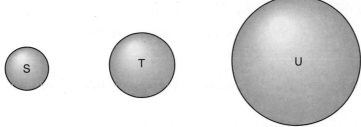

(a) What is the surface area and volume of sphere U with radius $2r$?

(b) What are the surface area and volume of sphere S with radius $\frac{2}{3}r$?

(c) (i) Give the ratio   Surface area of S : Surface area of U

     (ii) Give the ratio   Volume of S : Volume of U

4. A cone is divided into three parts of equal height:

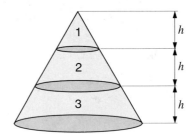

(a) If the area of the base of the top cone 1 is A, what is the area of the base of the whole cone?

(b) What is the ratio of:

area of base of cone 1 : area of base of whole cone?

(c) Parts 1 and 2 together make a middle-sized cone. What is the area of the base of this cone?

What is the ratio of:

area of base of cone 1 : area of base of cone 2 : area of base of cone 3?

(d) If the volume of the top cone 1 is V, find the volumes of the middle-sized cone and the whole cone.

(e) What is the ratio of: volume of cone 1 : volume of cones 1 + 2 (middle-sized cone) : volume of cones 1 + 2 + 3 (whole cone)?

(f) What is the ratio of:

volume of cone 1 : volume of cone 2 : volume of cone 3?

5. The formula for the volume of a square based pyramid of side x and height h is: $V = \frac{1}{3}x^2h$

(a) Calculate the volume of a pyramid with a square base of side 4 cm and height 6 cm.

(b) Write down the volume of a similar pyramid:

     (i) 12 cm high.

     (ii) 36 cm high.

Exercise 17.7: Summary exercise

1. A square of side 2 cm is enlarged by scale factor 5
   (a) What are the lengths of the sides of the enlargement?
   (b) What is the area of the enlargement?
   (c) What is the ratio of the area of the original square to the area of the enlargement?

2. A cube of sides 3 cm is enlarged by scale factor 2
   (a) What is the volume of the original cube?
   (b) What is the volume of the enlarged cube?
   (c) What is the ratio of the volume of the original cube to the volume of the enlargement?

3. A cube has been enlarged by scale factor 5
   The enlarged cube has a volume of 750 cm³. What is the volume of the original cube?

4. Find the value of k and hence find x, y, and z in this enlargement.

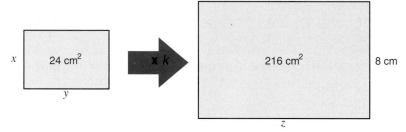

5. If £10 is worth 14 Euros:
   (a) how many Euros will I get for £25?
   (b) how many £s will I get for 40 Euros?

6. A cone has a smaller cone cut off its tip. The small cone has height one quarter the height of the whole cone.
   (a) If the smaller cone has height h cm, what is the height of the whole cone?
   (b) If the small cone has a surface area of A cm², what is the surface area of the whole cone?
   (c) Find the ratio of the volume of the small cone to volume of the original cone and hence the ratio of the volume of the small cone to the volume of the remaining piece.

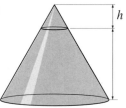

End of chapter 17 activity: Fibonacci and the Golden ratio

Artists use mathematics to develop pleasing ratios for art and architecture. The most famous of these dates back to at least the time of the Ancient Egyptians and is known as the **Golden ratio.**

The Greeks used the Golden ratio when designing and building the Parthenon. They stated the ratio as: 'the small is to the large, as the large is to the whole.'

The façade of the Parthenon is built so that the ratio of the height to the width is the same as the ratio of the width to the width plus the height – it is a Golden rectangle.

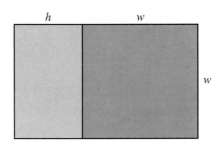

$$h : w = w : w + h$$

The Golden rectangle

Have you ever wondered why photographs are usually rectangles that are a little longer than they are wide?

Look at the following rectangles and decide which one has the shape that you like most:

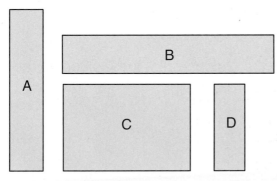

You probably chose rectangle C – it is a Golden rectangle.

If the short side is 1 unit, the long side is 1.618 units, the ratio of the long side to the sum of the sides is 1.618 to 2.618 which simplifies to 1 : 1.618

The ratio of the lengths of the sides of a Golden rectangle is therefore 1 : 1.618

The Golden spiral

Draw a rectangle 10 cm by 16.2 cm
Mark out a square in the rectangle, as
shown. The part of the rectangle remaining
will be a golden rectangle.

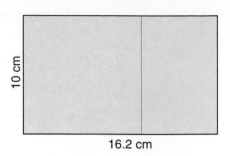

10 cm

16.2 cm

Now draw another line to make a square in
the new rectangle. Go on doing this until you
reach the stage as shown.

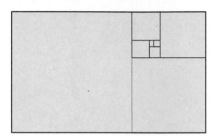

If you now draw a quarter of a circle in
each square, you will get a Golden spiral.

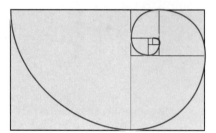

This spiral is the same as the shape of
the nautilus shell.

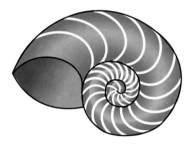

What do think the connection is between the Golden ratio, the Golden spiral
and the Fibonacci sequence 1, 1, 2, 3, 5, 8, 13, 21 etc?

Firstly, draw squares in the Fibonacci sequence so that they make the spiral as we saw on the previous page:

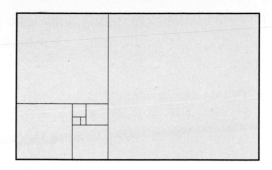

We can explore the ratios of the sides of the rectangles by dividing the length by the width, or each number in the sequence by the one before. When we do this we get the following series of numbers:

$$\frac{1}{1} = 1 \qquad \frac{2}{1} = 2 \qquad \frac{3}{2} = 1{\cdot}5 \qquad \frac{5}{3} = 1{\cdot}666 \ldots$$

$$\frac{8}{5} = 1{\cdot}6 \qquad \frac{13}{8} = 1{\cdot}625 \qquad \frac{21}{13} = 1{\cdot}61\ 538 \ldots$$

It is easier to see what is happening if we plot the ratios on a grid:

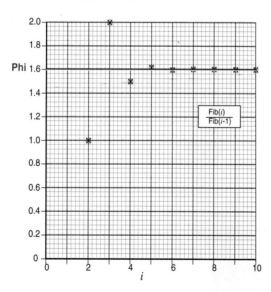

You can see that the results seem to be settling down to a particular value: **1·618** (or 1·618 034 to be more exact). You will recognise this as **the Golden ratio**.

The Golden ratio is often represented by the Greek letter **phi**.

Fibonacci numbers, the Golden ratio and the Golden spiral often occur in nature, as we saw with the nautilus shell. Here are some other places you could look:

- Petals on flowers
  Find some pictures of flowers and count their petals. How many have the same number as one of the Fibonacci numbers?

- Seed heads (poppies, sunflowers)

- Pine cones

- Some common trees which have a Fibonacci leaf arrangement (e.g. **1/2** elm, lime; **1/3** beech, blackberry; **2/5** oak, holly; **3/8** poplar, willow; **5/13** almond)

Are you a golden child?

Measure your height.

Now measure the distance from the floor to your navel.

If the ratio:
height : height of navel
is
1.618 : 1
then you are a golden child!

Chapter 18: Introducing trigonometry

What is trigonometry

When we studied Pythagoras' theorem, we saw that there was a fixed relationship between the lengths of the sides of a right-angled triangle. Trigonometry takes this a stage further and is the branch of mathematics that deals with the relationships between the sides and angles of triangles.

The history of trigonometry goes back first to ancient Babylon, where the angle was divided into 360 degrees, and then into smaller sixtieths, called minutes, and then again into seconds.

Trigonometry was then taken further by the ancient Egyptians. Have you ever wondered how they managed to design the pyramids? Well, they used trigonometry!

There are many mysteries surrounding the pyramids and their construction. One amazing achievement was that because the Egyptians were able to calculate with such precision, they could design the pyramids so that the mystical stars shone directly into the royal burial chambers:

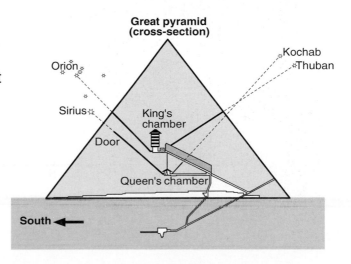

The earliest applications of trigonometry were in the fields of navigation, surveying and astronomy. Nowadays we also use applications of trigonometry in physics, chemistry and in almost all branches of engineering.

Simple trigonometry uses the relationship between the size of an angle and the lengths of the sides in a right-angled triangle.

Look at these right-angle triangles, all of base 5 cm:

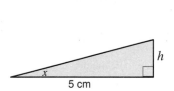 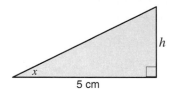 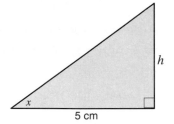

You can see that as the angle marked x increases, so the height of the triangle increases. There would appear to be a relationship between the size of the angle and the lengths of the sides of the triangle.

Exercise 18.1

1. (a) Draw a large right-angled triangle *ABC* in your book, with the right-angle at *B*. It does not matter what size the other two angles are. In fact for this investigation it is a good idea if everybody in the class draws different shapes of triangles.

    (b) Now divide your triangle into smaller triangles like this:

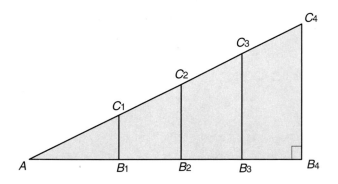

2. Draw a table like this :

Triangle	AB	BC	$\frac{BC}{AB}$	angle BAC
AB_1C_1				
AB_2C_2				
AB_3C_3				
AB_4C_4				

Fill in the *AB* and *BC* columns by measuring the lines in your drawing.

3. Calculate *BC* ÷ *AB*. If you have measured accurately, all the values in this column will be the same.

4. Measure the angle *BAC*.

5. To investigate the relationship between *BC* and *AB* you will need a scientific calculator. When you turn it on make sure that the memory is clear and that it is in DEGREE mode (shown by the word DEG at the top of the display). If it is not in this mode change it using the mode buttons.

The ratio we are investigating is known as the TANGENT of an angle – find the TAN (or tan) button on your calculator. If you have a new style DAL calculator, press the TAN (or tan) button and then enter the size of the angle you measured. If you have an older style calculator, enter the angle first and then enter TAN.

In either case, the figure that you have should be about the same as your ratio $\frac{BC}{AB}$.

If it is not, check it again or ask your teacher.

Terminology

When looking at the sides of a right-angled triangle we need to relate them to a marked angle. The angle here is marked with an arc. You are familiar with the **hypotenuse** – the longest side, opposite the right-angle. The side opposite the marked angle is the **opposite** and the side touching the right-angle and the marked angle is the **adjacent.** The sides of the triangle can then be marked H, O and A to determine which is which.

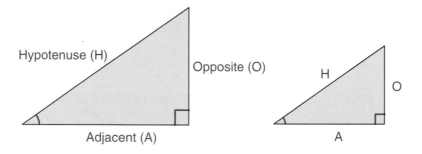

In the right-angled triangle *ABC*:

$$\text{Tangent of angle } A = \frac{\text{opposite side}}{\text{adjacent side}}$$

$$\text{or } \tan A = \frac{\text{opp}}{\text{adj}}$$

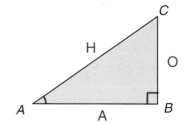

There are two principal trigonometric relationships (ratios): the tangent and the sine. The tangent is notably related to **gnomonics**, the science of sundials. The tangent, in particular, relates to the shade that a gnomon (a pole fixed perpendicularly on a vertical wall) projects onto a wall for a given height of the sun.

Calculating the tangent

Use your calculator to find the tangents of various angles. Give your answers to three significant figures:

> Example: Find the tangent of 30°
>
> $$tan\ 30° = 0.57\ 735\ ...$$
> $$= 0.577\ (to\ 3\ s.f.)$$

Exercise 18.2

Use your calculator to find the tangents of these angles. Give your answer to 3 s.f.

1.	60°	**5.**	20°	**9.**	72.5°
2.	45°	**6.**	27.5°	**10.**	5°
3.	80°	**7.**	65°	**11.**	33.35°
4.	15°	**8.**	67.5°	**12.**	43.71°

Calculating the angle

If you know the tangent and need to find the angle, use the second function on your calculator marked tan^{-1} or possibly 'inverse tan'.

> Example:
>
> Find the angle whose tangent is 1.37
>
> Give your answer to one decimal place:
>
> $$tan\ x = 1.37$$
> $$x = 53.873\ ...$$
> $$= 53.9°\ (to\ 1\ d.p.)$$

Exercise 18.3

Use your calculator to find the angles whose tangents are given below, giving your answers to 1 d.p.

1.	1.5	**5.**	0.5	**9.**	4.5
2.	2.3	**6.**	1.75	**10.**	88.9
3.	0.72	**7.**	0.89	**11.**	0.05
4.	0.14	**8.**	0.37	**12.**	0.32

Finding the opposite side

We can calculate the tangent of an angle by using a formula. We can use our calculators to help us. When using a formula remember to follow the steps we learned in *So you really want to learn Maths* Book 1:

> Write the **formula**
> **substitute** known values
> **calculate**
> write the **answer**
> and remember the **units**.

Remember, you should always draw a diagram. Label the hypotenuse with H, and then label the opposite and adjacent sides with O and A, just as we did when we solved problems using Pythagoras' theorem. This may seem unnecessary now, but it is a good habit to get into and you will find it very useful once the problems become more challenging.

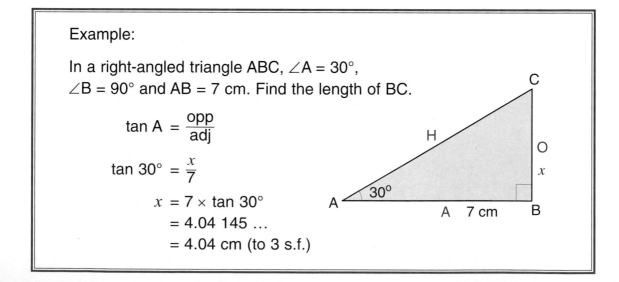

Example:

In a right-angled triangle ABC, $\angle A = 30°$, $\angle B = 90°$ and AB = 7 cm. Find the length of BC.

$$\tan A = \frac{opp}{adj}$$

$$\tan 30° = \frac{x}{7}$$

$$x = 7 \times \tan 30°$$
$$= 4.04\,145 \ldots$$
$$= 4.04 \text{ cm (to 3 s.f.)}$$

Exercise 18.4

Find the side indicated by a letter in the following questions. Always start by drawing the diagram and labelling the sides H, O and A. Give your answers correct to 3 significant figures:

1.

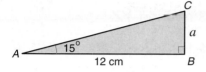

2.

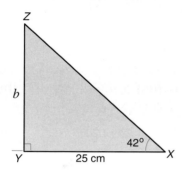

3.

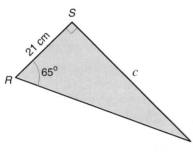

4.

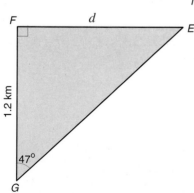

5.

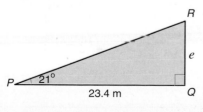

6.

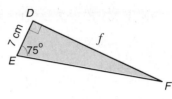

7.

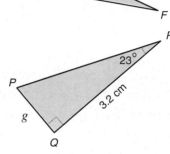

8.

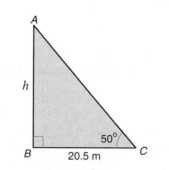

9.

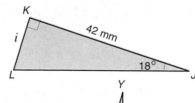

10.

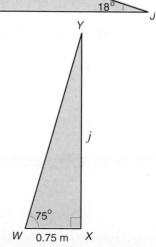

In the next five questions it is important to draw the triangle first, taking care when labelling the sides H, O and A.

11. In $\triangle ABC$, $\angle A = 42°$, $\angle B = 90°$ and $AB = 7.2$ cm. Find BC.

12. In $\triangle DEF$, $\angle D = 83°$, $\angle F = 90°$ and $DF = 105$ m. Find EF.

13. In $\triangle XYZ$, $\angle Z = 90°$, $\angle X = 42°$ and $XZ = 53$ m. Find YZ.

14. In $\triangle PQR$, $\angle P = 21°$, $\angle R = 90°$ and $PR = 4.1$ m. Find QR.

15. In $\triangle STU$, $\angle S = 90°$, $\angle U = 71°$ and $SU = 37$ m. Find ST.

Finding the adjacent side

The simplest way to calculate the adjacent side is first to calculate the third angle of the triangle and then use that as the marked angle. You can then label your triangle O, A and H as before. Alternatively you can use the method below:

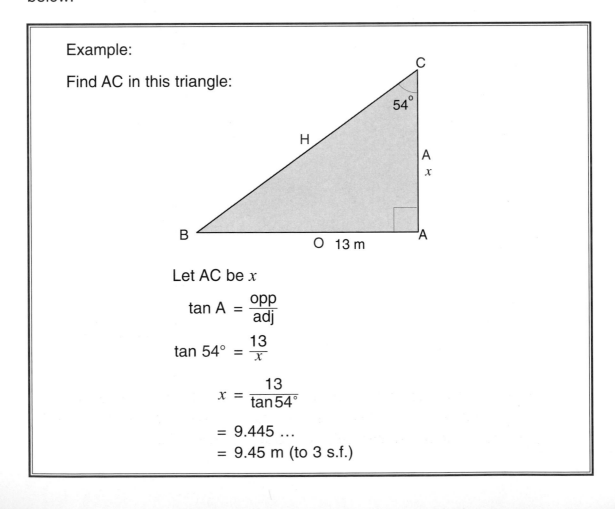

Example:

Find AC in this triangle:

Let AC be x

$$\tan A = \frac{\text{opp}}{\text{adj}}$$

$$\tan 54° = \frac{13}{x}$$

$$x = \frac{13}{\tan 54°}$$

$$= 9.445 \ldots$$
$$= 9.45 \text{ m (to 3 s.f.)}$$

Exercise 18.5

Find the side indicated by a letter in the following questions. Always start by drawing the diagram and labelling the sides O, A and H. Give your answers correct to 3 significant figures:

1.

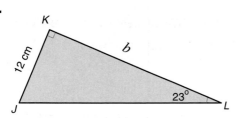

5.

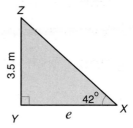

2.

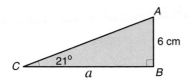

6.

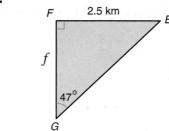

3.

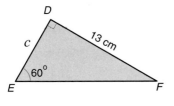

7.

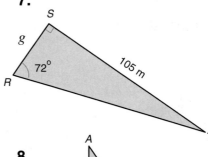

4.

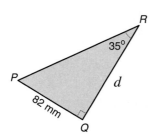

8.

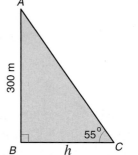

The remainder of the questions in this exercise are mixed. Sometimes, the side marked is the opposite side and sometimes it is the adjacent side. It is particularly important to take care when labelling O, A and H.

9.

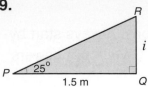

12.

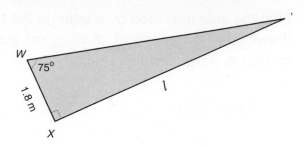

10.

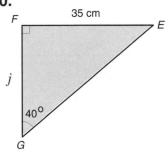

13.

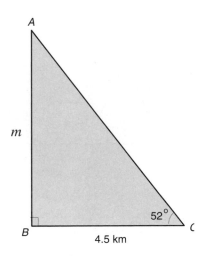

11.

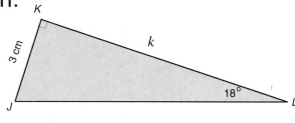

14.

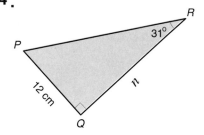

In the next 4 questions it is important to draw the triangle first, and again to take care when labelling the sides H, O and A.

15. In △ *ABC*, ∠*A* = 75°, ∠*B* = 90° and *AB* = 25 cm. Find *BC*.

16. In △ *DEF*, ∠*D* = 17°, ∠*F* = 90° and *EF* = 6 m. Find *DF*.

17. In △ *XYZ*, ∠*Z* = 90°, ∠*X* = 67° and *YZ* = 3.2 km. Find *XZ*.

18. In △ *PQR*, ∠*P* = 17°, ∠*R* = 90° and *PR* = 12 m. Find *QR*.

Finding the angle

Remember to use the second function on your calculator to find the angle:

Example:

Find ∠B in this triangle, giving your answer correct to 1 d.p.

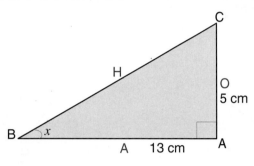

$$\tan \angle B = \frac{\text{opp}}{\text{adj}}$$

$$\tan \angle B = \frac{5}{13}$$

$$\angle B = 21.0375 \ldots$$
$$= 21.0° \text{ (to 1 d.p.)}$$

Exercise 18.6

Find the angle indicated by a letter in these questions. Always start by drawing the diagram and labelling the sides *O, A* and *H*. Give your answers correct to 1 decimal place:

1.

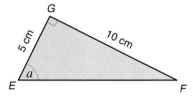

2.

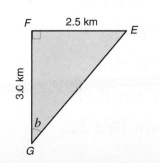

3.

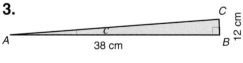

4.

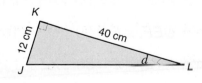

5.

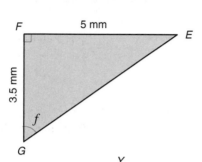

6.

7.

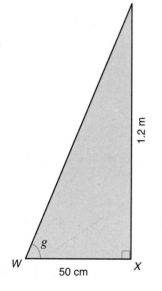

8.

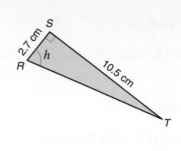

9.

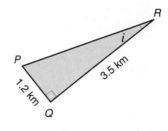

10.

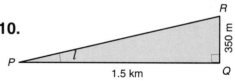

11. In △ *ABC*, ∠*B* = 90°, *AB* = 2 cm and *BC* = 5 cm. Find ∠*A*.

12. In △ *DEF*, ∠*F* = 90°, *DF* = 16 m and *EF* = 25 m. Find ∠*D*.

13. In △ *XYZ*, ∠*Z* = 90°, *XZ* = 1.2 km and *XY* = 600 m. Find ∠*X*.

14. In △ *PQR*, ∠*R* = 90°, *PR* = 25 mm and *QR* = 37 mm. Find ∠*P*.

15. In △ *ABC*, ∠*A* = 90°, *AB* = 12 km and *AC* = 25 km. Find ∠*C*.

Angles of elevation and depression

If you are standing some distance from a tall object such as a building or a tree, the angle between the line of sight to the top of the object and the ground is called the 'angle of elevation':

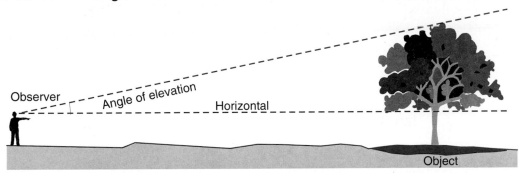

If you are standing above an object, when on top of a cliff for example, the angle between the line of sight and the horizontal is known as the 'angle of depression':

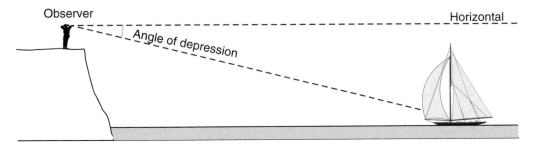

Exercise 18.7

To solve the following problems you will first have to draw a diagram. Make sure it is a simple, clear 2-dimensional diagram. Label it with all the information that you are given. Carefully label H, O and A and then, and only then, try to solve the problem.

Give non-exact answers correct to 3 significant figures.

Example:

The angle of elevation of the top of a building 12 m away is 65°.
Calculate the height of the building, to 3 significant figures:

$$\tan A = \frac{\text{opp}}{\text{adj}}$$

$$\tan 65° = \frac{x}{12}$$

$$x = 12 \times \tan 65°$$
$$= 25.73\,408\,...$$
$$= 25.7 \text{ m (to 3 s.f.)}$$

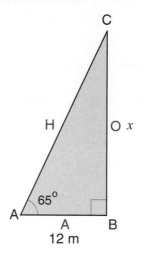

1. The angle of elevation of the top of a flagpole from a point 50 m away from its base on horizontal ground is 5°. How tall is the flagpole?

2. The angle of elevation of the top of a tree from a point 45 m away on horizontal ground is 9°. Calculate the height of the tree.

3. From a point on a cliff 17 m above sea level the angle of depression of a yacht is 12°. How far is the yacht from the base of the cliff?

4. A plane at *A* is flying 500 m above the ground. The angle of depression of a point *C* is 45° and of a point *B* is 23°. Calculate the distance between *B* and *C*.

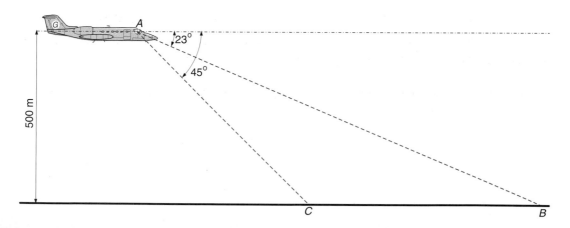

5. A line passes through the points *A*(3, 5) and *B*(−2, 9). Find the angle the line makes with the *x*-axis.

6. Draw a sketch of the line *y* = 3*x* + 2, carefully showing where it crosses the *x*-axis and the *y*-axis. Calculate the angle the line makes with the *y*-axis.

Exercise 18.8: Extension questions

The word tangent comes from the Latin *tangere* – to touch, and is the same word that is used to describe the line that touches the circumference of a circle:

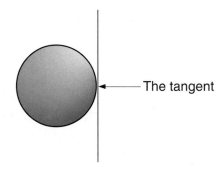

The tangent

The early use of trigonometry in astronomy is understandable if you think about the link with circles or the celestial spheres.

Let us put more detail into our circle:

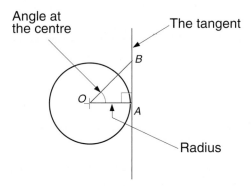

We have used a calculator to work out the answers to various problems, but early mathematicians had to work out tables of values. They built up their tables using the diagram above and taking the length of the radius as 60 units.

1. Without using a calculator and using the diagram above work out the length of *AB* when the angle at the centre is 45°.

2. Draw a circle of radius 60 mm. Draw a tangent to the circle. By careful drawing and measurement, complete this table of values:

Angle *AOB*	*AB*	$\dfrac{AB}{60}$
15°		
30°		
45°		
60°		
75°		

3. The third column gives the tangent.
What do you think will be the tangent of (i) 85° (ii) 89° (iii) 90°?

4. Draw a graph of the tangent against the angle and then, from your graph, find the tangents of these angles:

(a) 20°   (b) 55°   (c) 65°   (d) 80°

5. Now check your answers with your calculator. How accurate were you?

Exercise 18.9: Summary exercise

Give non-exact answers to 3 significant figures, unless instructed otherwise.

1. Find the values of these:
(a) tan 24°   (b) tan 52°   (c) tan 72°

2. Find x when:
(a) tan x = 0.6   (b) tan x = 1.24   (c) tan x = 3.7

3. Find a and b in these diagrams:

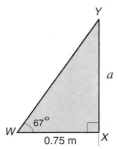

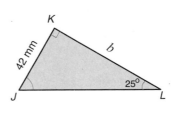

4. Find angle *C*:

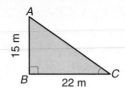

5. In △ *XYZ*, ∠*Z* = 90°, ∠*X* = 35° and *YZ* = 15 cm. Find *XZ*.

6. In △ *ABC*, ∠*A* = 36°, ∠*B* = 90° and *AB* = 2.4 m. Find *BC*.

7. In △ *DEF*, ∠*F* = 90°, *DF* = 12 m and *EF* = 25 m. Find ∠*D*.

8. From a yacht the angle of elevation of a lighthouse 7 m tall is 6°. How far is the yacht from the lighthouse?

End of chapter 18 activity: The cube root trick

This trick lets you find the cube root of any number instantly and is guaranteed to impress your maths teacher.

Before you can do the trick you will have to learn the first nine cubes:

1, 8, 27, 64, 125, 216, 343, 512, 729

Now remember the last digit of each cube:

No.1   1
No.2   8
No.3   7
No.4   4
No.5   5
No.6   6
No.7   3
No.8   2
No.9   9

They are quite easy to remember because:
No.1 and No.9 are 1 and 9
No.4, No.5 and No.6 are 4, 5, and 6

And the others add up to 10:

No.2 is 8   No.7 is 3
No.3 is 7   No.8 is 2

Now the trick

Announce that you can work out the cube root of any number. Ask the person to think of any two digit number, calculate its cube and give you the number.

For example: 50 653   (the cube of 37) $37^3 = 50\,653$

To find the cube root follow these two steps:

Step 1:   Ignore the last three digits of the number (i.e. 653) and work out the largest cube contained in 50

In this case it is $3^3 = 27$ This tells us that the tens digit is 3

Step 2:   Go back to the last three digits (i.e. 65**3**) and look at the last digit, 3
3 is the same ending as 7^3 (No.7) so your units digit is 7

You can now reveal that the cube root of 50 653 is 37!

Look at one more example:

To find the cube root of 592 704

Step 1:   The nearest cube to 592 is $8^3 = 512$ So the tens digit is 8

Step 2:   The cube that ends in 4 is No. 4, therefore the cube root of 592 704 is 84

Now go and amaze your teacher!

The cube root of 592704 is 84

Chapter 19: More trigonometry

In chapter 18 we looked at the tangent of an angle. In this chapter we are going to meet the other principal trigonometrical ratios – the sine and, its associate, the cosine.

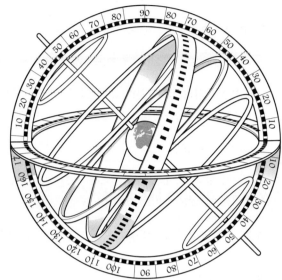

Trigonometry is now first taught using simple triangles, but its origins are based in astronomy and therefore spherical triangles. A spherical triangle is a shape formed on the surface of a sphere by three great circular arcs intersecting in three vertices. Before the sixteenth century, astronomers believed that the Earth was at the centre of a series of celestial spheres. To calculate the positions of stars or planets, they used concepts that we now refer to as trigonometry but were based on chords of a circle.

The Greek astronomer and mathematician Hipparchus produced the first known table of chords in 140 BC. He was followed by astronomers Menelaus (ca. AD 100) and Ptolemy (ca. AD 100) who used the angle notation of Babylon and wrote the original 'Almagest'.

Exercise 19.1: Sine and cosine

1. Draw another copy of the original triangle *ABC* that you drew in chapter 18:

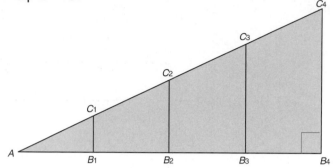

2. Now draw a table like this:

Triangle	AB	BC	AC	$\dfrac{BC}{AC}$	$\dfrac{AB}{AC}$	Angle BAC
AB_1C_1						
AB_2C_2						
AB_3C_3						
AB_4C_4						

The *AB*, *BC* and *AC* columns can be filled in by measuring the lines in your drawing.

3. (a) When you have done that, calculate $BC \div AC$. If you have measured accurately, all the values in this column will be the same.

   (b) Now calculate $AB \div AC$. Again all the values should be the same.

   (c) Measure the angle *BAC*.

4. Find the SIN button on your calculator and calculate the sine or SIN of the angle *BAC*.

   The figure that you have should be the same as your ratio $\dfrac{BC}{AC}$. If not check it again or ask your teacher.

5. Find the COS button on your calculator and calculate the cosine or COS of the angle *BAC*.

Remember the triangle we looked at in chapter 18

You can see that the ratio $\dfrac{BC}{AC}$ is $\dfrac{\text{opposite}}{\text{hypotenuse}}$

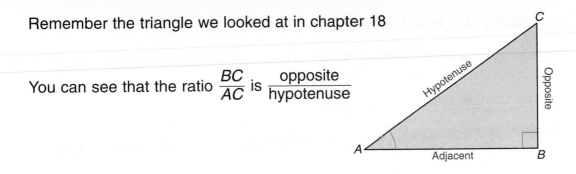

In the right-angled triangle *ABC*:

We say that the **sine of an angle** $= \dfrac{\text{opposite}}{\text{hypotenuse}}$

or $\sin A = \dfrac{\text{opp}}{\text{hyp}}$

The figure that you have calculated in your table, should be the same as your ratio $\dfrac{AB}{AC}$. If not check it again or ask your teacher.

You can see that the ratio $\dfrac{AB}{AC}$ is $\dfrac{\text{adjacent}}{\text{hypotenuse}}$

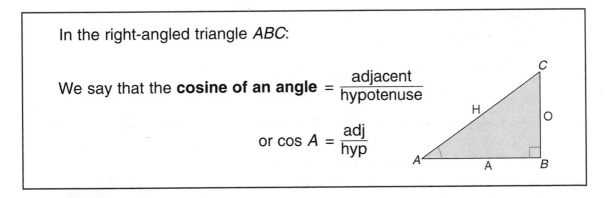

In the right-angled triangle *ABC*:

We say that the **cosine of an angle** $= \dfrac{\text{adjacent}}{\text{hypotenuse}}$

or $\cos A = \dfrac{\text{adj}}{\text{hyp}}$

Because triangle *ABC* is a right-angled triangle then $\angle C = 90° - \angle A$, which makes it possible to calculate the sides by doing the angle calculation first.

However, the cosine ratio has other uses and is almost as important as the sine.

Where does the word 'sine' come from?

Interestingly the history of the word 'sine' is not straightforward. It derives from lost manuscripts and mistranslation!

When Ptolemy wrote the 'Almagest' he considered the parts of a circle but this time, instead of looking at the tangent, he considered a chord. (A chord is a line joining two points on a curve and is often used to describe a line whose ends lie on a circle.)

Radius

B A chord

O A

C

Angle at the centre

In this circle *OB* is a radius, *BC* is a chord and *AB* is a 'half-chord'.

Ptolemy referred to what we call the sine, as half chord $O = \dfrac{AB}{OB}$

The original Greek 'Almagest' was lost but the Hindu mathematician and astronomer Aryabhata the Elder translated the original and correctly translated the sine ratio *ardha-jya* ('half-chord') which was later abbreviated to *jya* ('chord'). Arab translators turned this phonetically into *jiba* – a meaningless word in Arabic – which they wrote as *jb*, according to Arabic practice of omitting the vowels in writing.

In 1085 the Spanish king Alphonso the 6th captured Toledo from the Arabs and with it captured a large library with many Arab manuscripts, including translations of Greek books that had been lost and were unknown to the rest of Europe. Alphonso hired scholars who gradually translated those books into Latin.

In 1145 one of these translators, Robert of Chester, first encountered the word *jb* and, not realizing it was an Indian word transliterated into Arabic, looked up what its Arabic meaning might be. With appropriate vowels added, it meant 'bay', which in Latin was *sinus*. This was the word he wrote down and is the term still used today.

The word has the same origin as the word 'sinus' used in medicine (as in 'sinus headache') where it means the cavities extending from the nose towards the eyes.

Calculating the sine and cosine

Use your calculator to find, to 3 significant figures, the sine and cosine of various angles.

Example:

Find (i) sine 35° and (ii) cosine 45°, giving your answers to 3 s.f.

(i) sin 35° = 0.573 576 ...   (ii) cos 45° = 0.7071 ...
$\qquad\qquad$ = 0.574 (to 3 s.f.) $\qquad\qquad$ = 0.707 (to 3 s.f.)

Exercise 19.2

Use your calculator to find the sine and cosine of each of these angles, giving your answer to 3 s.f.

1.	cos 60°	**5.**	sin 20°	**9.**	cos 12.5°
2.	sin 15°	**6.**	cos 37.5°	**10.**	sin 5°
3.	cos 80°	**7.**	sin 85°	**11.**	cos 73.25°
4.	cos 25°	**8.**	sin 77.5°	**12.**	sin 63.71°

Calculating the angle

If you know the sine and need to find the angle, use the second function on your calculator marked $\sin^{-1}$ or possibly 'inverse sin'.

Example:

Find the angle whose sine is 0.45, giving your answer to 1 decimal place.

$$\sin x = 0.45$$
$$x = 26.743 \ldots$$
$$x = 26.7° \text{ (to 1 d.p.)}$$

N.B. Look carefully at this example.
See how we have described the angle
whose sine is 0.45 as: $\sin x = 0.45$

We find the angle x by calculating:
$$x = \sin^{-1}(0.45)$$

Never write sin⁻¹ in your answers to these exercises!

Exercise 19.3

1. Use your calculator to find the angles whose sines are given below. Give your answers to 1 decimal place.

(a) 0.7   (e) 0.75   (i) 0.567
(b) 0.9   (f) 0.12   (j) 0.345
(c) 0.5   (g) 0.89   (k) 0.055
(d) 0.2   (h) 0.37   (l) 0.382

2. Now find the angles whose cosines are the values given above in (a) – (l).

3. Compare the angles found in q.2 with the angles found in q.1 What do you notice?

This leads to a useful fact about sine and cosine:

$$\sin x° = \cos (90 - x)°$$

Finding opposite and adjacent sides using sine and cosine

In the right-angled triangle *ABC*:

$$\sin A = \frac{\text{opp}}{\text{hyp}} \qquad \text{and} \qquad \cos A = \frac{\text{adj}}{\text{hyp}}$$

The sides are calculated in the same manner as when we used the tangent.

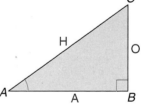

In the examples below we still label the three sides H, O and A, but the side not being used in the fraction is crossed out. This helps us to avoid errors caused by using the wrong fraction.

Example:

Find the values of x in these two triangles:

(i)

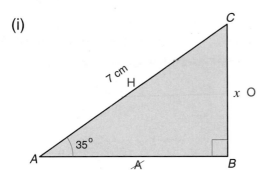

(ii)

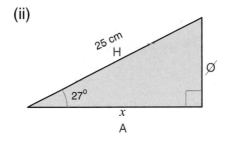

$$\sin A = \frac{\text{opp}}{\text{hyp}}$$

$$\sin 35° = \frac{x}{7}$$

$$x = 7 \times \sin 35°$$
$$= 4.0150 \dots$$
$$= 4.02 \text{ cm (to 3 s.f.)}$$

$$\cos A = \frac{\text{adj}}{\text{hyp}}$$

$$\cos 27° = \frac{x}{25}$$

$$x = 25 \times \cos 27°$$
$$= 22.275 \dots$$
$$= 22.3 \text{ cm (to 3 s.f.)}$$

Exercise 19.4

Find the side indicated by a letter in each of these questions. Always start by drawing the diagram and labelling the sides H, O and A. Give your answers correct to 3 significant figures:

The first four questions all involve the sine ratio:

1.

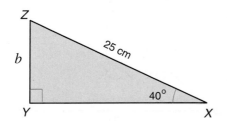

2.

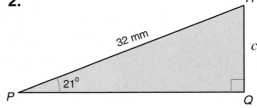

3.

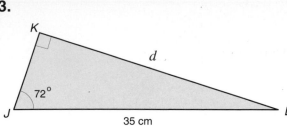

4.

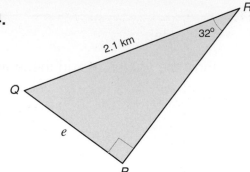

The next four questions all involve the cosine ratio:

5.

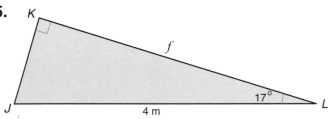

7.

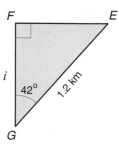

6.

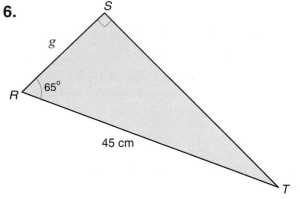

8.

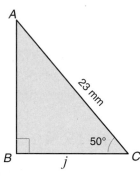

The next few questions involve either sine or cosine:

9.

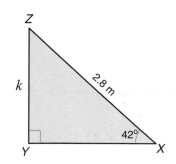

10.

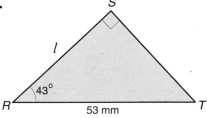

11.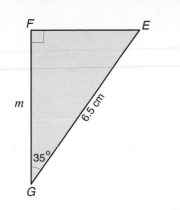

13.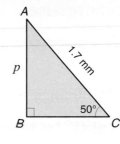

12.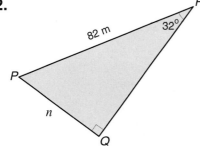

14.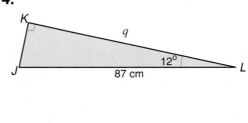

The next 6 questions involve a mixture of sine, cosine and tangent. It is important to draw the triangle first, taking care when labelling the sides O, A and H. Take time to make sure that you are using the correct ratio.

15. In △ *ABC*, ∠*A* = 37°, ∠*B* = 90° and *AC* = 3.2 km. Find *AB*.

16. In △ *DEF*, ∠*D* = 83°, ∠*E* = 90° and *DF* = 55 m. Find *DE*.

17. In △ *XYZ*, ∠*Z* = 90°, ∠*X* = 65° and *XZ* = 12 cm. Find *YZ*.

18. In △ *JKL*, ∠*J* = 25°, ∠*K* = 90° and *JL* = 104 m. Find *KL*.

19. In △ *PQR*, ∠*P* = 71°, ∠*R* = 90° and *PR* = 53 mm. Find *RQ*.

20. In △ *STU*, ∠*S* = 90°, ∠*U* = 36° and *TU* = 3 m. Find *SU*.

Finding the hypotenuse

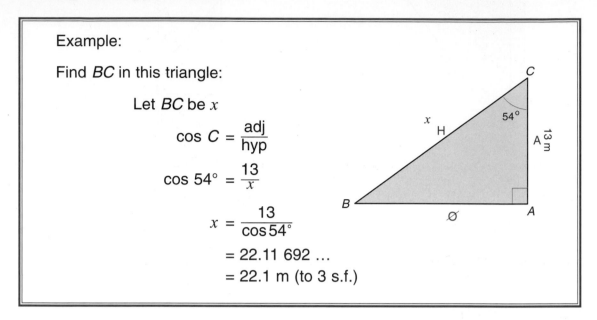

Example:

Find *BC* in this triangle:

Let *BC* be x

$$\cos C = \frac{\text{adj}}{\text{hyp}}$$

$$\cos 54° = \frac{13}{x}$$

$$x = \frac{13}{\cos 54°}$$

$$= 22.11\ 692\ ...$$

$$= 22.1 \text{ m (to 3 s.f.)}$$

Exercise 19.5

Find the hypotenuse in these questions. There is a mixture requiring either sine or cosine. Take time to make sure that you are using the correct ratio.

Give your answers correct to 3 significant figures.

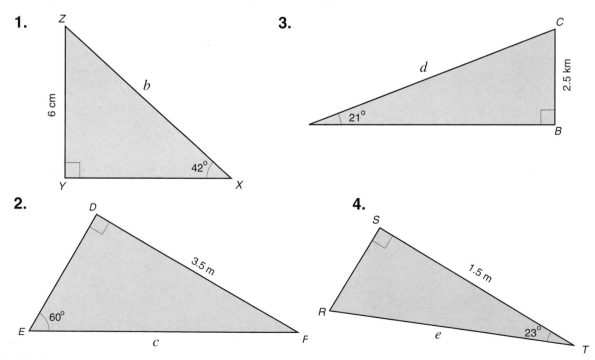

1.

2.

3.

4.

5.

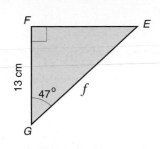

6.

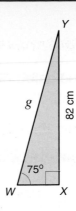

7. In △ *ABC*, ∠*A* = 12°, ∠*B* = 90° and *AB* = 45 cm. Find *AC*.

8. In △ *DEF*, ∠*D* = 65°, ∠*F* = 90° and *EF* = 12 m. Find *DE*.

9. In △ *XYZ*, ∠*Z* = 90°, ∠*X* = 42° and *YZ* = 4.2 km. Find *XY*.

10. In △ *PQR*, ∠*P* = 37°, ∠*R* = 90° and *PR* = 27 mm. Find *PQ*.

Finding the angle

Remember to use the second function on your calculator to find the angle:

Example:

Find angle x in this triangle, giving your answer correct to 1 d.p.

$$\sin x = \frac{\text{opp}}{\text{hyp}}$$

$$\sin x = \frac{5}{13}$$

$$x = 22.619 \ldots$$

$$= 22.6° \text{ (to 1 d.p.)}$$

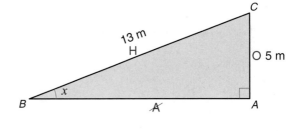

Exercise 19.6

Find the angles indicated by letters in these questions. Always start by drawing the diagram and labelling the sides H, O and A. Give your answers correct to 1 decimal place:

The first four all use the sine ratio:

1.

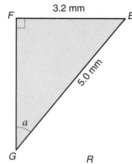

2.

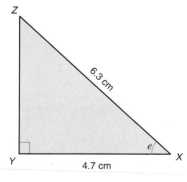

3.

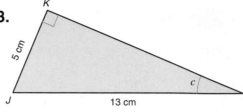

4.

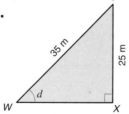

The next two use the cosine ratio:

5.

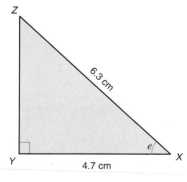

6.

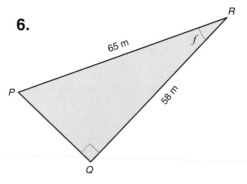

The last few questions are a mixture of tangent, sine and cosine problems.

It is particularly important to take care when labelling H, O and A.

7.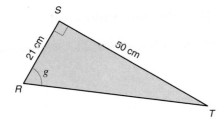

8.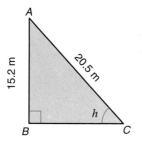

9.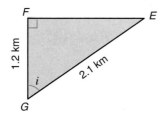

10.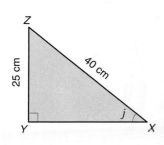

11.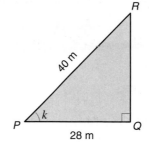

12.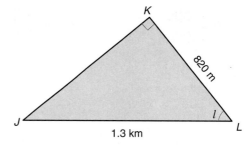

13.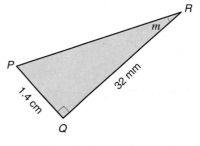

14.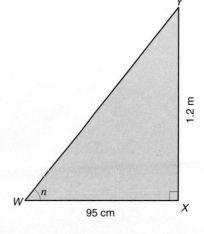

15. In △ *ABC*, ∠*B* = 90°, *AB* = 25 cm and *AC* = 35 cm. Find ∠*A*.

16. In △ *DEF*, ∠*F* = 90°, *DF* = 12 m and *EF* = 29 m. Find ∠*D*.

17. In △ *XYZ*, ∠*X* = 90°, *YZ* = 3.6 km and *XY* = 700 m. Find ∠*Y*.

18. In △ *PQR*, ∠*R* = 90°, *PQ* = 52 mm and *QR* = 25 mm. Find ∠*P*.

Solving problems using trigonometry

When dealing with problems in trigonometry, it can be a help to use the mnemonic SOHCAHTOA, which is made up of the three formulae SOH CAH TOA

$$\sin = \frac{\text{opp}}{\text{hyp}} \qquad \cos = \frac{\text{adj}}{\text{hyp}} \qquad \tan = \frac{\text{opp}}{\text{adj}}$$

or

$$S = \frac{O}{H} \qquad C = \frac{A}{H} \qquad T = \frac{O}{A}$$

Here are some other rhymes and phrases that may help:

- Some Of Her Children Are Having Trouble Over Algebra.

- Saddle Our Horses, Canter Away Happily, To Other Adventures.

- Some Old Hairy
  Camels Are Hairier
  Than Others Are.

As with problems using Pythagoras' theorem, it is important to draw the right-angled triangle; indeed some problems may require Pythagoras' theorem to solve them.

Example:

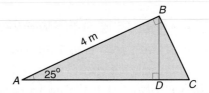

ABCD is a cross-section through a roof truss.

Find (a) *BD* (b) *AD* (c) *AC*

(a) Let *BD* be x

$$\sin A = \frac{\text{opp}}{\text{hyp}}$$

$$\sin 25° = \frac{x}{4}$$

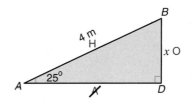

$$x = 4 \times \sin 25°$$

$$= 1.690\ 47\ \ldots$$

$$BD = 1.69 \text{ m (to 3 s.f.)}$$

(b) In △ *ABD*:

$$AB^2 = AD^2 + BD^2 \qquad \text{(Pythagoras' theorem)}$$

$$4^2 = AD^2 + (1.69\ 047\ \ldots)^2$$

$$AD^2 = 16 - (1.69\ 047\ \ldots)^2$$

$$= 13.142\ 311$$

$$AD = 3.625\ 23\ \ldots$$

$$= 3.63 \text{ m (to 3 s.f.)}$$

(c) Let *AC* be y

$$\cos A = \frac{\text{adj}}{\text{hyp}}$$

$$\cos 25° = \frac{4}{y}$$

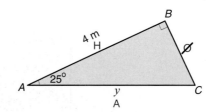

$$y = \frac{4}{\cos 25°}$$

$$= 4.4135\ \ldots$$

$$= 4.41 \text{ m (to 3 s.f.)}$$

Exercise 19.7

1. The princess is at the window 12 m above the ground. The prince has to rescue her with a ladder, but he knows that it is unsafe to have a ladder at an angle of more than 75° with the ground. What is the shortest ladder he will need to be able to reach the bottom of the window safely?

2. A hunter walks 4 km due East and then changes course to a bearing of 202°. How far must he walk until he is due South of his starting point?

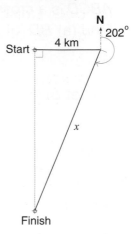

3. A plane flew 100 km on a bearing of 125°. How far West must it then fly to be due South of its starting point?

4. From a point *A* a bird *B* can be seen on a bearing of 72° and a cat *C* can be seen on a bearing of 162°. *AC* is 5 m and *AB* is 7.2 m. Find the bearing and distance of *C* from *B*.

5. A line passes through the points *A*(5, ‾6) and *B*(‾4, 12). Find the angle the line makes with the *x*-axis and the distance *AB*.

6. This is a section through a roof truss *WXYZ*. $\angle XZY = \angle WXY = 90°$, $\angle XWZ = 55°$ and $XY = 7.5$ m.

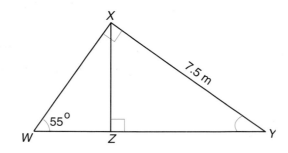

Find: (a) *WY*　　(b) $\angle XYZ$　　(c) *XZ*　　(d) *WX*

7. (a) A ship set sail on a bearing of 290° and sailed for 500 miles. Draw a sketch of this journey and calculate how far North and West the ship was from the starting point.
    (b) The ship then changed course and sailed another 500 miles on a bearing of 215°. Draw a sketch of this part of the journey and calculate how far the ship sailed West and South on this part of the journey.
    (c) Draw a diagram of the total voyage so far. Mark clearly on the diagram all the distances you have calculated.
    (d) At this point the crew mutiny. They throw the captain overboard and set sail for home. On what bearing should they sail and how far from home are they?

Exercise 19.8: Extension questions

In this exercise we are going to look at the sines, cosines and tangents of angles in common right-angled triangles.

1. (a) Sketch an equilateral triangle of side 2 units.
    (b) Use Pythagoras' theorem to calculate the height of the triangle. Leave your answer as a square root.
    (c) Use your answer to part (b) to find the values of sin 30°, cos 30° and tan 30°. Leave your answers as fractions with square roots if necessary.
    (d) Use your answer to part (b) to find the values of sin 60°, cos 60° and tan 60°. Leave your answers as fractions with square roots if necessary.

2. (a) Sketch an isosceles triangle with base angles of 45° and two equal sides of one unit.
    (b) Use Pythagoras' theorem to calculate the length of the third side. Leave your answer as a square root.
    (c) Use your answer to part (b) to find the values of sin 45°, cos 45° and tan 45°. Leave your answers as fractions with square roots if necessary.

3. Here are two special right-angled triangles.

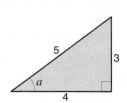 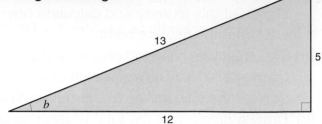

Write down the values of sin a, cos a and tan a and sin b, *cos b* and tan b. Leave your answers as fractions.

Now use your answers to the first three questions to solve the following problems. Some of the triangles are the same as the ones in the earlier questions and some are similar (e.g. the lengths may be doubled but the angles, and therefore the ratios, are the same).

You should calculate in fractions, leaving values as square roots if necessary:

4. Find all the remaining lengths in this cross-section:

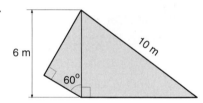

5. From a point A the angle of depression to a point C is 45°.
AD is 100 m and BD is 240 m.
Calculate the distance between B and C.

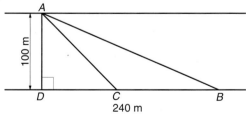

6. From a point B the angle of elevation of the top of a building D is 60°. If AC is 240 m and CD is 100 m, calculate the distance between A and B, and the distance AD.

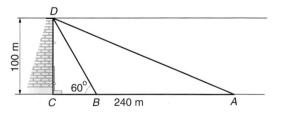

Exercise 19.9: Summary exercise

Give any non-exact answers to 3 significant figures.

1. Find the value of:
   (a) tan 48°   (b) sin 52°   (c) cos 62°

2. Find x when:
   (a) tan x = 1.5   (b) sin x = 0.785   (c) cos x = 0.632

3. Find the sides marked with letters in these triangles:

(a)
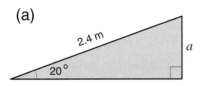

(c)
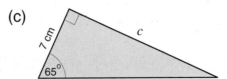

(b)
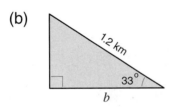

(d)
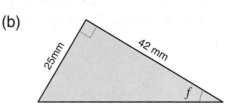

4. Find angles marked with letters in these triangles:

(a)
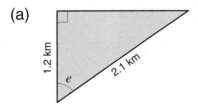

(b)
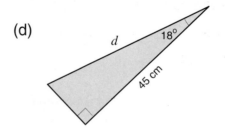

5. In Δ *JKL*, ∠*J* = 25°, ∠*K* = 90° and *JL* = 104 m. Find *KL*.

6. In Δ *DEF*, ∠*D* = 65°, ∠*F* = 90° and *DF* = 12 m. Find *DE*.

7. In Δ *XYZ*, ∠*X* = 90°, *YZ* = 3.6 km and *XY* = 700 m. Find ∠*Y*.

8. A plane travels 200 km on a bearing of 65°. It then turns and heads West until it is due North of its starting point. How far away from its starting point is the plane?

End of chapter 19 activity: Binary arithmetic

You should by now have a good appreciation of how our decimal number system works on the base of ten.

This number system has served us very well for centuries. However, towards the end of the twentieth century, something changed – humans were not just confined to speaking to each other, they started to talk to machines – to telephones, calculators and computers. As technology advanced the machines started to talk to each other, and then to talk back to humans. Have you ever wondered how this is this possible?

Machines 'talk' to each other by a series of electronic pulses. These pulses have two states 'on' and 'off'. Let us write these as 1 and 0

When a machine needs to transmit a number it can only transmit a pulse. It would be very inefficient to transmit 1000 pulses to represent the number 1000, so how do they do it?

Consider our number system with 10 numerals, zero to nine. The value of each numeral is represented by its position:

H	T	U	or	10^2	10^1	10^0	
3	7	5		3	7	5	three hundred and seventy-five.

Using this idea, where the column represents the value of the digit, we can consider how a machine might operate. A machine only has numerals 1 and 0, and so the column headings must be in powers of 2:

2^2	2^1	2^0
1	0	1

Therefore 101 in binary becomes, in base 10, $(1 \times 4) + (1 \times 1) = 5$

This system of using 1s and 0s is known as the **binary system**. It was of interest to mathematicians before technology came into use but now is an essential part of any system design.

Here are some numbers written in binary, can you convert them to decimal numbers:

1. 110
2. 11
3. 1011
4. 10 101
5. 11 001

6. 1101
7. 111
8. 1010
9. 11 101
10. 111 111

Now convert these decimal numbers to binary form:

11. 8
12. 19
13. 50
14. 324
15. 429

16. 16
17. 20
18. 100
19. 171
20. 245

Now investigate binary arithmetic – addition, subtraction, multiplication and division.

Can you write an arithmetic book explaining how to use these numbers and calculate with them, include any 'algorithms' or rules that you can find?

Chapter 20: Looking at data

Charts and diagrams

Data can be collected in many forms. Sometimes it can be quite hard to interpret data when it is in a purely numerical format. Using graphs, charts or diagrams to display the data can help us to see and interpret it more easily.

In this country, we seem to be particularly concerned with the weather. You may well have found yourself having to interpret charts like these in Geography:

Last seven days weather

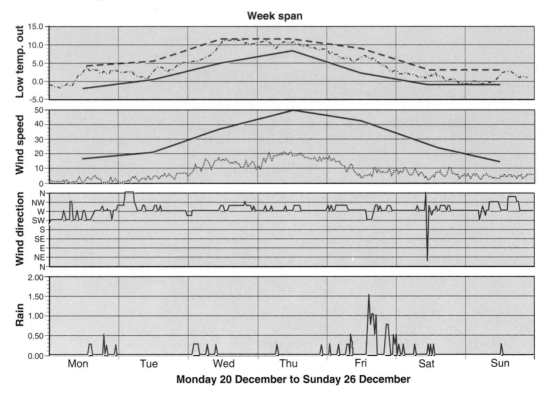

Monday 20 December to Sunday 26 December

There are various ways we could interpret the data displayed on this weather chart. You will be familiar with some of these, such as finding the mean, mode, median and range.

In this chapter we will summarise everything you should know about looking at and interpreting data.

Pie charts

A pie chart is used to show the proportion of various amounts that add up to a whole. If you are lucky then the angles will add up to 360°, but in real life they often do not:

Example:

A company has a total income of £150m. This is derived from the following sources:

Property : £36m   Retail: £53m   Catering: £27m
Interest: £13m   The remainder is 'miscellaneous' (misc).

Show this information on a pie diagram.

In this example £150m represents a full circle i.e. 360°

Therefore £1m can be represented by $\frac{360°}{150}$

The angles at the centre of the circle are therefore:

$$\text{Property} = \frac{360}{150} \times 36 = 86.4 \approx 86°$$

$$\text{Retail} = \frac{360}{150} \times 53 = 127.2 \approx 127°$$

$$\text{Catering} = \frac{360}{150} \times 27 = 64.8 \approx 65°$$

$$\text{Interest} = \frac{360}{150} \times 13 = 31.2 \approx 31°$$

$$\text{Misc} = \frac{360}{150} \times 21 = 50.4 \approx 50°$$

You should now check that the sum of these angles adds up to 360°

$$86 + 127 + 65 + 31 + 50 = 359$$

The check is important because the angles have been rounded up or down and the total may not be exactly 360°. In this case the total is 359°.

To resolve this difference you should try rounding the angles to the nearest half degree. They become:

Property 86.5°, Retail 127°, Catering 65°, Interest 31° and Misc 50.5°

This now totals 360°

The pie chart can now be drawn and labelled.

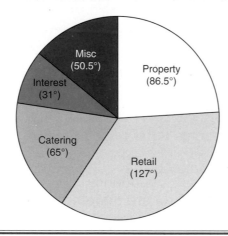

Exercise 20.1

1. In a survey of our local park we asked 168 people to tell us their most important reason for coming to the park. 52 came for the sports facilities, 41 came for the playground, 26 came just to go running, 35 came to walk and sit and the rest did not know. Draw a pie diagram to show the above data.

2. During the survey at the park we decided to pick up pieces of litter to see if it would help us to understand the users. 27% of the litter was empty bottles and cans, 35% of the litter was cigarette packets, 22% of the litter was crisp packets and sweet wrappers, and the rest we called miscellaneous.

   (a) Draw a pie chart to show this information.
   (b) How does the litter relate to the survey on the users?

Bar charts

The same information could have been shown on a bar chart, but bar charts are more usually used when comparing numbers or frequencies of occurrences. A bar chart often needs a tally table or frequency table to be drawn first.

Here is a set of raw data. The numbers represents the 'battery lives' of torch batteries, of the same brand, that we tested in the laboratory. The times are in hours:

24	18	22	19	30	11	23	25	29	10
17	21	27	31	14	26	25	22	18	29
22	32	17	26	31	23	27	14	24	26

These results can be recorded in a frequency table:

Time in hours	Tally	Frequency
6 – 10	I	1
11 – 15	III	3
16 – 20	⊬⊬	5
21 – 25	⊬⊬ ⊬⊬	10
26 – 30	⊬⊬ III	8
31 – 35	III	3
		30

Note how we have divided the hours into bands of the same length. This information can now be used to draw the frequency diagram.

A frequency diagram to show the 'battery lives' of torch batteries in a laboratory test

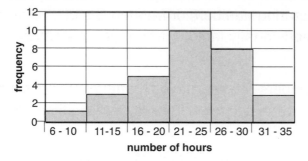

number of hours

Remember always to label a bar chart with a title and axis labels. Note that in a frequency diagram (a bar chart displaying frequency results), frequency is **always** on the vertical axis. Other bar charts are occasionally drawn with horizontal bars.

Exercise 20.2

1. We recorded the lengths of time 32 people spent in the park during the morning. These are our results in minutes:

5	12	25	4	2	55	17	8
12	8	46	22	9	12	50	32
6	14	8	32	45	9	3	5
26	34	16	9	5	17	12	8

    Draw a frequency diagram to show the above data. You will need to group the times into sensible divisions and draw a frequency table first.

2. We then recorded the lengths of time 32 people spent in the park in the early evening. These are our results in minutes:

7	22	25	15	10	56	7	38
41	34	86	45	12	5	19	36
72	53	41	12	6	29	32	36
9	12	57	5	42	6	35	15

    Draw a frequency diagram to show the above data. You will need to group the times into sensible divisions and draw a frequency table first.

3. Now compare your two diagrams. What can you say about the differences and what reasons do you think would explain them?

Scatter graphs

Scatter graphs plot one variable against another. They can be used to see if there is any relationship between the two sets of variables, for example height against shoe size. When all the points have been plotted it is sometimes possible to draw a line of best fit.

Example:

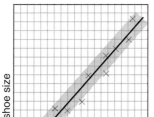

Positive correlation

Shoe size increases with height

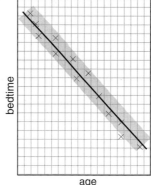

Negative correlation

Bedtime is earlier as adults get older

A line of best fit can be drawn by inspection but it can be quite hard to get it exactly right. Another way of drawing the line of best fit is to draw the narrowest possible rectangle that encloses all the points and then draw a line through the middle of that rectangle with the same number of points on either side of it.

Exercise 20.3

1. We asked people if they would pay to go into the park, so that the money could be used to maintain the facilities and to keep out vandals. These were our results:

Max price	Number of people
0p	25
20p	20
50p	18
75p	15
£1	20
£1.25	12
£1.50	10
£1.75	4
£2	2
£2.50	1

Show these results on a scatter graph and comment on the findings. Does your graph show positive or negative correlation?

2. Over a period of time we recorded the temperature at midday and then the number of people in the park in the early evening. These were our results:

Temp at midday	Number of people
5° C	25
10° C	40
15° C	47
17° C	52
20° C	63
22° C	85
25° C	107
27° C	116
30° C	124

(a) Show these results on a scatter graph and comment on the findings.

(b) Draw a line of best fit.

(c) Does your graph show positive or negative correlation?

(d) Use the line of best fit to estimate the number of people you might expect in the park in the evening following a midday temperature of 12°C.

Mean, median and mode

The average is a way of expressing the value of the mid point of a set of numbers. There are different ways of looking at an average:

- the one used most often is the **mean** of a set of numbers; or

- you can consider the middle value when the numbers are arranged in order of size, the **median**; or

- the value or group of values that occurs most often, which is known as the **mode** or **modal group**.

Range

The range, for a set of numerical data, refers to the difference between the largest value and the smallest value.

Mean

To find the mean of a set of values add up all the elements and divide by the number of elements:

To find the mean of 1, 3, 7, 5, 8, 4, 3

$$\text{Mean} = \frac{1 + 3 + 7 + 5 + 8 + 4 + 3}{7}$$

$$= \frac{31}{7}$$

$$= 4\frac{3}{7}$$

Note that the answer will not always be a whole number and some thought may have to be given as to how to treat the remainder. The answer above is given as a mixed number but could have been given as 4 (to the nearest whole number) or 4.4 (to 1 d.p.). Always read the question carefully to see what degree of accuracy is required. In general, answers given to 3 s.f. will be acceptable.

Median

A different way of looking at the average of values is to look at the **median** or 'middle' value. If there is no actual 'middle' term the median is taken as the mean of the two 'middle' values.

To find the median of 3, 6, 2, 5, 7, 9, 4, 6, 8, 3, 7

2, 3, 3, 4, 5, 6, 6, 7, 7, 8, 9   11 numbers
The median will be the 6th number (the middle number) i.e. 6

To find the median of 3, 9, 8, 5, 1, 5, 7, 6
1, 3, 5, 5, 6, 7, 8, 9   8 numbers

The median is the mean of the 4th and 5th = $\frac{5+6}{2}$ = 5.5

Mode

The **mode** is yet another way of looking at the average of a sample of data. It refers to the value that occurs most frequently or most often. If each value occurs only once, there is no mode. The group of items with value equal to the mode is called the **modal group.** The number of times each value appears is called the **frequency**. In the two examples above the mode would have been 3, 6 and 7 in the first and 5 in the second.

The mode is particularly useful when analysing measurements such as shoe size, where there is no value between one size and the next (i.e. there is no size 36.2)

Example: The daily rainfall in the month of April was recorded and the results, correct to the nearest 0.1 cm, are shown below.

1.2	0	0	0.8	2.4	1.8	0	0	0.4	0.2
0	0	1.5	1.2	2.1	2.6	3.1	1.8	0.5	0.2
0	2.1	1.8	0	1.5	1.7	2.5	2.4	0	0.7

(i) Give the range of values and calculate the mean, median and mode.

(ii) Group the data in appropriate bands and illustrate the distribution with a bar chart. Write a brief summary of your findings.

(i) Maximum value = 3.1   Minimum value = 0

Range = 3.1

Rainfall in cm	Tally	Frequency
0 – 0.4	‖‖ ‖‖ ‖	12
0.5 – 0.9	‖‖	3
1.0 – 1.4	‖	2
1.5 – 1.9	‖‖ ‖	6
2.0 – 2.4	‖‖‖	4
2.5 – 2.9	‖	2
3.0 – 3.4	‖	1
		30

Mean = (1.2 + 0.8 + 2.4 + 1.8 + 0.4 + 0.2 + 1.5 + 1.2 + 2.1 + 2.6 + 3.1 + 1.8 + 0.5 + 0.2 + 2.1 + 1.8 + 1.5 + 1.7 + 2.5 + 2.4 + 0.7) / 30

$$= \frac{32.5}{30}$$

$$= 1.0833 \ldots$$

Mean = 1.08 (to 3 s.f.)

Mode = 0

Median: There are 30 items, so when these are arranged in order of size there is no middle term. The median is therefore calculated as the mean of the 15th and 16th values:

0, 0, 0, 0, 0, 0, 0, 0, 0, 0.2, 0.2, 0.4, 0.5, 0.7, 0.8, 1.2, etc. ...

$$\textbf{Median} = \frac{(0.8 + 1.2)}{2} = 1$$

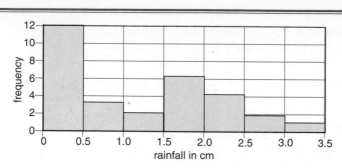

From our results we can see that the month of April was mostly dry with periods of no rain at all but when it did rain it rained hard. The distribution is therefore skewed towards zero, which is also the mode. The mean is 1.08 This reflects the heavy rainfall when it did occur but the median of 1 reflects the overall dryness of the month.

The above example is unusual as it shows a very uneven distribution with quite different values of mean, median and mode. The fact that these are different is interesting but the distribution is not really clear until the bar chart is considered.

Note the horizontal scale on the bar chart. This does not immediately reflect the groups of the frequency table. However the groups could have been written as:

$0 \leq x < 0.5$, $0.5 \leq x < 1.0$, $1.0 \leq x < 1.5$ and so on where x is the rainfall in cm.

Had the data been recorded more accurately, to one tenth of a millimetre perhaps, then this method of grouping the data would have been the most appropriate. This is reflected by the scale on the bar chart.

Finding the total

If the mean of a set of data is known, then the total can be calculated:
'There are 22 classes in the school, with an mean of 19.5 pupils per class.'

This means: $\dfrac{\text{total number of pupils}}{\text{number of classes}} = 19.5$

$$\text{Total number of pupils} = 19.5 \times 22$$

$$= 429$$

Note that averages (mean and median) can often look ridiculous (e.g. 19.5 pupils), but this is acceptable given the nature of the calculation.

Exercise 20.4

Give any non-exact answers correct to 3 significant figures.

1. Give the range, mean, mode and median of each of these sets of data:

(a) 1, 3, 4, 5, 2, 5, 2, 6, 7, 2, 1, 2

(b) 1.3, 2.3, 1.4, 1.2, 1.5, 1.2, 2.6, 1.7, 1.5, 2.1

(c) 75, 32, 53, 25, 65, 72, 78, 91, 56, 67, 70, 62, 83, 95, 43

(d) 34, 38, 39.5, 37.5, 36, 37.5, 42, 40, 39, 40.5, 41

2. Suggest what measurements each set of data in q.1 might represent.

3. My brother is 10 years old and my sister is 21
The mean of our three ages is 15 How old am I?

4. 40 boys have a mean height of 1.48 m. 60 girls have a mean height of 1.52 m. What is the mean height of all 100 children?

5. The daily rainfall in the month of September was recorded and the results, correct to the nearest 0.1 cm, are shown below in cm.

1.2	0	1.5	0.8	2.4	1.6	1.6	1.1	0.4	2.6
1.1	1.2	1.5	1.2	2.1	2.6	3.1	1.8	2.8	0.2
1.5	2.1	1.8	0	1.5	1.7	2.5	2.4	0	0.7

(a) Give the range of values and calculate the mean, median and mode.

(b) Group the data in appropriate bands and illustrate the distribution with a frequency diagram.

(c) Write a brief summary of your findings.

(d) Compare the rainfall this month with the rainfall in the month of April in the example on page 413.

6. In science we collected a number of seed pods and counted the number of seeds in each pod. These were our results:

2	4	6	3	5	3	5	3	4	5
3	5	6	4	7	4	4	5	3	5
5	4	2	5	3	6	4	5	4	4
4	5	5	3	6	4	5	5	5	3
6	7	3	5	4	4	6	7	5	3

(a) Draw up a frequency table to find the frequency of the number of seeds in each pod.

(b) This information is to be shown in a pie chart. Use the information in the frequency table to calculate each angle.

(c) Draw the pie chart.

(d) Comment on the results of this experiment.

7. Here is a pie chart showing the results of a similar sample of seed pods, but these were gathered in a wetter environment.

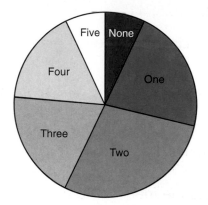

What can you say about the comparative results of these two surveys? (Compare all the information you have, including the range, mean, median and mode and the general distribution.)

8. (a) A supermarket is selling 2.5 kg of nectarines in a bag. The exact number of nectarines in each bag varies. A survey of 40 bags, looking at the number of nectarines contained in each, gave the following results:

20	18	22	19	23	18	20	21	22	19
20	23	21	20	21	21	19	22	21	21
23	22	20	21	20	21	19	21	20	22
20	21	21	18	21	19	22	21	21	20

Draw a frequency table to record this information and use this to draw a frequency diagram to show the distribution. Calculate the mean, median and mode.

(b) A sample of another 60 bags found that the mode and the median of this sample were both 20 and the mean was 19.6 nectarines per bag. Which, if any, of the mean, median and mode can you work out for the whole sample of 100 bags of nectarines?

9. A supermarket chain surveyed its total sales from its meat counters in two supermarkets A and B. Here are the results:

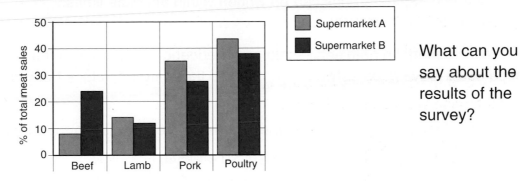

What can you say about the results of the survey?

10. If the bar chart in q.9 compared the sales in **one** supermarket during two months [Month x / Month y], what could you say about the results of the survey?

11. The manager of the supermarket chain wants to find out more about the customers that shop at each store. Draw up a list of ten questions that shoppers could be asked which would help the manager to draw better conclusions from the results of his survey.

12. Before the January exams we were all asked the total number of hours of revision we had done over the holidays. This information is recorded below with our final positions in the examinations.

No. of hours	18	24	13	11	10	14	20	10	18	8	10	20	24	20	19	21	9	18	21	16
Exam position	6	2	14	9	1	11	8	18	15	20	16	5	13	3	7	19	17	10	4	12

    (a) Record this information on a scatter graph. Draw a line of best fit and state whether these results show positive or negative correlation.

    (b) What quantities could have been compared that would have given the opposite correlation?

    (c) Some candidates have a result that does not fit the general pattern of the other results. Suggest as many reasons as you can for these.

Working with grouped data

Data is often presented in grouped form. A set of data that has distinct and separate values or observations i.e. they can be counted, e.g.: number of kittens in a litter is known as **discrete data**. Data that could take on any value, e.g. height, weight, temperature is known as **continuous data**.

Drawing bar charts

With discrete data, the groups can be written within absolute limits:

1 – 10, 11 – 20, 21 – 30, ...

When considering the horizontal scale on a frequency diagram, discrete groups could leave gaps between the bars, as there are no values between 10 and 11

When considering continuous data, the groups are best written in the form:

$0 \leq x < 10$, $10 \leq x < 20$, $20 \leq x < 30$, $30 \leq x < 40$

Exercise 20.5

Give non-exact answers correct to one decimal place.

1. Here are the results of a survey that looked at the ages of passengers taking the Eurostar train to Paris on a weekday:

Age	$0 \leq x < 10$	$10 \leq x < 20$	$20 \leq x < 30$	$30 \leq x < 40$	$40 \leq x < 50$	$50 \leq x < 60$	$60 \leq x < 70$	$70 \leq x < 100$
Frequency	5	23	55	42	25	18	50	32

(a) Draw a frequency diagram to show the distribution.
(b) Why do you think there were so few young passengers on the train?
(c) Why do you think there are so many passengers aged over 60 years old?

2. Here are the results of another survey of the ages of passengers taking the Eurostar train to Paris. This one was done at a weekend:

Age	$0 \leq x < 10$	$10 \leq x < 20$	$20 \leq x < 30$	$30 \leq x < 40$	$40 \leq x < 50$	$50 \leq x < 60$	$60 \leq x < 70$	$70 \leq x < 100$
Frequency	23	34	27	51	35	12	32	14

(a) Draw a frequency diagram to show the distribution.
(b) What difference is there between the ages of the passengers in the two surveys?

Exercise 20.6

The questions in the following exercise require you to think a bit harder.

1. Here are the results of a survey that I carried out looking at the numbers of people living in each house in our street. Unfortunately I opened a can of drink when I had finished and sprayed my page with Fizz. Some of the numbers and tallies have been washed away. Copy my results and fill in all the missing data.

No. in house	Tally	Frequency	Total people
2	||	. . . .	$2 \times 2 = 4$
3		4	$3 \times 4 = 12$
4		. . . .	. . . .
5	⊮ ||	7	$5 \times 7 = 35$
6	|||	. . . .	$6 \times 3 = 18$
7	|	1	. . . .
Total		. . . .	108

$$\text{Mean} = \frac{108}{\ldots} = 4.32$$
$$\text{Mode} = 4$$
$$\text{Median} = \ldots$$

2. Here are the results of a similar survey:

No. in House	2	3	4	5
Frequency	4	x	9	4

(a) What are the mode and median of this set of data if x is:
   (i) 8   (ii) 9   (iii) 10?

(b) In fact, the mean, to two decimal places, is 3.59
   What are x, the mode and the median?

3. Pupils in my school took part in a survey to find out how long their journey to school took them in the morning. The headmaster produced the results of the survey in the form of this frequency diagram:

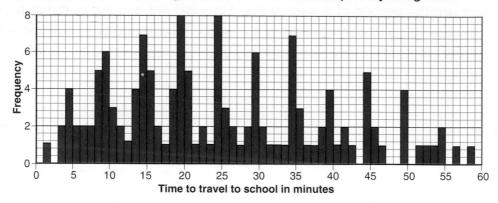

(a) What was the mode as shown by the headmaster's frequency diagram?

(b) What was the mean length of time taken to come to school?

(c) What was the median length of time?

The Head of Maths was shown this chart. He commented that it showed that most people had rounded their journey times to the nearest 5 minutes and suggested that it was re-drawn with the times in groups of 5 minutes.

(d) Draw a frequency table with the journey times in groups 0 – 5, 6 – 10, 11 – 15 etc.

(e) Draw the revised frequency diagram.

(f) How many pupils took part in the survey?

(g) What was the modal group in the survey?

4. As you know, teachers get quite long holidays. We asked the staff in our school how many days they spent abroad last year. Here are the results of our survey.

No. of days	0	1 – 7	8 – 14	15 – 21	22 – 28	29 – 40	41 – 100
Frequency	4	3	15	8	6	5	1

(a) Why do you think that we grouped the data in the way we did?

(b) What kind of teacher do you think might have spent between 41 and 100 days abroad last year?

(c) There is only one teacher in the last group of data. If this one teacher had spent 41 days abroad, what would you estimate the mean to be?

(d) If this teacher had spent 100 days abroad, what would you estimate the mean to be?

5. Last year 120 children in the school took part in a Readathon to raise money for charity. This frequency table shows how many children raised various amounts of money:

Amount in pounds	$0 \leq x < 10$	$10 \leq x < 20$	$20 \leq x < 30$	$30 \leq x < 40$	$40 \leq x < 50$
Frequency	8	22	47	34	9

(a) Draw a frequency diagram to show the distribution.

(b) How much money did the school raise in total? If you cannot tell exactly, how could you make an estimate?

Exercise 20.7: Summary exercise

1. Find the range and the mean, median and mode of these sets of data:

(a) 1, 3, 4, 1, 2, 3, 2, 1, 4, 5

(b) 3.4, 5.1, 1.2, 4.2, 1.8, 4.2, 5.1, 3.1, 4.7, 4.2, 2.9, 5.8

(c) $2\frac{1}{2}$, $3\frac{1}{4}$, $1\frac{3}{4}$, $2\frac{1}{4}$, $3\frac{1}{2}$

2. My team are practising for the relay race on sports day. Our times have been:

12 min 40 s, 11 min 55 s, 12 min 25 s, 11 min 50 s, 12 min 35 s and 11 min 47 s.

(a) What is our mean time?

(b) On the day we did not beat our best time, but our mean time was improved by 2 seconds. In what time did we run our race?

3. My class have been growing bean plants from seeds. After a month we measured and recorded their heights correct to the nearest cm.

    | 48 | 22 | 34 | 26 | 0 | 41 | 25 | 34 | 37 | 25 |
    | 37 | 16 | 23 | 42 | 0 | 0 | 35 | 46 | 24 | 36 |
    | 27 | 0 | 20 | 31 | 37 | 29 | 19 | 0 | 33 | 18 |

    (a) Draw a frequency table to record this information. (You will need to group the data in suitable bands.) Use this to draw a frequency diagram to show the distribution. Calculate the mean, median and modal group of the sample.

    (b) What can you say about your survey?

    (c) 5 plants did not grow at all. If you leave these 5 out of your calculations, what difference does this make to the mean, median and modal group?

    (d) Do you think that these 5 plants should have been included in the results or not?

4. In a manufacturing company 18 employees earn £14 000 per annum, 15 employees earn £22 000 per annum, 3 employees earn £32 000 per annum and the chairman earns £75 000 per annum. Calculate the mean, median and modal earnings of the company. Which measure of the average would you use if:

    (a) you wished to negotiate a pay rise?

    (b) you were the company secretary and were writing the annual report?

    (c) you wished to recruit more workers to the company?

5. (a) You have to write a marketing brief for the school. Look at these statistics and write a sentence or short paragraph about each – remember the idea is to attract parents and pupils to the school!
    - there is 2% unauthorised absence.
    - 4 out of 5 pupils study 2 languages.
    - 48% of pupils learn an instrument.
    - a small percentage of pupils have packed lunch.

    (b) Funnily enough, there is no mention of academic results in the school statistics. Make up some statistics that you think would attract parents to the school.

    (c) Now make up any statistics that you think would attract pupils to the school.

End of chapter 20 activity: Data collection

When preparing a report it is necessary to collect and analyse data. In this chapter we have dealt with various ways of analysing data. Let us now look at ways data can be collected in the first place.

Data can come in 3 forms:

1. **Measured data**
    This is typically collected from an experiment and consists of measurements of whatever variable or physical condition is being measured. This could be, for example, temperature, height, distance or, time.

2. **Absolute data**
    This is data, which is factual. For example your age is an absolute value and is not measured, but calculated from your birth date. The number of people living in an area at a fixed time is also an exact value and not a measurement.

3. **Opinion**
    This is the hardest type of data to collect. If you are asked your opinion about something then there are several variables that could affect your reply. For example: how you feel that day, what information you last heard, whether you like the person asking the question, and so on.

Your favourite subject

Here are several versions of a question that you might ask, in order to find out about someone's favourite subject:

Is Maths your favourite subject?
What is your favourite subject?
What is your least favourite subject?
Rank your subjects in order of preference with 1 being your favourite.

Which of these do you think would give you the most reliable answer?

Which do you think would get the least helpful answer?

Your political preferences

Here are three versions of the same question:

> Will you vote Labour at the next election?
> Who will you vote for at the next election?
> Will you vote for the government at the next election?

Which of these questions do you think would give you the most reliable answer?

Which question do you think would get the least helpful answer?

Your own questionnaire

Compile a brief questionnaire to canvass opinions on a subject that interests you. It could be on local issues, environmental issues or something to do with your school. Work with a friend. Each of you should compile a questionnaire on the same subject but with questions phrased in different ways.

Collect your results from the same group of people and then compare them. Have you both got the same results?

Index

Addition 50

Adjacent side 372

Algebra 117, 135-151

Angle 369, 387

Angles of depression 377

Angles of elevation 377

Area 34, 183, 226-251, 353
   Comparing area and volume 349

Average speed.192

Brackets 14, 141, 293-307

Calculator 11, 39
   Calculator problems 16
   Using index functions on the calculator 74
   Using the memory 15, 78

Charts 404
   Bar charts 407
   Drawing bar charts 418

Circles 226
   Circle problems 230
   Parts of circles: Perimeter 227

Compound interest 108

Cosine 384, 387
   Finding opposite and adjacent sides using cosine 388

Curves 287

Data 404-422

Decimal places 37

Decimals 26-41
   Dividing by decimals 31
   Dividing decimals 30

Degree of accuracy 37

Diagrams 404
   Drawing diagrams to help solve problems 321

Distance 189

Distance, speed and time formulae 189

Division 136
   Combining multiplication and division 139
   Dividing by decimals 31

Dividing decimals 30
   Long division 2-3

Elimination method 261

End of chapter activities
   3D fractals 176-7
   A literary genius 272
   Binary arithmetic 402-3
   Calculator puzzles and games 23-5
   Chain letters 91-2
   Data collection 423-4
   Experiments and graphs 291-2
   Fibonacci and the Golden Ratio 361-4
   Fraction, decimal and percentage dominoes 65
   Hexaflexagons 347-8
   My Great Uncle's bequest 152-4
   Packaging the litre 251-2
   Perigal's dissection 200-1
   Polyhedral numbers 133-4
   Probability experiments 324-8
   The cube root trick 381-2
   The dragon curve or Jurassic Park fractal 308-10
   The national elf problem 41-2
   The trading game 112-4
   Truthful twins? 223-5

Enlargements 339
   Volumes of enlargements 352

Equations 115-133, 293-307
   Equations and brackets 293
   Equations and Inequations 115
   Equations with fractions 122
   Equations with two fractions 124
   From equations to graphs 280
   Solving equations by factorising 301
   Solving equations with x2 71

What is an equation? 253
   Writing equations in two variables 253

Estimating 36

Factorising 143
   Factorising algebraic expressions 294
   Solving problems with factorising 302

Factors 7

Finding a side other than the hypotenuse 208

Finding an unknown quantity 185

Finding the adjacent side 372

Finding the angle 375, 393

Finding the hypotenuse 204, 392

Finding the opposite side 370

Finding the original amount 106

Finding the radius 229

Finding the total 414

Formula 178-200

Fractions 5, 43-64
   A fraction of an amount 52, 95
   Adding fractions 47
   Dividing with fractions 56
   Fractions on the calculator 60
   Multiplying fractions 54
   Subtracting fractions 49

Geometric sequences and numbers 168170

Graphical method 259

Graphs 273-290
   Everyday graphs 277
   From equations to graphs 280
   Graphs of curves 282
   Scatter graphs 409
   Travel graphs 273
   Using graphs to solve problems 254

Grouped data 417

Highest common factors 9

Hypotenuse 204, 208, 392

Income tax 102

Index functions 16, 76
    Using index functions on the
    calculator 74
Index numbers 66-91, 138
    Index numbers as fractions
    138
Indices 135-151
    Indices and algebra 135
    Indices and brackets 141
    Negative indices 69
    Roots as indices 86
Inequalities 127
Inexact answers 126
Integers 5
Isosceles triangles 212
Large numbers 79
Long division 2-3
Long multiplication 2-3
Lowest common multiples 9
Mean 411
Median 411
Metric units 33
Mixed addition 50
Mixed operations 59
Mixed problems 217
Mixed subtraction 50
Mode 13, 411
Money 28
Multiples 7
Multiplying 29, 135
    Combining multiplication and
    division 139
    Long multiplication 2-3
    Multiplying fractions 54
Natural numbers 1
Negative indices 69
Negative numbers 13
    Negative index numbers 136
Numbers 1-25
Opposite side 370
Other roots 74

Percentages 93-112
    Percentage decrease 99-100
    Percentage increase 99-100
    Percentage as a decimal 97
    Percentage change 104
Perimeter 227
Pie charts 405
Points of intersection 285
Polygon formulae 187
Possibility space for combined
    events 318
Power 0 136
Powers 86,137
Prime factors 7
    Using prime factors to find
    square roots 73
Prime numbers 7
Probability 311-324
    Probability with two events
    315
    Using theoretical probability
    313
Product 8
Proportion 349-360
Pythagoras' theorem 202-223
Pythagorean triplets 221
Quadratic sequences 162
Radius 229
Ratio 349-360
Re-arrangement and substitution
    methods 264
Rearranging formulae 194, 197
Reciprocal 57
Reciprocal curve 287
Reflections 330-1
Roots 74, 86
Roots as indices 86
Rotational symmetry 335
Rotations 333
Rules of conversion 94
Scale factor 263

Scatter graphs 409
Second function 14, 76
Sequence notation 160
Sequences 155-175
    Fibonacci type number
    pattern 157
    Square numbers 156
    Times table 156
    Triangle numbers 157
Significant figures 37
Simple index functions 16
Simultaneous equations 253-271
Sine 384, 387-388
Small numbers 79
Special triangles 213
Speed 189
Square roots 87, 71, 149
    Using prime factors to find
    square roots 73
Squares 71, 299
Standard index form 82
Substituting into formulae 180
Subtraction 217
Surface area of a cylinder 239
Tangent 369
Terminology 368
The Penny and the first taxation
    26
Time 189
Time formulae 189
Transformations 329-346
Translations 336
Trial and improvement 144
Triangles 213
Trigonometry 365-381, 383-401
Units of formulae 195
Volume 226-251, 243, 353
    Volume formulae 183
    Volume of a cylinder 237
    Volumes of enlargements 352